Affect Regulation Training

Matthias Berking • Brian Whitley

Affect Regulation Training

A Practitioners' Manual

 Springer

Matthias Berking
Department of Clinical Psychology
and Psychotherapy
Friedrich-Alexander-University
Erlangen-Nuremberg
Erlangen, Germany

Brian Whitley
Private Practice
Irvine, CA, USA

Translation from the German language edition: Training emotionaler Kompetenzen by Matthias Berking, © Springer-Verlag Berlin Heidelberg 2008, 2010

ISBN 978-1-4939-1021-2   ISBN 978-1-4939-1022-9 (eBook)
DOI 10.1007/978-1-4939-1022-9
Springer New York Heidelberg Dordrecht London

Library of Congress Control Number: 2014941915

Printed on acid-free paper

Springer is part of Springer Science+Business Media (www.springer.com)

Preface

The ability to perceive, identify, accept, and regulate intense emotions is an important contributor to health and well-being. Unfortunately, not everyone has been given the chance to acquire these complex skills. The Affect Regulation Training (ART) program was designed to foster emotion regulation skills in individuals who suffer from mental disorders, are at-risk for developing such disorders, or simply want to learn how to cope with challenging emotions in their daily life.

It took several years to develop ART. First, the research literature was thoroughly reviewed to identify emotion regulation skills deficits that are linked to the development and maintenance of mental disorders. Second, a theoretical model was developed to conceptualize the critical components of *adaptive* emotion regulation. Third, building upon this theoretical framework, the most effective emotion regulation techniques from a broad range of psychotherapeutic approaches were identified and integrated into a beta version of ART. This initial version of the training program went through an extensive testing phase in which clinical feasibility was scrutinized. The current version of ART incorporates feedback from this testing phase.

ART has now been used successfully for several years in various treatment centers. Results from pilot research studies indicate that ART, used as an adjunctive intervention, enhances the effectiveness of empirically based treatments (such as cognitive behavior therapy) and that ART can also be effectively applied as a stand-alone, first-step intervention. Numerous therapists have been trained to deliver the ART curriculum. The positive feedback we have received from these therapists and from the participants who have attended ART classes has been very encouraging.

The ART manual was originally published in the German language. As ART was presented in lectures and workshops in the United States and the United Kingdom, there were numerous requests for an English version of the ART manual, so work began with Brian Whitley to develop an updated, English version. Since some of the expressions in the original German version did not translate well into English, the translation process was difficult at times. However, with perseverance and determination, the task was completed with the valuable help of numerous native speakers from the United States, the United Kingdom, New Zealand, and Australia.

We would like to give special thanks, posthumously, to Dr. Klaus Grawe. While developing ART, he provided tremendous support, inspiration, and motivation. We also want to thank the German Research Association and the Swiss National Science Foundation for funding the research on which the training is based.

Additionally, we would like to mention the numerous advisors, physicians, therapists, colleagues, students, and trainees who contributed to this manual in many different ways, particularly Tiffany Calvert, Kristen Ellard, Nicholas Salsman, and Peggilee Wupperman. Last but not least, we are grateful to our wives and children, who had to cope with our frequent absence during the work on this manual. Without their support and understanding, this book never could have been made.

Erlangen, Germany   Matthias Berking
Irvine, CA, USA   Brian Whitley

Contents

Part I
Theoretical Overview
and Conceptualizations

Chapter 1
Introduction

I do a lot of things, like use drugs, for no reason.

If I start crying, I am afraid I will not be able to stop. This is why I always fight back my tears!

When my spouse says that to me, I instantly lose control!

Have you heard statements like these in your clinical practice? Have you found that many patients have difficulties perceiving, labeling, accepting, and regulating their emotions in healthy ways? Have you seen how these difficulties contribute to the development and maintenance of your patients' problems? Do you believe emotion regulation difficulties are often responsible for the development and maintenance of mental disorders? Do you believe that enhancing emotion regulation skills could be a promising transdiagnostic target in the treatment of various disorders? Have you had trouble finding techniques to enhance your patients' general emotion regulation skills among the myriad disorder-specific treatment manuals? If your answer to these questions is "Yes!", then you share the experiences that originally served as the starting point for the manual you are now holding in your hands.

After seeing the negative impact of emotion regulation deficits in our own patients, we embarked on a search for ways we could help patients develop these important skills. First, more than 100 scientific studies were analyzed and summarized for what is known about the relationship between emotion regulation deficits and mental disorders. Building on these findings, theoretical frameworks were created that outlined the development of emotion regulation deficits and conceptualized adaptive emotion regulation. Additionally, we explored potential pathways between emotion regulation skills and mental health. In *Part 1* of this manual, we present these findings and theories and discuss the implications for clinical practice.

Following the foundational work, a comprehensive, group-training program was developed to teach emotion regulation skills that could be used with a wide range of populations. This training program became known as Affect Regulation Training (ART). In *Part 2* of this manual, we describe the training in detail in order to equip therapists to deliver ART themselves. In *Part 3*, the final section, we discuss clinical experiences with the ART curriculum, present empirical evidence for the effectiveness of ART, and describe current efforts to expand and enhance the ART program.

M. Berking and B. Whitley, *Affect Regulation Training: A Practitioners' Manual*,
DOI 10.1007/978-1-4939-1022-9_1, © Springer Science+Business Media New York 2014

Chapter 2
Emotion Regulation: Definition and Relevance for Mental Health

2.1 Defining Important Concepts

Although the term emotion is frequently used in our daily life, it is not easily defined. In the scientific literature, emotions are described as coordinated sets of responses to internal or external events which have a particular significance for the organism (e.g., Lazarus, 1993). These response sets may involve cognitive, behavioral, physiological, and neural mechanisms and aim to orchestrate the best possible response to significant events. The subjective experience of an emotion is often called a feeling. Emotions and feelings refer to distinct and rather brief phenomena. In contrast, moods refer to less specific and longer-lasting experiences. Stress is a term to describe a less distinct alarm response, which may eventually turn into specific emotions. In the scientific language, affect is an encompassing term which includes emotions, feelings, motivational impulses, and moods together (Gross, 2014). In everyday language, the terms affect, emotions, and feelings are often used interchangeably, so to enhance the readability of this manual we will do the same.

In the past two decades, the topic of emotion regulation has become quite popular in psychological research and clinical psychology and commonly refers to measures taken by an individual to modify the natural course of affective responses. For example, Thompson (1994) defined emotion regulation as "...the extrinsic and intrinsic processes responsible for monitoring, evaluating, and modifying emotional reactions, especially their intensive and temporal features, to accomplish one's goals" (pp. 27–28). To date, numerous studies have investigated the association between the ability to regulate one's emotions and various aspects of mental health. The findings that will be reviewed in the following chapter suggest two important points. First, the inability to effectively regulate emotions poses serious risks to a person's mental health, and second, enhancing effective emotion regulation skills is a promising way of fostering or restoring mental health.

M. Berking and B. Whitley, *Affect Regulation Training: A Practitioners' Manual*,
DOI 10.1007/978-1-4939-1022-9_2, © Springer Science+Business Media New York 2014

2.2 Emotion Regulation Deficits and Mental Disorders

Evidence for a significant association between the ability to effectively regulate undesired affective states and mental health has been found across almost all mental disorders included in the Diagnostic and Statistical Manual for Mental Disorders (DSM-5; APA, 2013). For example, individuals suffering from depression, one of the most prevalent mental health problems of our time, often report difficulties identifying their emotions (Honkalampi, Saarinen, Hintikka, Virtanen, & Viinamaki, 1999; Rude & McCarthy, 2003), accepting and tolerating negative[1] emotions (Brody, Haaga, Kirk, & Solomon, 1999; Campbell-Sills, Barlow, Brown, & Hofmann, 2006; Conway, Csank, Holm, & Blake, 2000; Hayes et al., 2004), compassionately supporting themselves when suffering from negative emotions (Gilbert, Baldwin, Irons, Baccus, & Palmer, 2006; Hofmann, Grossman, & Hinton, 2011), and effectively modifying their emotions (Catanzaro, Wasch, Kirsch, & Mearns, 2000; Ehring, Fischer, Schnülle, Bösterling, & Tuschen-Caffier, 2008; Kassel, Bornovalova, & Mehta, 2007). Moreover, it has been shown that symptoms of depression are positively associated with ruminating/brooding, catastrophizing, and expressional suppression (Aldao, Nolen-Hoeksema, & Schweizer, 2010; Conway et al., 2000; Ehring, Tuschen-Caffier, Schnülle, Fischer, & Gross, 2010; Garnefski & Kraaij, 2006; Kraaij, Pruymboom, & Garnefski, 2002; Morrow & Nolen-Hoeksema, 1990), which have been conceptualized as ineffective attempts to avoid negative emotions (Berking & Wupperman, 2012; Moulds, Kandris, Starr, & Wong, 2007).

Cross-sectional findings such as these provide preliminary evidence for the hypothesis that emotion regulation deficits have a negative impact on mental health. However, cross-sectional findings do not clarify whether such deficits are the cause of or the effect of mental disorders. In order to clarify whether regulation difficulties actually contribute to the development of mental disorders, such as depression, we must look at the longitudinal and experimental research.

Longitudinal research has found that a person's positive belief in their ability to successfully modify their own negative affect can predict future reductions in depression (Kassel et al., 2007), and the use of regulation strategies generally considered to be maladaptive can predict depressive symptoms (Aldao & Nolen-Hoeksema, 2012; Kraaij et al., 2002). Moreover, studies using daily diaries (i.e., ecological momentary assessments) have shown that responses of negative affect to aversive events persisted longer in depressed individuals than in nondepressed controls (Peeters, Nicolson, Berkhof, Delespaul, & deVries, 2003), and the tendency to respond to aversive events with negative affect predicted depressive symptoms 2 months after the initial assessment in college students (O'Neill, Cohen, Tolpin, & Gunthert, 2004). Similarly, tendencies to respond to aversive events with negative affect and negative mood-regulation expectancies have been shown to predict less symptom reduction during cognitive behavior therapy (CBT) for major

---

[1] When we refer to emotions as *negative*, we are referring to the aversive, undesired or challenging aspects of these emotions. We are not implying that these emotions are bad or wrong in any way.

depressive disorder (Backenstrass et al., 2006; Cohen, Gunthert, Butler, O'Neill, & Tolpin, 2005). Finally, dampening of positive affect was found to predict depressive symptoms 3 and 5 months later, even when controlling for ruminative responses to negative affect and depressive symptoms at initial assessment (Raes, Smets, Nelis, & Schoofs, 2012).

Further evidence for the causal effect of emotion regulation on mental health problems, such as depression, comes from experimental studies which systematically manipulate emotion regulation and assess potential effects on depressive symptoms. In such studies, it has been shown that maladaptive responses to dysphoric mood states (e.g., rumination or suppression) impair the recovery from such states in individuals vulnerable to depression (Campbell-Sills et al., 2006; Ehring et al., 2010; Liverant, Brown, Barlow, & Roemer, 2008; Morrow & Nolen-Hoeksema, 1990), and that individuals with depression are more likely to utilize such strategies than healthy controls (Ehring et al., 2010).

Similar to the research involving depression, numerous studies are also finding that emotion regulation skill deficits contribute to the development and maintenance of anxiety disorders (Aldao & Nolen-Hoeksema, 2012; Aldao et al., 2010; Amstadter, 2008; Berking & Wupperman, 2012; Campbell-Sills, Ellard, & Barlow, 2014; Cisler, Olatunji, Feldner, & Forsyth, 2010; Kashdan, Zvolensky, & McLeish, 2008; Suveg, Morelen, Brewer, & Thomassin, 2010). For example, in a *nonclinical* sample of 631 participants, emotion regulation skill deficits significantly predicted subsequent anxiety symptom severity during a 2-week interval (Berking, Orth, Wupperman, Meier, & Caspar, 2008). In another nonclinical sample, the participants' belief that they could successfully cope with negative moods predicted subsequent anxiety symptom severity over an 8-week period (Kassel et al., 2007). Additionally, in a nonclinical sample of adolescents, unsuccessful emotion regulation predicted anxiety symptom severity after 7 months (McLaughlin, Hatzenbuehler, Mennin, & Nolen-Hoeksema, 2011), and in a sample of college students, difficulties describing and identifying emotions predicted increases in anxiety symptom severity 1 year later (Ciarrochi & Scott, 2006). Finally, in a nonclinical sample of 131 participants, emotion regulation skills negatively predicted anxiety symptom severity during a 5-year period, while anxiety symptom severity did not predict subsequent emotion regulation (Wirtz, Hofmann, Riper, & Berking, 2013).

Research involving *clinical* samples has found that individuals suffering from generalized anxiety disorder (GAD) display deficits in emotional clarity, a poorer understanding of emotions, greater negative reactivity to emotions, as well as less acceptance and less successful management of emotions (McLaughlin, Mennin, & Farach, 2007; Mennin, Heimberg, Turk, & Fresco, 2005; Salters-Pedneault, Roemer, Tull, Rucker, & Mennin, 2006; Turk, Heimberg, Luterek, Mennin, & Fresco, 2005). In addition, emotion regulation skill deficits have been found to mediate the effect of preexisting generalized anxiety disorder on psychological distress during the year following the terrorist attacks of 9/11 in a sample of New York University students that were directly affected by the event (Farach, Mennin, Smith, & Mandelbaum, 2008).

Research on clinical samples also indicates that individuals meeting criteria for panic disorder report difficulties identifying, labeling, accepting, and tolerating undesired emotions (Baker, Holloway, Thomas, Thomas, & Owens, 2004; Naragon-Gainey, 2010; Parker, Taylor, Bagby, & Acklin, 1993; Shear, Cooper, Lerman, Busch, & Shapiro, 1993). Further evidence indicates these individuals also tend to use avoidant strategies when trying to cope with anxiety-provoking or other types of aversive experiences (Tull & Roemer, 2007), and the use of these avoidant strategies may paradoxically increase anxiety (Eifert & Heffner, 2003; Feldner, Zvolensky, Eifert, & Spira, 2003; Feldner, Zvolensky, Stickle, Bonn-Miller, & Leen-Feldner, 2006; Karekla, Forsyth, & Kelly, 2004; Spira, Zvolensky, Eifert, & Feldner, 2004), thus contributing to the development and maintenance of anxiety disorders (Craske, Miller, Rotunda, & Barlow, 1990; Hino, Takeuchi, & Yamanouchi, 2002; Levitt, Brown, Orsillo, & Barlow, 2004).

When compared to healthy controls, individuals meeting criteria for social anxiety disorder have been found to have more difficulty describing and identifying emotions (Turk et al., 2005), experience higher levels of shame (Fergus, Valentiner, McGrath, & Jencius, 2010), and display greater difficulty accepting emotional experiences when they are confronted with negative events (Kashdan & Steger, 2006). Individuals suffering from specific phobias report high use of avoidance, self-accusation, rumination, catastrophizing, and low reliance on positive reappraisals when trying to manage challenging experiences (Davey, Burgess, & Rashes, 1995; Kraaij, Garnefski, & Van Gerwen, 2003).

Similarly, in individuals suffering from posttraumatic stress disorder (PTSD), symptom severity and impairment have been associated with a lack of emotional clarity, a lack of emotional acceptance, and difficulties engaging in goal-directed behavior and effective emotion regulation strategies (Cloitre, Miranda, Stovall-McClough, & Han, 2005; Ehring & Quack, 2010; Roemer, Litz, Orsillo, & Wagner, 2001; Tull, Barrett, McMillan, & Roemer, 2007; Weiss et al., 2012). Emotion regulation difficulties have also been shown to mediate the association between PTSD symptom severity and substance abuse in patients with histories of childhood abuse (Staiger, Melville, Hides, Kambouropoulos, & Lubman, 2009).

Further research has shown that patients with eating disorders tend to experience emotions more intensely than controls (Overton, Selway, Strongman, & Houston, 2005; Svaldi, Griepenstroh, Tuschen-Caffier, & Ehring, 2012). For example, increased feelings of fear, anxiety, tension, and nervousness have been found in patients with eating disorders (McClenny, 1998). These patients also tend to avoid experiencing emotions, have difficulties accepting and managing their emotions (Corstorphine, Mountford, Tomlinson, Waller, & Meyer, 2007; Whiteside et al., 2007), and have a decreased capacity for emotional awareness (Bydlowski et al., 2005; Carano et al., 2006; Svaldi, Caffier, & Tuschen-Caffier, 2010).

When compared to nonclinical controls, patients with bulimia nervosa were found to be deficient in their ability to be aware of and identify their internal emotional state (Sim, 2002; Sim & Zeman, 2004). Additionally, research using the Difficulties in Emotion Regulation Scale (DERS; Gratz & Roemer, 2004) found that a sample of women with anorexia nervosa reported significantly more difficulties in all of the subscales of the DERS than did nonpsychiatric controls (Harrison, Sullivan, Tchanturia, & Treasure, 2009). Moreover, in a meta-analysis, rumination and suppression were associated with more severe eating disorder symptoms (Aldao et al., 2010). In longitudinal studies, negative mood predicted binge eating in binge eating disorder (Chua, Touyz, & Hill, 2004; Hilbert & Tuschen-Caffier, 2007; Stein et al., 2007; Wild et al., 2007) as well as binging and purging in bulimia nervosa (Crosby et al., 2009; Smyth et al., 2007, 2009).

Evidence for the causal effect that emotion regulation may have on eating disorders comes from experimental studies indicating that the induction of negative mood or stress increases subsequent food intake and/or the likelihood of binge eating in individuals with binge eating disorder (Agras & Telch, 1998; Chua et al., 2004; Laessle & Schulz, 2009). However, conflicting findings were found in another experimental study (Dingemans, Martijn, Jansen, & van Furth, 2009), in which participants received instructions either to suppress emotions or to react naturally to a sadness-inducing film clip. Results of this study revealed the two different responses to the film clip did not significantly affect subsequent food intake. This conflicting finding demonstrates that it is difficult to absolutely define certain regulatory strategies as "maladaptive" or "effective" (Bonanno, Papa, Lalande, Westphal, & Coifman, 2004).

The use of drugs and alcohol in substance-related disorders are widely regarded as an effort to regulate or avoid negative emotions (Baker, Piper, McCarthy, Majeskie, & Fiore, 2004; Cooper, Frone, Russell, & Mudar, 1995; Weiss, Griffin, & Mirin, 1992; Wupperman et al., 2012). Since negative emotions serve as important triggers for relapse (Cooney, Litt, Morse, Bauer, & Gaupp, 1997; ElSheikh & Bashir, 2004; Isenhart, 1991), the availability of effective emotion regulation skills should help a person to maintain sobriety even in the presence of such emotions (Berking et al., 2011). Preliminary evidence for this hypothesis comes from studies showing that patients meeting criteria for the so-called emotional disorders (affective and anxiety disorders; Ellard, Fairholme, Boisseau, Farchione, & Barlow, 2010) as well as borderline personality disorders often also meet criteria for substance disorders (Hasin, Stinson, Ogburn, & Grant, 2007) and display significantly higher rates of relapse after treatment (Bradizza, Stasiewicz, & Paas, 2006). Additionally, low levels of "emotional intelligence," defined by Salovey and Mayer (1990), p. 189, as the "ability to monitor one's own and others' feelings and emotions, to discriminate among them, and to use this information to guide one's thinking and actions," has consistently been found to be associated with more intensive levels of drug and alcohol use (Kun & Demetrovics, 2010). Individuals with substance disorders also often report more emotion regulation difficulties than do healthy controls, especially during periods of abstinence (Berking et al., 2011; Fox, Axelrod, Paliwal, Sleeper, & Sinha, 2007).

Additionally, in several longitudinal studies, negative affect predicted future drinking levels and the desire to drink (Falk, Yi, & Hilton, 2008; Gamble et al., 2010; Hodgins, El-Guebaly, & Armstrong, 1995; Swendsen et al., 2000; Willinger et al., 2002), and deficits in adaptive emotion regulation predicted relapse during and after inpatient treatment for alcohol dependence (Berking et al., 2011). Additionally, experimental research has found that an induction of negative affect leads to increased urges to drink (Birch et al., 2004; Cooney et al., 1997; Sinha et al., 2009). Finally, interventions that target symptoms of depression and anxiety in patients with substance abuse issues have been found to decrease both relapse and the severity of substance use (Brown, Evans, Miller, Burgess, & Mueler, 1997; Watt, Stewart, Birch, & Bernier, 2006).

A substantial amount of research points to emotion dysregulation as a core concept underlying borderline personality disorder (Linehan, 1993). This disorder is partly defined and characterized (APA, 2013) by intense and unstable mood states (Austin, Riniolo, & Porges, 2007; Kuo & Linehan, 2009; Weinberg, Klonsky, & Hajcak, 2009). Patients meeting criteria for this personality disorder have been found to experience less emotional awareness and clarity (Leible & Snell, 2004; Svaldi et al., 2012; Wolff, Stiglmayr, Bretz, Lammers, & Auckenthaler, 2007) and are less able to tolerate distress when working toward a goal (Gratz, Rosenthal, Tull, Lejuez, & Gunderson, 2006). These patients also tend to utilize avoidant (Berking, Neacsiu, Comtois, & Linehan, 2009) and harmful emotion regulation strategies (e.g., self-injurious behavior) when distressed (Wupperman, Neumann, Whitman, & Axelrod, 2009), and their regulatory attempts have been found to be less successful than those of healthy controls, despite exerting more regulatory effort (Gruber, Harvey, & Gross, 2012). Additionally, research has found that borderline patients have deficits in their ability to use reappraisal to regulate their emotions (Schulze et al., 2011). In a longitudinal study Tragesser and colleagues found that emotion dysregulation predicted future borderline features better than impulsivity, supporting a causal effect that emotion regulation may have on this personality disorder (Tragesser, Solhan, Schwartz-Mette, & Trull, 2007).

It has also been hypothesized that difficulties in correctly identifying emotions place individuals at risk for developing somatoform disorders, as they misinterpret the somatic components of an emotion as serious health problems (Nemiah & Sifneos, 1970; Sifneos, 1973). In accordance with this theory, several studies have found evidence for associations between somatoform disorders and emotion regulation deficits, such as the abilities to consciously experience and tolerate emotions, correctly identify emotions, and accurately link emotions to sensations occurring in the body (De Gucht & Heiser, 2003; Lumley, Stettner, & Wehmer, 1996; Schweinhardt et al., 2008; Subic-Wrana et al., 2002; Subic-Wrana, Beutel, Knebel, & Lane, 2010; Subic-Wrana, Bruder, Thomas, Lane, & Köhle, 2005; Waller & Scheidt, 2004, 2006).

Finally, a number of studies from the developmental literature have found a significant relationship between emotion regulation deficits and childhood psychopathology, including attention-deficit/hyperactivity disorder (Walcott & Landau, 2004) and a variety of internalizing (e.g., social withdrawal, depression, and anxiety) and externalizing behaviors (e.g., aggression, anger, and behavior problems) (Calkins & Howse, 2004; Kim & Cicchetti, 2010; McLaughlin et al., 2011). Children and adolescents diagnosed with anxiety disorders have been found to have a significantly lower perceived ability to control anxious reactions as compared to child and adolescent controls (Weems, Silverman, Rapee, & Pina, 2003).

In summary, there is strong empirical evidence that emotion regulation deficits are associated with mental disorders and that emotion regulation deficits contribute significantly to the development and maintenance of these disorders. Based on these findings, we attempted to develop a conceptualization model of adaptive emotion regulation. The following chapter will describe this model in detail.

References

Agras, W. S., & Telch, C. F. (1998). The effects of caloric deprivation and negative affect on binge eating in obese binge-eating disordered women. *Behavior Therapy, 29*(3), 491–503.

Aldao, A., & Nolen-Hoeksema, S. (2012). When are adaptive strategies most predictive of psychopathology? *Journal of Abnormal Psychology, 121*(1), 276–281.

Aldao, A., Nolen-Hoeksema, S., & Schweizer, S. (2010). Emotion-regulation strategies across psychopathology: A meta-analytic review. *Clinical Psychology Review, 30*(2), 217–237.

American Psychiatric Association. (2013). *Diagnostic and statistical manual of mental disorders* (5th ed.). Washington, DC: Author.

Amstadter, A. (2008). Emotion regulation and anxiety disorders. *Journal of Anxiety Disorders, 22*(2), 211–221.

Austin, M. A., Riniolo, T. C., & Porges, S. W. (2007). Borderline personality disorder and emotion regulation: Insights from the polyvagal theory. *Brain and Cognition, 65*(1), 69–76.

Backenstrass, M., Schwarz, T., Fiedler, P., Joest, K., Reck, C., Mundt, C., & Kronmueller, K. T. (2006). Negative mood regulation expectancies, self-efficacy beliefs, and locus of control orientation: Moderators or mediators of change in the treatment of depression? *Psychotherapy Research, 16*(2), 250–258.

Baker, R., Holloway, J., Thomas, P. W., Thomas, S., & Owens, M. (2004). Emotional processing and panic. *Behaviour Research and Therapy, 42*(11), 1271–1287.

Baker, T. B., Piper, M. E., McCarthy, D. E., Majeskie, M. R., & Fiore, M. C. (2004). Addiction motivation reformulated: An affective processing model of negative reinforcement. *Psychological Review, 111*(1), 33–51.

Berking, M., Margraf, M., Ebert, D., Wupperman, P., Hofmann, S. G., & Junghanns, K. (2011). Deficits in emotion-regulation skills predict alcohol use during and after cognitive-behavioral therapy for alcohol dependence. *Journal of Consulting and Clinical Psychology, 79*(3), 307–318.

Berking, M., Neacsiu, A., Comtois, K. A., & Linehan, M. M. (2009). The impact of experiential avoidance on the reduction of depression in treatment for borderline personality disorder. *Behaviour Research and Therapy, 47*(8), 663–670.

Berking, M., Orth, U., Wupperman, P., Meier, L., & Caspar, F. (2008). Prospective effects of emotion regulation on emotional adjustment. *Journal of Counseling Psychology, 55*(4), 485–494.

Berking, M., & Wupperman, P. (2012). Emotion regulation and mental health: Recent findings, current challenges, and future directions. *Current Opinion in Psychiatry, 25*(2), 128–134.

Birch, C. D., Stewart, S. H., Wall, A. M., McKee, S. A., Eisnor, S. J., & Theakston, J. A. (2004). Mood-induced increases in alcohol expectancy strength in internally motivated drinkers. *Psychology of Addictive Behaviors, 18*(3), 231–238.

Bonanno, G., Papa, A., Lalande, K., Westphal, M., & Coifman, K. (2004). The importance of being flexible: The ability to both enhance and suppress emotional expression predicts long-term adjustment. *Psychological Science, 15*, 482–487.

Bradizza, C. M., Stasiewicz, P. R., & Paas, N. D. (2006). Relapse to alcohol and drug use among individuals diagnosed with co-occurring mental health and substance use disorders: A review. *Clinical Psychology Review, 26*(2), 162–178.

Brody, C. L., Haaga, D. A., Kirk, L., & Solomon, A. (1999). Experiences of anger in people who have recovered from depression and never-depressed people. *The Journal of Nervous and Mental Disease, 187*(7), 400–405.

Brown, R. A., Evans, D. M., Miller, I. W., Burgess, E. S., & Mueler, T. I. (1997). Cognitive-behavioral treatment for depression in alcoholism. *Journal of Consulting and Clinical Psychology, 65*(5), 715–726.

Bydlowski, S., Corcos, M., Jeammet, P., Paterniti, S., Berthoz, S., Laurier, C., Chambry, J., et al. (2005). Emotion-processing deficits in eating disorders. *The International Journal of Eating Disorders, 37*(4), 321–329.

Calkins, S. D., & Howse, R. B. (2004). Individual differences in self-regulation: Implications for childhood adjustment. In R. Feldman & P. Philippot (Eds.), *The regulation of emotion* (pp. 307–332). Mahwah, NJ: Erlbaum.

Campbell-Sills, L., Barlow, D. H., Brown, T. A., & Hofmann, S. G. (2006). Effects of suppression and acceptance on emotional responses of individuals with anxiety and mood disorders. *Behaviour Research and Therapy, 44*, 1251–1263.

Campbell-Sills, L., Ellard, K., & Barlow, D. H. (2014). Emotion regulation in anxiety disorders. In J. J. Gross (Ed.), *Handbook of emotion regulation* (2nd ed., pp. 393–412). New York, NY: Guilford Press.

Carano, A., De Berardis, D., Gambi, F., Di Paolo, C., Campanella, D., Pelusi, L., … Ferro, F. M. (2006). Alexithymia and body image in adult outpatients with binge eating disorder. *The International Journal of Eating Disorders, 39*(4), 332–340.

Catanzaro, S. J., Wasch, H. H., Kirsch, I., & Mearns, J. (2000). Coping related expectancies and dispositions as prospective predictors of coping responses and symptoms. *Journal of Personality, 68*(4), 757–788.

Chua, J. L., Touyz, S., & Hill, A. J. (2004). Negative mood-induced overeating in obese binge eaters: An experimental study. *International Journal of Obesity and Related Metabolic Disorders, 28*(4), 606–610.

Ciarrochi, J., & Scott, G. (2006). The link between emotional competence and well-being: A longitudinal study. *British Journal of Guidance and Counselling, 34*(2), 231–243.

Cisler, J., Olatunji, B., Feldner, M., & Forsyth, J. (2010). Emotion regulation and the anxiety disorders: An integrative review. *Journal of Psychopathology and Behavioral Assessment, 32*, 68–82.

Cloitre, M., Miranda, R., Stovall-McClough, K. C., & Han, H. (2005). Beyond PTSD: Emotion regulation and inter-personal problems as predictors of functional impairment in survivors of childhood abuse. *Behavior Therapy, 36*(2), 119–124.

Cohen, L. H., Gunthert, K. C., Butler, A. C., O'Neill, S. C., & Tolpin, L. H. (2005). Daily affective reactivity as a prospective predictor of depressive symptoms. *Journal of Personality, 73*(6), 1687–1714.

Conway, M., Csank, P. A. R., Holm, S. L., & Blake, C. K. (2000). On assessing individual differences in rumination on sadness. *Journal of Personality Assessment, 75*(3), 404–425.

Cooney, N. L., Litt, M. D., Morse, P. A., Bauer, L. O., & Gaupp, L. (1997). Alcohol cue reactivity, negative-mood reactivity, and relapse in treated alcoholic men. *Journal of Abnormal Psychology, 106*(2), 243–250.

Cooper, M. L., Frone, M. R., Russell, M., & Mudar, P. (1995). Drinking to regulate positive and negative emotions: A motivational model of alcohol use. *Journal of Personality and Social Psychology, 69*(5), 990–1005.

Corstorphine, E., Mountford, V., Tomlinson, S., Waller, G., & Meyer, C. (2007). Distress tolerance in the eating disorders. *Eating Behaviors, 8*(1), 91–97.

Craske, M. G., Miller, P. P., Rotunda, R., & Barlow, D. H. (1990). A descriptive report of features of initial unexpected panic attacks in minimal and extensive avoiders. *Behaviour Research and Therapy, 28*(5), 395–400.

Crosby, R. D., Wonderlich, S. A., Engel, S. G., Simonich, H., Smyth, J., & Mitchell, J. E. (2009). Daily mood patterns and bulimic behaviors in the natural environment. *Behaviour Research and Therapy, 47*(3), 181–188.

Davey, G. C., Burgess, I., & Rashes, R. (1995). Coping strategies and phobias: The relationship between fears, phobias and methods of coping with stressors. *British Journal of Clinical Psychology, 34*(3), 423–434.

De Gucht, V., & Heiser, W. (2003). Alexithymia and somatisation: A quantitative review of the literature. *Journal of Psychosomatic Research, 54*(5), 425–434.

Dingemans, A. E., Martijn, C., Jansen, A., & van Furth, E. F. (2009). The effect of suppressing negative emotions on eating behavior in binge eating disorder. *Appetite, 52*(1), 51–57.

Ehring, T., Fischer, S., Schnülle, J., Bösterling, A., & Tuschen-Caffier, B. (2008). Characteristics of emotion regulation in recovered depressed versus never depressed individuals. *Personality and Individual Differences, 44*(7), 1574–1584.

Ehring, T., & Quack, D. (2010). Emotion regulation difficulties in trauma survivors: The role of trauma type and PTSD symptom severity. *Behavior Therapy, 41*(4), 587–598.

Ehring, T., Tuschen-Caffier, B., Schnülle, J., Fischer, S., & Gross, J. J. (2010). Emotion regulation and vulnerability to depression: Spontaneous versus instructed use of emotion suppression and reappraisal. *Emotion, 10*(4), 563–572.

Eifert, G. H., & Heffner, M. (2003). The effects of acceptance versus control contexts on avoidance of panic-related symptoms. *Journal of Behavior Therapy and Experimental Psychiatry, 34*(3), 293–312.

Ellard, K. K., Fairholme, C. P., Boisseau, C. L., Farchione, T. J., & Barlow, D. H. (2010). Unified protocol for the transdiagnostic treatment of emotional disorders: Protocol development and initial outcome data. *Cognitive and Behavioral Practice, 17*(1), 88–101.

ElSheikh, S. E. G., & Bashir, T. Z. (2004). High risk relapse situations and self-efficacy: Comparison between alcoholics and heroin addicts. *Addictive Behaviors, 29*(4), 753–758.

Falk, D., Yi, H., & Hilton, M. (2008). Age of onset and temporal sequencing of lifetime DSM-IV alcohol use disorders relative to comorbid mood and anxiety disorders. *Drug and Alcohol Dependence, 94*(1–3), 234–245.

Farach, F. J., Mennin, D. S., Smith, R. L., & Mandelbaum, M. (2008). The impact of pretrauma analogue GAD and posttraumatic emotional reactivity following exposure to the September 11 terrorist attacks: A longitudinal study. *Behavior Therapy, 39*(3), 262–276.

Feldner, M. T., Zvolensky, M. J., Eifert, G. H., & Spira, A. P. (2003). Emotional avoidance: An experimental test of individual differences and response suppression using biological challenge. *Behaviour Research and Therapy, 41*(4), 403–411.

Feldner, M. T., Zvolensky, M. J., Stickle, T. R., Bonn-Miller, M. O., & Leen-Feldner, E. (2006). Anxiety sensitivity—Physical concerns as moderator of the emotional consequences of emotion suppression during biological challenge: An experimental test using individual growth curve analysis. *Behaviour Research and Therapy, 44*(2), 249–272.

Fergus, T. A., Valentiner, D. P., McGrath, P. B., & Jencius, S. (2010). Shame-and guilt-proneness: Relationships with anxiety disorder symptoms in a clinical sample. *Journal of Anxiety Disorders, 24*(8), 811–815.

Fox, H. C., Axelrod, S. R., Paliwal, P., Sleeper, J., & Sinha, R. (2007). Difficulties in emotion regulation and impulse control during cocaine abstinence. *Drug and Alcohol Dependence, 89*(2–3), 298–301.

Gamble, S. A., Conner, K. R., Talbot, N. L., Yu, Q., Tu, X. M., & Connors, G. J. (2010). Effects of pretreatment and posttreatment depressive symptoms on alcohol consumption following treatment in project MATCH. *Journal of Studies on Alcohol and Drugs, 71*(1), 71–77.

Garnefski, N., & Kraaij, V. (2006). Relationships between cognitive emotion regulation strategies and depressive symptoms: A comparative study of five specific samples. *Personality and Individual Differences, 40*(8), 1659–1669.

Gilbert, P., Baldwin, M. W., Irons, C., Baccus, J. R., & Palmer, M. (2006). Self-criticism and self-warmth: An imagery study exploring their relation to depression. *Journal of Cognitive Psychotherapy, 20*(2), 183–200.

Gratz, K. L., & Roemer, L. (2004). Multidimensional assessment of emotion regulation and dysregulation: Development, factor structure, and initial validation of the Difficulties in Emotion Regulation Scale. *Journal of Psychopathology and Behavioral Assessment, 26*, 41–54.

Gratz, K. L., Rosenthal, M. Z., Tull, M. T., Lejuez, C. W., & Gunderson, J. G. (2006). An experimental investigation of emotion dysregulation in borderline personality disorder. *Journal of Abnormal Psychology, 115*(4), 850–855.

Gross, J. J. (2014). Emotion regulation: Conceptual and empirical foundations. In J. J. Gross (Ed.), *Handbook of emotion regulation* (2nd ed., pp. 3–20). New York, NY: Guilford Press.

Gruber, J., Harvey, A. G., & Gross, J. J. (2012). When trying is not enough: Emotion regulation and the effort–success gap in bipolar disorder. *Emotion, 12*(5), 997–1003.

Harrison, A., Sullivan, S., Tchanturia, K., & Treasure, J. (2009). Emotion recognition and regulation in anorexia nervosa. *Clinical Psychology & Psychotherapy, 16*(4), 348–356.

Hasin, D. S., Stinson, F. S., Ogburn, E., & Grant, B. F. (2007). Prevalence, correlates, disability, and comorbidity of DSM-IV alcohol abuse and dependence in the United States: Results from the national epidemiologic survey on alcohol and related conditions. *Archives of General Psychiatry, 64*(7), 830–842.

Hayes, S. C., Strosahl, K., Wilson, K. G., Bissett, R. T., Pistorello, J., Toarmino, D., … McCurry, S. M. (2004). Measuring experiential avoidance: A preliminary test of a working model. *Psychological Record, 54*(4), 553–578.

Hilbert, A., & Tuschen-Caffier, B. (2007). Maintenance of binge eating through negative mood: A naturalistic comparison of binge eating disorder and bulimia nervosa. *The International Journal of Eating Disorders, 40*(6), 521–530.

Hino, T., Takeuchi, T., & Yamanouchi, N. (2002). A 1-year follow-up study of coping in patients with panic disorder. *Comprehensive Psychiatry, 43*(4), 279–284.

Hodgins, D. C., El-Guebaly, N., & Armstrong, S. (1995). Prospective and retrospective reports of mood states before relapse to substance use. *Journal of Consulting and Clinical Psychology, 63*(3), 400–407.

Hofmann, S. G., Grossman, P., & Hinton, D. E. (2011). Loving-kindness and compassion meditation: Potential for psychological interventions. *Clinical Psychology Review, 31*(7), 1126–1132.

Honkalampi, K., Saarinen, P., Hintikka, J., Virtanen, J., & Viinamaki, H. (1999). Factors associated with alexithymia in patients suffering from depression. *Psychotherapy and Psychosomatics, 68*(5), 270–275.

Isenhart, C. E. (1991). Factor structure of the inventory of drinking situations. *Journal of Substance Abuse, 3*(1), 59–71.

Karekla, M., Forsyth, J. P., & Kelly, M. M. (2004). Emotional avoidance and panicogenic responding to a biological challenge procedure. *Behavior Therapy, 35*(4), 725–746.

Kashdan, T. B., & Steger, M. F. (2006). Expanding the topography of social anxiety: An experience-sampling assessment of positive emotions, positive events, and emotion suppression. *Psychological Science, 17*(2), 120–128.

Kashdan, T. B., Zvolensky, M. J., & McLeish, A. C. (2008). Anxiety sensitivity and affect regulatory strategies: Individual and interactive risk factors for anxiety-related symptoms. *Journal of Anxiety Disorders, 22*(3), 429–440.

Kassel, J. D., Bornovalova, M., & Mehta, N. (2007). Generalized expectancies for negative mood regulation predict change in anxiety and depression among college students. *Behaviour Research and Therapy, 45*(5), 939–950.

Kim, J., & Cicchetti, D. (2010). Longitudinal pathways linking child maltreatment, emotion regulation, peer relations, and psychopathology. *Journal of Child Psychology and Psychiatry, 51*(6), 706–716.

Kraaij, V., Garnefski, N., & Van Gerwen, L. (2003). Cognitive coping and anxiety symptoms among people who seek help for fear of flying. *Aviation, Space, and Environmental Medicine, 74*(3), 273–277.

Kraaij, V., Pruymboom, E., & Garnefski, N. (2002). Cognitive coping and depressive symptoms in the elderly: A longitudinal study. *Aging and Mental Health, 6*(3), 275–281.

Kun, B., & Demetrovics, Z. (2010). Emotional intelligence and addictions: A systematic review. *Substance Use & Misuse, 45*, 1131–1160.

Kuo, J. R., & Linehan, M. M. (2009). Disentangling emotion processes in borderline personality disorder: Physiological and self-reported assessment of biological vulnerability, baseline intensity, and reactivity to emotionally evocative stimuli. *Journal of Abnormal Psychology, 118*(3), 531–544.

Laessle, R. G., & Schulz, S. (2009). Stress-induced laboratory eating behavior in obese women with binge eating disorder. *International Journal of Eating Disorders, 42*(6), 505–510.

Lazarus, R. S. (1993). From psychological stress to emotions. *Annual Review of Psychology, 44*, 1–21.

Leible, T. L., & Snell, W. E., Jr. (2004). Borderline personality disorder and multiple aspects of emotional intelligence. *Personality and Individual Differences, 37*(2), 393–404.

Levitt, J. T., Brown, T. A., Orsillo, S. M., & Barlow, D. H. (2004). The effects of acceptance versus suppression of emotion on subjective and psychophysiological response to carbon dioxide challenge in patients with panic disorder. *Behavior Therapy, 35*(4), 747–766.

Linehan, M. M. (1993). *Cognitive-behavioral treatment of borderline personality disorder.* New York, NY: Guilford.

Liverant, G. I., Brown, T. A., Barlow, D. H., & Roemer, L. (2008). Emotion regulation in unipolar depression: The effects of acceptance and suppression of subjective emotional experience on the intensity and duration of sadness and negative affect. *Behaviour Research and Therapy, 46*(11), 1201–1209.

Lumley, M. A., Stettner, L., & Wehmer, F. (1996). How are alexithymia and physical illness linked? A review and critique of pathways. *Journal of Psychosomatic Research, 41*(6), 505–518.

McClenny, B. D. (1998). Emotion regulation in bulimia nervosa: Neuro-physiological correlates of reactivity and self-regulation (Ph.D. dissertation, University of Maryland College Park, Maryland, United States). Retrieved December 1, 2011, from Dissertations & Theses: Full Text. (Publication No. AAT 9836444).

McLaughlin, K. A., Hatzenbuehler, M. L., Mennin, D. S., & Nolen-Hoeksema, S. (2011). Emotion dysregulation and adolescent psychopathology: A prospective study. *Behaviour Research and Therapy, 49*(9), 544–554.

McLaughlin, K. A., Mennin, D. S., & Farach, F. J. (2007). The contributory role of worry in emotion generation and dysregulation in generalized anxiety disorder. *Behaviour Research and Therapy, 45*(8), 1735–1752.

Mennin, D. S., Heimberg, R. G., Turk, C. L., & Fresco, D. M. (2005). Preliminary evidence for an emotion regulation deficit model of generalized anxiety disorder. *Behaviour Research and Therapy, 43*(10), 1281–1310.

Morrow, J., & Nolen-Hoeksema, S. (1990). Effects of responses to depression on the remediation of depressive affect. *Journal of Personality and Social Psychology, 58*(3), 519–527.

Moulds, M. L., Kandris, E., Starr, S., & Wong, A. (2007). The relationship between rumination, avoidance and depression in a non-clinical sample. *Behaviour Research and Therapy, 45*(2), 251–261.

Naragon-Gainey, K. (2010). Meta-analysis of the relations of anxiety sensitivity to the depressive and anxiety disorders. *Psychological Bulletin, 136*(1), 128.

Nemiah, J. C., & Sifneos, P. E. (1970). Psychosomatic illness: A problem in communication. *Psychotherapy and Psychosomatics, 18*(1–6), 154–160.

O'Neill, S. C., Cohen, L. H., Tolpin, L. H., & Gunthert, K. C. (2004). Affective reactivity to daily interpersonal stressors as a prospective predictor of depressive symptoms. *Journal of Social and Clinical Psychology, 23*(2), 172–194.

Overton, A., Selway, S., Strongman, K., & Houston, M. (2005). Eating disorders—The regulation of positive as well as negative emotion experience. *Journal of Clinical Psychology in Medical Settings, 12*(1), 39–56.

Parker, J. D. A., Taylor, G. J., Bagby, R. M., & Acklin, M. W. (1993). Alexithymia in panic disorder and simple phobia: A comparative study. *The American Journal of Psychiatry, 150*(7), 1105–1107.

Peeters, F., Nicolson, N. A., Berkhof, J., Delespaul, P., & deVries, M. (2003). Effects of daily events on mood states in major depressive disorder. *Journal of Abnormal Psychology, 112*(2), 203–211.

Raes, F., Smets, J., Nelis, S., & Schoofs, H. (2012). Dampening of positive affect prospectively predicts depressive symptoms in non-clinical samples. *Cognition and Emotion, 26*(1), 75–82.

Roemer, L., Litz, B. T., Orsillo, S. M., & Wagner, A. W. (2001). A preliminary investigation of the role of strategic withholding of emotions in PTSD. *Journal of Traumatic Stress, 14*(1), 149–156.

Rude, S. S., & McCarthy, C. T. (2003). Emotional functioning in depressed and depression vulnerable college students. *Cognition and Emotion, 17*(5), 799–806.

Salovey, P., & Mayer, J. D. (1990). Emotional intelligence. *Imagination, Cognition, and Personality, 9*(3), 185–211.

Salters-Pedneault, K., Roemer, L., Tull, M. T., Rucker, L., & Mennin, D. S. (2006). Evidence of broad deficits in emotion regulation associated with chronic worry and generalized anxiety disorder. *Cognitive Therapy and Research, 30*(4), 469–480.

Schulze, L., Domes, G., Krüger, A., Berger, C., Fleischer, M., Prehn, K., … Herpertz, S. C. (2011). Neuronal correlates of cognitive reappraisal in borderline patients with affective instability. *Biological Psychiatry, 69*(6), 564–573.

Schweinhardt, P., Kalk, N., Wartolowska, K., Chessell, I., Wordsworth, P., & Tracey, I. (2008). Investigation into the neural correlates of emotional augmentation of clinical pain. *NeuroImage, 40*(2), 759–766.

Shear, M. K., Cooper, A. M., Lerman, G. L., Busch, F. N., & Shapiro, T. (1993). A psychodynamic model of panic disorder. *The American Journal of Psychiatry, 150*(6), 859–866.

Sifneos, P. E. (1973). The prevalence of 'alexithymic' characteristics in psychosomatic patients. *Psychotherapy and Psychosomatics, 22*(2–6), 255–262.

Sim, L. A. (2002). Emotion regulation in adolescent females with bulimia nervosa: An information processing perspective (Ph.D. dissertation, The University of Maine, Main, United States). Retrieved December 1, 2011, from Dissertations & Theses: Full Text. (Publication No. AAT 3057876).

Sim, L., & Zeman, J. (2004). Emotion awareness and identification skills in adolescent girls with bulimia nervosa. *Journal of Clinical Child and Adolescent Psychology, 33*(4), 760–771.

Sinha, R., Fox, H. C., Hong, K. A., Bergquist, K., Bhagwagar, Z., & Siedlarz, K. M. (2009). Enhanced negative emotion and alcohol craving, and altered physiological responses following stress and cue exposure in alcohol dependent individuals. *Neuropsychopharmacology, 34*(5), 1198–1208.

Smyth, J. M., Wonderlich, S. A., Heron, K. E., Sliwinski, M. J., Crosby, R. D., Mitchell, J. E., & Engel, S. G. (2007). Daily and momentary mood and stress are associated with binge eating and vomiting in bulimia nervosa patients in the natural environment. *Journal of Consulting and Clinical Psychology, 75*(4), 629–638.

Smyth, J. M., Wonderlich, S. A., Sliwinski, M. J., Crosby, R. D., Engel, S. G., & Mitchell, J. E. (2009). Ecological momentary assessment of affect, stress, and binge-purge behaviors: Day of week and time of day effects in the natural environment. *The International Journal of Eating Disorders, 42*(5), 429–436.

Spira, A. P., Zvolensky, M. J., Eifert, G. H., & Feldner, M. T. (2004). Avoidance-oriented coping as a predictor of panic-related distress: A test using biological challenge. *Journal of Anxiety Disorders, 18*(3), 309–323.

Staiger, P. K., Melville, F., Hides, L., Kambouropoulos, N., & Lubman, D. I. (2009). Can emotion-focused coping help explain the link between posttraumatic stress disorder severity and triggers for substance use in young adults? *Journal of Substance Abuse Treatment, 36*(2), 220–226.

Stein, R. I., Kenardy, J., Wiseman, C. V., Dounchis, J. Z., Arnow, B. A., & Wilfley, D. E. (2007). What's driving the binge in binge eating disorder? A prospective examination of precursors and consequences. *The International Journal of Eating Disorders, 40*(3), 195–203.

Subic-Wrana, C., Beutel, M. E., Knebel, A., & Lane, R. D. (2010). Theory of mind and emotional awareness deficits in patients with somatoform disorders. *Psychosomatic Medicine, 72*(4), 404–411.

Subic-Wrana, C., Bruder, S., Thomas, W., Gaus, E., Merkle, W., & Kohle, K. (2002). Distribution of alexithymia as a personality-trait in psychosomatically ill in-patients: Measured with TAS-20 and LEAS. *Psychotherapie, Psychosomatik, Medizinische Psychologie, 52*(11), 454–460.

Subic-Wrana, C., Bruder, S., Thomas, W., Lane, R. D., & Köhle, K. (2005). Emotional awareness deficits in inpatients of a psychosomatic ward: A comparison of two different measures of alexithymia. *Psychosomatic Medicine, 67*(3), 483–489.

Suveg, C., Morelen, D., Brewer, G. A., & Thomassin, K. (2010). The emotion dysregulation model of anxiety: A preliminary path analytic examination. *Journal of Anxiety Disorders, 24*(8), 924–930.

Svaldi, J., Caffier, D., & Tuschen-Caffier, B. (2010). Emotion suppression but not reappraisal increases desire to binge in women with binge eating disorder. *Psychotherapy and Psychosomatics, 79*(3), 188–190.

Svaldi, J., Griepenstroh, J., Tuschen-Caffier, B., & Ehring, T. (2012). Emotion regulation deficits in eating disorders: A marker of eating pathology or general psychopathology? *Psychiatry Research, 197*(1), 103–111.

Swendsen, J. D., Tennen, H., Carney, M. A., Affleck, G., Willard, A., & Hromi, A. (2000). Mood and alcohol consumption: An experience sampling test of the self-medication hypothesis. *Journal of Abnormal Psychology, 109*(2), 198–204.

Thompson, R. A. (1994). Emotion regulation: A theme in search of a definition. *Monographs of the Society for Research in Child Development, 59*(2/3), 25–52.

Tragesser, S. L., Solhan, M., Schwartz-Mette, R., & Trull, T. J. (2007). The role of affective instability and impulsivity in predicting future BPD features. *Journal of Personality Disorders, 21*(6), 603–614.

Tull, M. T., Barrett, H. M., McMillan, E. S., & Roemer, L. (2007). A preliminary investigation of the relationship between emotion regulation difficulties and posttraumatic stress symptoms. *Behavior Therapy, 38*(3), 303–313.

Tull, M. T., & Roemer, L. (2007). Emotion regulation difficulties associated with the experience of uncued panic attacks: Evidence of experiential avoidance, emotional nonacceptance, and decreased emotional clarity. *Behavior Therapy, 38*(4), 378–391.

Turk, C. L., Heimberg, R. G., Luterek, J. A., Mennin, D. S., & Fresco, D. M. (2005). Emotion dysregulation in generalized anxiety disorder: A comparison with social anxiety disorder. *Cognitive Therapy and Research, 29*(1), 89–106.

Walcott, C. M., & Landau, S. (2004). The relation between disinhibition and emotion regulation in boys with attention deficit hyperactivity disorder. *Journal of Clinical Child and Adolescent Psychology, 33*(4), 772–782.

Waller, E., & Scheidt, C. E. (2004). Somatoform disorders as disorders of affect regulation: A study comparing the TAS-20 with non-self-report measures of alexithymia. *Journal of Psychosomatic Research, 57*(3), 239–247.

Waller, E., & Scheidt, C. E. (2006). Somatoform disorders as disorders of affect regulation: A development perspective. *International Review of Psychiatry, 18*(1), 13–24.

Watt, M., Stewart, S., Birch, C., & Bernier, D. (2006). Brief CBT for high anxiety sensitivity decreases drinking problems, relief alcohol outcome expectancies, and conformity drinking motives: Evidence from a randomized controlled trial. *Journal of Mental Health, 15*(6), 683–695.

Weems, C. F., Silverman, W. K., Rapee, R. M., & Pina, A. A. (2003). The role of control in childhood anxiety disorders. *Cognitive Therapy and Research, 27*(5), 557–568.

Weinberg, A., Klonsky, E. D., & Hajcak, G. (2009). Autonomic impairment in borderline personality disorder: A laboratory investigation. *Brain and Cognition, 71*(3), 279–286.

Weiss, R. D., Griffin, M. L., & Mirin, S. M. (1992). Drug abuse as self-medication for depression: An empirical study. *The American Journal of Drug and Alcohol Abuse, 18*(2), 121–129.

Weiss, N. H., Tull, M. T., Davis, L. T., Dehon, E. E., Fulton, J. J., & Gratz, K. L. (2012). Examining the association between emotion regulation difficulties and probable posttraumatic stress disorder within a sample of African Americans. *Cognitive Behaviour Therapy, 41*(1), 5–14.

Whiteside, U., Chen, E., Neighbors, C., Hunter, D., Lo, T., & Larimer, M. (2007). Difficulties regulating emotions: Do binge eaters have fewer strategies to modulate and tolerate negative affect? *Eating Behaviors, 8*(2), 162–169.

Wild, B., Eichler, M., Feiler, S., Friederich, H. C., Hartmann, M., Herzog, W., & Zipfel, S. (2007). Dynamic analysis of electronic diary data of obese patients with and without binge eating disorder. *Psychotherapy and Psychosomatics, 76*(4), 250–252.

Willinger, U., Lenzinger, E., Hornik, K., Fischer, G., Schönbeck, G., Aschauer, H. N., ... European Fluvoxamine in Alcoholism Study Group. (2002). Anxiety as a predictor of relapse in detoxified alcohol-dependent clients. *Alcohol and Alcoholism, 37*(6), 609–612.

Wirtz, C. M., Hofmann, S. G., Riper, H., & Berking, M. (2013). Emotion regulation predicts anxiety over a five-year interval: A cross-lagged panel analysis. *Depression and Anxiety, 30*(11), 1–9.

Wolff, S., Stiglmayr, C., Bretz, H. J., Lammers, C. H., & Auckenthaler, A. (2007). Emotion identification and tension in female patients with borderline personality disorder. *The British Journal of Clinical Psychology, 46*(Pt 3), 347–360.

Wupperman, P., Marlatt, G. A., Cunningham, A., Bown, S., Berking, M., Mulvihill-Rivera, N., & Easton, C. (2012). Mindfulness and modification therapy for behavior dysregulation: Results from a pilot study targeting alcohol use and aggression in women. *Journal of Clinical Psychology, 68*(1), 50–66.

Wupperman, P., Neumann, C. S., Whitman, J. B., & Axelrod, S. R. (2009). The role of mindfulness in borderline personality disorder features. *The Journal of Nervous and Mental Disease, 197*(10), 766–771.

Chapter 3
The Adaptive Coping with Emotions Model (ACE Model)

3.1 Search for a Model of Adaptive Emotion Regulation

After reviewing the evidence for the impact of emotion regulation deficits on mental health, we began looking for a theory of adaptive emotion regulation. It was hoped that such a theory would help identify the key components of emotion regulation that are essential for mental health, which would serve as treatment targets for a broad range of mental health problems. Theoretical models we reviewed for this purpose included theories proposed by Eisenberg and Spinrad (2004), Gottman and Katz (1989), Gross (1998, 2014), Larsen (2000), Lazarus (1991), Leahy (2002), Saarni (1999), Salovey and Mayer (1990), and many others. Each of these theories offered helpful insight into the dynamics of emotion regulation and how adaptive emotion regulation can be conceptualized. However, for the specific purpose of understanding regulation deficits typically found in individuals suffering from mental disorders and developing treatments to help these individuals, none of the available theories of emotion regulation seemed completely satisfying to us. Thus, we developed a new and arguably more helpful model for our clinical purposes. The development of this model was based on the theories just mentioned, empirical research findings, our clinical experience, and reports from numerous patient interviews regarding their difficulties with emotion regulation. This model was named the Adaptive Coping with Emotions (ACE) Model.

3.2 Description of the Adaptive Coping with Emotions Model (ACE Model)

The Adaptive Coping with Emotions Model (ACE Model) was developed to provide a conceptualization of adaptive emotion regulation. By defining healthy emotion regulation, the model helps explain how emotion dysregulation can occur and provides directions for interventions that enhance effective emotion regulation.

M. Berking and B. Whitley, *Affect Regulation Training: A Practitioners' Manual*,
DOI 10.1007/978-1-4939-1022-9_3, © Springer Science+Business Media New York 2014

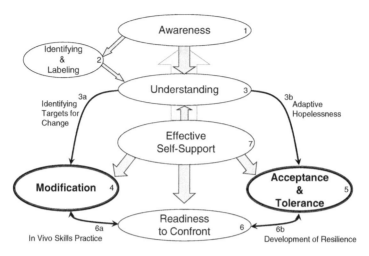

Fig. 3.1 The adaptive coping with emotions model

In this model (see Fig. 3.1), adaptive emotion regulation is conceptualized as a situation-dependent interaction between seven emotion regulation skills.

1. *The ability to be consciously aware of emotions* (Fig. 3.1; Item 1)

    Emotion regulation typically occurs via unconscious automatic processes, as long as affective states remain within a person's comfort zone (Gyurak & Etkin, 2014; Koole & Rothermund, 2011). If, however, aversive emotions cannot be regulated through unconscious processes alone, conscious activities, such as labeling and analyzing emotions, are initiated in order to either solve the problem that triggered the emotion or regulate the emotion when the problem eliciting the emotion cannot be solved (Mauss & Tamir, 2014). Such conscious and effortful processes of emotion regulation are severely impeded when a person has difficulties becoming consciously aware of the emotions they are experiencing. Thus, a lack of conscious emotional awareness can impair effective emotion regulation and contribute to the maintenance of negative emotions (e.g., Sifneos, 1973).

2. *The ability to identify and correctly label emotions* (Fig. 3.1; Item 2)

    Identifying and labeling affective states refers to matching emotional experiences with the appropriate semantic categories (e.g., *This feeling I am experiencing is anger.*). The availability of differentiated cognitive representations of affective states and the ability to correctly assign experiences to these specific categories are helpful for adaptive regulation. For example, recognizing an emotion as anger provides information regarding the purpose of the emotion (e.g., enhancing assertive behavior), its potential risks (cueing aggression that may lead to sanctions through others) and benefits (getting what I want, even if I have to fight for it), as well as information on regulation strategies that are likely to be effective (e.g., distraction, relaxation, reappraisal, and compassion) and strategies that are likely to be ineffective (e.g., prolonged exposure). Thus, accurately identifying and labeling an emotion fosters effective affect regulation and hence mental health and well-being (Barrett, Gross, Christensen, & Benvenuto, 2001).

3. *The ability to identify what causes and maintains an emotion* (Fig. 3.1; Item 3a)
There are several important benefits that come from understanding the various factors that elicit and maintain an affective state. First, identifying what causes and maintains an emotion helps us find meaning in an aversive experience, thereby making it easier to bear. It also clarifies the issue of whether an emotion can or cannot be changed and, if it cannot be changed, encourages acceptance of the emotion as a regulatory strategy. Finally, identifying the causes and maintaining factors of an affective state point to ways in which it can be modified, including changing the internal or external situation that triggered the emotion, modifying the appraisal of the situation, or revising the desires, beliefs, and goals related to the situation (Roseman & Smith, 2001).

4. *The ability to actively modify emotions in an adaptive manner* (Fig. 3.1; Item 4)
The ability to actively modify emotions in an adaptive manner involves changing the quality, intensity, and/or duration of an emotion in a desired manner through the use of strategies that do not have unwanted consequences. This ability reduces the use of dysfunctional regulation strategies that tend to have negative consequences. Being able to modify emotions increases emotional self-efficacy, which reduces anxiety and avoidance about future aversive events and emotions. Empirical research has shown strong associations between peoples' beliefs in their ability to modify their emotions and their mental health (Catanzaro & Greenwood, 1994; Kassel, Bornovalova, & Mehta, 2007). Finally, emotional self-efficacy, which comes from being able to modify emotions, facilitates a willingness to experience emotionally challenging situations that provide additional opportunities to strengthen and reinforce their regulation skills.

5. *The ability to accept and tolerate negative emotions when necessary* (Fig. 3.1; Item 3b/5)
Acceptance and tolerance of unwanted emotions is a crucial skill to have in situations where affective states cannot be changed (at least for the moment) or when changing them would come at too high a price (e.g., time, energy, etc.). While confidence in the ability to modify emotions is important in facilitating a person's well-being, acknowledging that affective states are often very difficult to modify or cannot be modified at all is important as well (Hayes, Wilson, Gifford, Follette, & Strosahl, 1996). Controlling emotions by sheer willpower is difficult because the limbic system (associated with emotional experiencing) has retained a great degree of autonomy from areas of the brain related to purposeful action. Difficulties modifying an emotion can cause a person to feel out of control, resulting in the use of dysfunctional regulation strategies to regain control. Having the ability to accept and tolerate negative emotions, however, reduces the need to use maladaptive strategies to regain control (e.g., Wupperman, Neumann, Whitman, & Axelrod, 2009).

6. *The ability to approach and confront situations likely to trigger negative emotions* (Fig. 3.1; Item 6)

In order to accomplish important personal goals, one must generally be willing to approach and confront situations that are likely to trigger negative emotions (Hayes, Strosahl, & Wilson, 1999). Becoming involved in situations that evoke negative emotions also provides valuable opportunities to hone existing emotion regulation skills while also developing new ones (Fig. 3.1; Item 6a/6b). A willingness to approach and confront difficult situations therefore strengthens emotion regulation capacities that can be applied during times of distress.

7. *The ability to provide effective self-support in distressing situations* (Fig. 3.1; Item 7)

In our clinical work, we frequently witnessed that patients who tried to regulate their emotions with the skills in the Adaptive Coping with Emotions Model often became stuck in the regulation process. Eventually these patients fell back into familiar and dysfunctional strategies to regulate their emotions. When we started thinking about why this happens so frequently, it occurred to us that each of the skills in this model has the potential to *increase* emotional suffering in the short term. For example, conscious awareness of negative emotions commonly results in experiencing painful emotions more intensely. Identifying feelings with labels such as fear, anger, sadness, guilt, etc. tends to evoke distressing emotions that are related to these words. Trying to understand what causes or maintains an emotion often leads to painful acknowledgment of these factors and the many barriers to resolving them. Efforts to modify negative emotions are often unsuccessful, or at least not as successful as expected or desired, which is likely to trigger emotions such as disappointment, frustration, and eventually despair. Accepting and tolerating a negative emotion, instead of fighting against it, can cause feelings of helplessness and cue unrealistic fears of catastrophic consequences of unregulated emotions. Finally, confronting situations that cue negative emotions will of course lead to experiencing distress.

Thus, trying to apply potentially adaptive emotion regulation skills can lead to short-term mood deterioration that some may feel is intolerable. This could compel them to revert to impulsive and dysfunctional ways of emotion regulation that focus on instant relief at the cost of unwanted mid- and long-term consequences (Tice, Bratslavsky, & Baumeister, 2001). Therefore, stabilizing one's mood during the process of emotion regulation seems crucial. In the Adaptive Coping with Emotions Model, we refer to this ability as "effective self-support." In the context of emotion regulation, this skill includes mental or behavioral activities that help keep one's mood within the "window of tolerance" (Siegel, 2012), which enables the individual to persistently utilize skills that are initially aversive but necessary for sustained emotional relief. People certainly differ in how they adaptively manage mood deterioration during the process of emotion regulation. However, based on the scientific literature and our clinical experience we propose three important components of effective self-support.

(a) **Self-compassion:** Compassion can be defined as a warm and strong feeling of empathy that is associated with a desire to help someone who is perceived to be suffering (e.g., Weissman & Weissman, 1996; see also Gilbert, 2009, 2011; Gilbert & Procter, 2006; Neff, 2003). A person can feel compassion toward others or oneself. *Self-compassion* is experienced by a person's "observing self" toward the person's "suffering self." For several reasons, self-compassion can be considered an effective mood stabilizing strategy. First, self-compassion cues empathy toward the self. Empathy is a cognitive-affective state that helps create helpful distance between the observing self and the suffering self. By taking the perspective of the observing self, a person can feel as though it is not him or her who is suffering, but instead it is someone else who is in pain. Second, since self-compassion involves empathy for the suffering self, self-compassion inhibits self-criticism and negative emotions such as guilt or shame that often contribute to mood deterioration during emotion regulation. Third, unlike other emotion regulation strategies, self-compassion may become *easier* to utilize as a person's suffering increases. The reason for this is that it is easier for the observing self to become more compassionate as the suffering self experiences increasing levels of emotional anguish. On the other hand, regulation strategies, such as cognitive reappraisal and acceptance, usually become more difficult to utilize as a person's suffering intensifies, since increasingly higher levels of negative affect likely impede positive reappraisals and the utilization of acceptance. Finally, self-compassion is an effective mood stabilizing strategy because it motivates the observing self to help the suffering self. Such a motivational boost is often needed to successfully engage in further mood stabilizing activities.[1]

(b) **Self-soothing and self-encouragement:** In ART, self-compassion is seen as a motivational force that encourages a person to engage in self-supportive actions through *self-soothing and self-encouragement*. As a kind of inner-cheerleading, self-soothing and self-encouragement involve supportive, sympathetic, friendly, and warm self-talk that (a) empathically validates the emotional reaction and the feeling that the current situation is indeed difficult, (b) offers support, and (c) gives reminders that he/she has successfully coped with difficult emotions in the past. The focus of self-soothing and self-encouragement is on improving one's mood in order to provide the energy and motivation needed for future actions.

(c) **Active self-coaching:** The third component of effective self-support is *active self-coaching*. In active self-coaching, the "observing self" assumes the role of an internalized coach who takes the "suffering self" by the hand and guides it to take helpful actions. While the focus of *self-compassion* and *self-soothing and*

---

[1] Since we consider compassion to be a core component for effective self-support, we have used the term "compassionate self-support" in prior publications.

self-encouragement is on relieving emotional distress by providing validation and emotional support, the focus of active *self-coaching* is on lovingly guiding the suffering self to take actions that are needed in order to solve problems, even if these actions initially cue some negative feelings. For example, the observing self could make statements toward the suffering self such as "Okay, now let's try to find a way out of this! What helpful actions could we take in this situation? What would be a good first step? Okay, then let's go for it one step at a time!"

In addition to this list of skills, the descriptions of how the skills interact, and the rationale for the importance of each skill, the Adaptive Coping with Emotions Model (ACE Model) includes the hypothesis that the skills of **accepting and tolerating negative emotions** and **modifying negative emotions** are the most critical for mental health. The other skills included in the model, such as awareness, are thought to foster mental health only by *facilitating* the successful application of the acceptance/tolerance and modification skills.

While this hypothesis has been confirmed through our research (see next section), it was initially based on our clinical observation that patients often remained dysregulated despite consciously experiencing their emotions and understanding the underlying causes of them. In fact, the use of these regulation strategies often appeared to maintain patients' pathology. For example, we observed that patients who constantly dwelled on their depression and anxiety were already acutely "aware" of their distress. Mere awareness of their distressed states did not appear to help move them out of their suffering. In fact, the constant focus on their negative feelings seemed to intensify these patients' distress and maintained their emotional anguish. We found that only when awareness was used as a stepping stone toward the ultimate goal of acceptance/tolerance or modification did awareness facilitate successful coping (Berking et al., 2012).

The distinction between the two critical skills (acceptance/tolerance and modification) and the other "supportive" skills has important implications for treatment. For example, a frequent goal in psychotherapy is to help patients become more *aware* of their emotions. In fact, television shows and movies often depict psychotherapists badgering their patients with the phrase "And how does this make you feel?" However, a strong therapeutic focus on fostering the skill of emotional awareness may not necessarily improve patients' acceptance/tolerance and modification skills. Thus, therapists should at least assess to what extent the focus on emotional awareness also facilitates acceptance/tolerance and modification capacities. If there is no progress with regard to the latter, therapists may choose to reconsider their approach and perhaps utilize additional techniques that more directly enhance the critical skills of acceptance/tolerance and modification.

An inflexible focus on emotional awareness may be particularly problematic with patients who have great difficulty becoming aware of their emotions, using bodily sensations to deduce what they are feeling, and finding correct labels for their affective states (referred to as "alexithymia" by Sifneos, 1972). Many therapists would automatically consider these deficits an important target in treatment. However, this could result in difficult situations for both the therapist and patient.

**Pitfalls of an inflexible "How does that make you feel?"
approach with an alexithymic patient**

Therapist: How are you feeling?
Patient: Well, … not so good.
Therapist: How would you describe your feelings?
Patient: I don't know … just … not well
Therapist: You said you feel so tense, does this mean you are anxious?
Patient: No, that's not it.
Therapist: What about depressed or angry?
Patient: No, it's not that either.
Therapist: So, what is it then? What are you feeling?
Patient: Well, I don't know. It is just … awful … I mean … not good at all.
Therapist: Well, let's go back to your body. How do you feel in your body?
Patient: Just somehow … awful.
Therapist: Are there emotions connected to the awful feelings you have in your body?
Patient: I am not sure. As I said, I don't feel so well.
Therapist: I am wondering what specific emotions you are experiencing?
Patient: As I said, I don't know.

As the therapist in this scenario continues to explore the patient's feelings, the patient likely will become frustrated at not being able to answer the therapist's questions. If the therapist in this scenario keeps trying to help the patient increase "awareness" of his[2] emotions, chances are the patient will feel like a failure and will start to focus on protecting himself from the aversive therapeutic situation. This will prevent the patient from openly exploring his inner experiences and putting his inner experiences into words. If, in this situation, the therapist does not change tactics, the treatment is unlikely to be successful.

To prevent this scenario, it is helpful to remember that while awareness is an important skill, it is only important in that it facilitates the skills of acceptance/tolerance and modification. Keeping this in mind, the therapist can continue to encourage increased awareness but also work with the level of awareness at which the patient is capable and using even the patient's vague labels for his emotional states (e.g., "not good," "bad," "the

---

[2] To make this manual easier to read, we will alternate the use of masculine and feminine pronouns throughout the manual even though all of the concepts that are discussed apply equally to both genders.

(continued)

(continued)

feeling I cannot identify," etc.). Even with such unspecific labels, all of the other skills of the Adaptive Coping with Emotions Model (ACE Model) can still be practiced and mastered. For example, patients can learn to accept this "awful feeling," to compassionately support themselves when they feel "awful," and to analyze when and why they typically feel "awful" in order to modify this emotion so they feel "better." Therefore, it is important for therapists not to get stuck in a patient's awareness difficulties by using the patient's level of awareness as the therapist helps the patient enhance all of the other regulation skills. As the patient acquires newfound regulation abilities and gains confidence in them, he will eventually feel more comfortable exploring his emotions in greater detail, leading to increased emotional awareness. At the end of such a process, we often experience dialogues similar to the following:

Patient: *Dr. Berking, I started thinking the other day … that the feeling … you know? The feeling we are talking about in here all the time? That maybe this feeling has a lot in common with … a little bit of … I mean, not necessarily anxiety, exactly, but maybe just a little. I think I may feel a little bit anxious. Do you know what I mean?*

Dr. Berking: *Ah, that's very interesting! What about your feeling leads you to believe this might be anxiety?*

3.3   Empirical Evidence for the Adaptive Coping with Emotions Model (ACE Model)

After the Adaptive Coping with Emotions Model had been conceptualized, we developed the Emotion Regulation Skills Questionnaire (ERSQ; Berking & Znoj, 2008) in order to assess the skills included in the model. In numerous studies, the ERSQ (Appendix A) displayed adequate to good internal consistencies (Cronbach's $\alpha = 0.82$–0.94 for the subscales). Results from exploratory and confirmatory factor analyses provide support for the assumed dimensionality of the measure. Additionally, sensitivity to change has been demonstrated in multiple samples of patients undergoing psychotherapy. All of the scales of the ERSQ have demonstrated positive associations with measures of well-being and mental health and negative associations with measures of psychopathology and emotion regulation deficits (Berking, Ebert, Cuijpers, & Hofmann, 2013; Berking et al., 2011, 2012; Berking, Meier, & Wupperman, 2010; Berking, Orth, Wupperman, Meier, & Caspar, 2008; Berking, Wupperman, et al., 2008; Berking & Znoj, 2008; Ebert, Christ, & Berking, 2013; Radkovsky, McArdle, Bockting, & Berking, 2014; Wirtz, Hofmann, Riper, & Berking, 2013).

The use of the ERSQ has shown cross-sectional associations between all of the skills in the Adaptive Coping with Emotions Model and mental health in nonclinical samples (Berking et al., 2012; Berking, Wupperman, et al., 2008; Berking & Znoj, 2008). Moreover, assessments using the ERSQ have shown that clinical patient samples report less successful application of the skills than do nonclinical controls (Berking et al., 2011, 2013; Berking, Wupperman, et al., 2008). Additionally, an increase in successful application of the model skills during cognitive behavior therapy, as measured by the ERSQ, was shown to be associated with greater symptom reduction (Berking, Wupperman, et al., 2008). The differences and correlations reported in these studies were particularly strong for modification and acceptance and tolerance. This finding provides preliminary support for the assumption that these two skills are particularly important for mental health. Moreover, multivariate regression analyses identified that only these two skill areas made a unique contribution when predicting treatment outcome from changes in affect regulation skills (e.g., Berking, Wupperman, et al., 2008).

Finally, in both a clinical and nonclinical sample, the ability to modify emotions completely mediated the associations between symptom severity and all of the skills of the Adaptive Coping with Emotions Model except for the skill of acceptance and tolerance of negative emotions. Only acceptance and tolerance was significantly associated with reduced symptom severity when the mediating effect of modifying emotions was controlled (Berking et al., 2012). The findings of this study suggest that the ability to accept and tolerate negative emotions may contribute significantly to maintaining mental health whether or not acceptance and tolerance facilitates the modification of undesired affective states.

Other studies utilizing the ERSQ as an assessment tool have pointed to the causal effect of emotion regulation deficits on mental health. These studies found that affect regulation skills predicted subsequent indicators of psychopathology over a 2-week and a 5-year period, whereas these indicators did not predict subsequent success in applying affect regulation skills (Berking, Orth, et al., 2008; Berking, Wirtz, Svaldi, & Hofmann 2014; Wirtz et al., 2013). In two additional studies, affect regulation skills assessed through the ERSQ predicted relapse during and after inpatient treatment for alcohol dependency (Berking et al., 2011) as well as the reduction of depressive symptoms in patients treated for major depressive disorder (Radkovsky et al., 2014).

In summary, a large body of evidence supports the hypotheses that the skills included in the Adaptive Coping with Emotions Model help maintain or restore mental health and that the abilities to modify and to accept and tolerate aversive emotions are the most important regulatory skills.

References

Barrett, L. F., Gross, J., Christensen, T. C., & Benvenuto, M. (2001). Knowing what you're feeling and knowing what to do about it: Mapping the relation between emotion differentiation and emotion regulation. *Cognition and Emotion, 15*(6), 713–724.

Berking, M., Ebert, D., Cuijpers, P., & Hofmann, S. G. (2013). Emotion regulation skills training enhances the efficacy of inpatient cognitive behavioral therapy for major depressive disorder: A randomized controlled trial. *Psychotherapy and Psychosomatics, 82*(4), 234–245.

Berking, M., Margraf, M., Ebert, D., Wupperman, P., Hofmann, S. G., & Junghanns, K. (2011). Deficits in emotion-regulation skills predict alcohol use during and after cognitive-behavioral therapy for alcohol dependence. *Journal of Consulting and Clinical Psychology, 79*(3), 307–318.

Berking, M., Meier, C., & Wupperman, P. (2010). Enhancing emotion-regulation skills in police officers: Results of a pilot controlled study. *Behavior Therapy, 41*(3), 329–339.

Berking, M., Orth, U., Wupperman, P., Meier, L., & Caspar, F. (2008). Prospective effects of emotion regulation on emotional adjustment. *Journal of Counseling Psychology, 55*(4), 485–494.

Berking, M., Poppe, C., Luhmann, M., Wupperman, P., Jaggi, V., & Seifritz, E. (2012). Is the association between various emotion-regulation skills and mental health mediated by the ability to modify emotions? Results from two cross-sectional studies. *Journal of Behavior Therapy and Experimental Psychiatry, 43*(3), 931–937.

Berking, M., Wirtz, C. M., Svaldi, J., & Hofmann, S. G. (2014). Emotion regulation predicts depression over five years. *Behaviour Research and Therapy, 57*, 13–20.

Berking, M., Wupperman, P., Reichardt, A., Pejic, T., Dippel, A., & Znoj, H. (2008). Emotion-regulation skills as a treatment target in psychotherapy. *Behaviour Research and Therapy, 46*(11), 1230–1237.

Berking, M., & Znoj, H. (2008). Entwicklung und Validierung eines Fragebogens zur standardisierten Selbsteinschätzung emotionaler Kompetenzen [Development and validation of a self-report measure for the assessment of emotion-regulation skills]. *Zeitschrift für Psychiatrie, Psychologie und Psychotherapie, 56*, 141–152.

Catanzaro, S. J., & Greenwood, G. (1994). Expectancies for negative mood regulation, coping, and dysphoria among college students. *Journal of Counseling Psychology, 41*(1), 34–44.

Ebert, D., Christ, O., & Berking, M. (2013). Entwicklung und validierung eines fragebogens zur emotionsspezifischen selbsteinschätzung emotionaler kompetenzen (SEK-ES). [Development and validation of a self-report instrument for the assessment of emotion-specific regulation skills]. *Diagnostica, 59*(1), 17–32.

Eisenberg, N., & Spinrad, T. L. (2004). Emotion-related regulation: Sharpening the definition. *Child Development, 75*(2), 334–339.

Gilbert, P. (2009). Introducing compassion-focused therapy. *Advances in Psychiatric Treatment, 15*(3), 199–208.

Gilbert, P. (2011). *Compassion focused therapy: The distinctive features*. London: Routledge.

Gilbert, P., & Procter, S. (2006). Compassionate mind training for people with high shame and self-criticism: Overview and pilot study of a group therapy approach. *Clinical Psychology and Psychotherapy, 13*(6), 353–379.

Gottman, J. M., & Katz, L. F. (1989). Effects of marital discord on young children's peer interaction and health. *Developmental Psychology, 25*(3), 373–381.

Gross, J. J. (1998). The emerging field of emotion regulation: An integrative review. *Review of General Psychology, 2*(3), 271–299.

Gross, J. J. (2014). Emotion regulation: Conceptual and empirical foundations. In J. J. Gross (Ed.), *Handbook of emotion regulation* (2nd ed., pp. 3–20). New York, NY: Guilford Press.

Gyurak, A., & Etkin, A. (2014). A neurobiological model of implicit and explicit emotion regulation. In J. J. Gross (Ed.), *Handbook of emotion regulation* (2nd ed., pp. 23–42). New York, NY: Guilford Press.

Hayes, S. C., Strosahl, K. D., & Wilson, K. G. (1999). *Acceptance and commitment therapy. An experiential approach to behavior change*. New York, NY: Guilford Press.

Hayes, S. C., Wilson, K. G., Gifford, E. V., Follette, V. M., & Strosahl, K. (1996). Experiential avoidance and behavioral disorders: A functional dimensional approach to diagnosis and treatment. *Journal of Consulting and Clinical Psychology, 64*(6), 1152–1168.

Kassel, J. D., Bornovalova, M., & Mehta, N. (2007). Generalized expectancies for negative mood regulation predict change in anxiety and depression among college students. *Behaviour Research and Therapy, 45*(5), 939–950.

Koole, S. L., & Rothermund, K. (2011). "I feel better but I don't know why": The psychology of implicit emotion regulation. *Cognition and Emotion, 25*(3), 389–399.

Larsen, R. J. (2000). Toward a science of mood regulation. *Psychological Inquiry, 11*(3), 129–141.

Lazarus, R. S. (1991). *Emotion and adaption*. New York, NY: Oxford University Press.

Leahy, R. L. (2002). A model of emotional schemas. *Cognitive and Behavioral Practice, 9*(3), 177–190.

Mauss, I. B., & Tamir, M. (2014). Emotion goals: How their content, structure, and operation shape emotion regulation. In J. J. Gross (Ed.), *Handbook of emotion regulation* (2nd ed., pp. 350–370). New York, NY: Guilford Press.

Neff, K. (2003). Self-compassion: An alternative conceptualization of a healthy attitude toward oneself. *Self and Identity, 2*(2), 85–101.

Radkovsky, A., McArdle, J. J., Bockting, C. L. H., & Berking, M. (2014). Successful emotion regulation skills application predicts subsequent reduction of symptom severity during treatment of major depressive disorder. *Journal of Consulting and Clinical Psychology*. Advance online publication. http://dx.doi.org/10.1037/a0035828

Roseman, I. J., & Smith, C. A. (2001). Appraisal theory: Overview, assumptions, varieties, controversies. In K. R. Scherer, A. Schorr, & T. Johnstone (Eds.), *Appraisal processes in emotion: Theory, methods, research* (Series in affective science, pp. 3–19). New York, NY: Oxford University Press.

Saarni, C. (1999). *The development of emotional competence*. New York, NY: Guilford Press.

Salovey, P., & Mayer, J. D. (1990). Emotional intelligence. *Imagination, Cognition, and Personality, 9*(3), 185–211.

Siegel, D. J. (2012). *The developing mind: How relationships and the brain interact to shape who we are* (2nd ed.). New York, NY: Guilford Press.

Sifneos, P. E. (1972). *Short-term psychotherapy and emotional crisis*. Cambridge, MA: Harvard University Press.

Sifneos, P. E. (1973). The prevalence of 'alexithymic' characteristics in psychosomatic patients. *Psychotherapy and Psychosomatics, 22*(2–6), 255–262.

Tice, D. M., Bratslavsky, E., & Baumeister, R. F. (2001). Emotional distress regulation takes precedence over impulse control: If you feel bad, do it! *Journal of Personality and Social Psychology, 80*(1), 53–67.

Weissman, S., & Weissman, R. (1996). *Meditation, compassion & loving kindness. An approach to vipassana practice*. York Beach, ME: Samuel Weiser.

Wirtz, C., Hofmann, S. G., Riper, H., & Berking, M. (2013). Emotion regulation predicts anxiety over a five-year interval: A cross-lagged panel analysis. *Depression and Anxiety, 30*(11), 1–9.

Wupperman, P., Neumann, C. S., Whitman, J. B., & Axelrod, S. R. (2009). The role of mindfulness in borderline personality disorder features. *The Journal of Nervous and Mental Disease, 197*(10), 766–771.

Chapter 4
How Do Emotion Regulation Deficits Result in Mental Health Problems?

4.1 Likely Pathways by Which Emotion Regulation Deficits Lead to Mental Disorders

In the previous chapter, we presented a model that describes adaptive emotion regulation. In this chapter we would like to briefly explore the processes involved when deficits in emotion regulation lead to mental disorders. Across various mental disorders, we consider the following pathways to be particularly relevant:

1. Emotion regulation deficits result in negative affective states that are intensified and/or maintained.
   The most straightforward pathway, by which emotion regulation deficits lead to mental disorders, occurs when these deficits result in undesired affective states that reach levels of intensity and duration that meet diagnostic criteria. For example, dysphoria and depressed mood are affective states that, if inadequately regulated, could eventually meet DSM-5 (APA, 2013) criteria for major depressive disorder.

2. Emotion regulation deficits trigger dysfunctional strategies that are included in the diagnostic criteria of mental disorders.
   When faced with an emotionally challenging situation, someone without adequate regulation skills experiences distress not only from their negative emotions but also from a lack of control over their emotions. The need to regain control may eventually trigger dysfunctional cognitive or behavioral strategies intended to immediately reduce the negative emotions, regardless of the long-term consequences of these maladaptive strategies. For example, individuals who are unable to adaptively cope with anxiety commonly utilize avoidant strategies (e.g., withdrawal from feared situations or people) to reduce anxiety. Individuals who are unable to effectively manage feelings of loneliness may drink heavily, and individuals who have difficulties with boredom may engage in overeating. In these cases, the dysfunctional regulation strategy (i.e., behavioral avoidance, alcohol use, overeating) could lead to the development of social phobia, alcohol

M. Berking and B. Whitley, *Affect Regulation Training: A Practitioners' Manual*,
DOI 10.1007/978-1-4939-1022-9_4, © Springer Science+Business Media New York 2014

use disorder, and binge eating disorder, respectively. In this manner, many behavioral and cognitive symptoms of mental disorders can be conceptualized as dysfunctional attempts to attain instant relief from seemingly unbearable emotions in the absence of more adaptive strategies.

3. Emotion regulation deficits result in unregulated emotions that impede self-help attempts to regulate other emotions that are related to mental disorders.
   The third pathway by which emotion regulation deficits can lead to mental disorders occurs when certain unregulated emotions impede efforts to regulate other emotions that eventually meet diagnostic criteria for mental disorders. For example, feelings of hopelessness are often experienced by individuals who suffer from anxiety. If hopelessness is not managed effectively, it can significantly reduce a person's capacity to confront feared situations and thus contribute to the development of an anxiety disorder. Likewise, feelings of anxiety often co-occur with depression. If anxiety is not effectively regulated, these feelings can impede a person's engagement in mood-enhancing, positive activities, such as social events, and thus contribute to the development of major depressive disorder.

In this section, we explored three broad, causal pathways by which emotion regulation difficulties can lead to mental disorders. In the following sections, we will explore these processes in more detail from a biographical perspective.

4.2   ART Developmental Model of Emotion Regulation Deficits

Neither regulation deficits nor mental disorders appear out of nowhere. Instead, they develop over time and under certain circumstances. In order to understand and explain this process more clearly, we devised the ART Developmental Model of Emotion Regulation Deficits, which is based on Klaus Grawe's *Consistency Theory* (Grawe, 2007, pp. 165–348). The model outlines the formation of emotion regulation deficits over the course of a person's life and shows how these deficits can lead to the development of a mental disorder (see Fig. 4.1).

In the biographical perspective used in this model, the *time* axis runs from left to right, with a person's birth on the upper left side, and the first appearance of a mental disorder on the lower right side. The model lists multiple risk factors for the development of mental disorders. Generally, the more risk factors a person has, the greater the likelihood the person will develop a mental disorder.

4.2.1   Early Stage Vulnerabilities: The Influence of Genetics

A person's genetic heritage (Fig. 4.1; Box 1) can set the stage for the future development of a mental disorder, since to a large extent, genes determine the brain's structural development and hence the outcome of information processing involving these

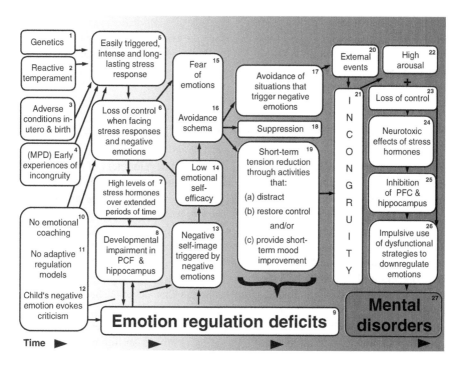

Fig. 4.1 ART developmental model of emotion regulation deficits

structures (Thompson et al., 2001). Although mental disorders cannot be solely attributable to a person's genetic makeup, current research has identified particular genes (e.g., *DRD4, 5-HTTLPR*, etc.) related to various systems in the brain, such as the dopamine and serotonin systems, which likely affect a person's mental health. The findings from this research suggest that when a person with these specific genes experiences environmental stress, such as childhood abuse, they are at greater risk for developing mental disorders (Belsky & Pluess, 2009; Ellis, Boyce, Belsky, Bakermans-Kranenburg, & Van Izendoorn, 2011).

Genetic inheritance determines to a great extent an individual's *temperament* (Fig. 4.1; Box 2), commonly defined as the core of individual differences in style of approach and response to the environment that is stable across time and situations (e.g., van den Akker, Deković, Prinzie, & Asscher, 2010, p. 485). Differences in temperament can be observed very early in life. Some infants are calm, even-tempered, and cheerful by nature. Others tend to have more intense and longer stress reactions. Reactive infants tend to be more easily provoked and more difficult to soothe.

It is important to note that a reactive temperament should not be viewed as inherently dysfunctional. Research suggests that in *unsupportive* environments, children with reactive temperaments have greater *decreases* in functioning than children who have lower reactivity scores (Belsky & Pluess, 2009). Thankfully, however, the same studies also suggest that when children are in *supportive* environments, the ones with reactive temperaments have greater *increases* in functioning than children with lower reactivity scores. Similar findings have also been found in animal research (Suomi, 1991).

4.2.2 Early Environmental Influences

Early environmental influence also plays a role in the development of future mental disorders. Evidence from neuroscience suggests that maternal stress during pregnancy and complications during birth (Fig. 4.1; Box 3) can affect the development of central brain systems responsible for emotion regulation in newborns (e.g., Viltart et al., 2006; Wurmser et al., 2006), causing them to be more emotionally reactive. The process by which these newborns become more emotionally reactive can be viewed as adaptive, since maternal stress probably indicates the child's postnatal environment will be hostile or dangerous. Heightened affect sensitivity in this case could help the child better manage future threats that occur in her environment (Weaver, 2007).

In addition to a child's genetic heritage and experiences in utero, the primary caregiver's behavior and attunement toward the child has an important impact on the development of the child's capacity to regulate her emotion. If the caregiver does not respond appropriately to the child's needs, the child will experience a discrepancy between her needs, wishes, or goals and her perceptions regarding the current fulfillment of her needs, wishes, or goals. We will refer to this discrepancy as "Motivation-Perception Discrepancy" (MPD) (Fig. 4.1; Box 4). For example, MPD would occur when a child wants to feel loved by her parents but instead feels unloved (Grawe, 2004, 2007).

Partly depending on the genetically and environmentally acquired emotional reactivity, MPD can lead to intense stress reactions that mobilize the body and the mind to reduce the discrepancy (Fig. 4.1; Box 5). If attachment figures respond appropriately to the MPD signals of the child (e.g., by satisfying the child's need for nourishment, stimulation, attention, praise, etc.), the stress response is terminated, or at least lessened, by this "external interference." In other words, by reducing the MPD, the attachment figure reduces the *negative affect* that was initiated by the MPD. Young children are highly dependent upon this external regulation of their emotions. Results of developmental psychology and neuroscience research suggest that such external emotion regulation is crucial for the development of neuronal structures that will later help the child self-regulate her emotions (e.g., Hofer, 1984, 1987; Ogawa et al., 1994; Schore & Schore, 2008).

If the child does not receive external regulation support in times of MPD, despite desperate attempts (e.g., crying) to seek support from her caregiver, the child may feel that she cannot control her environment. Physiologically, the experience of *uncontrollable* stress (Fig. 4.1; Box 6) initiates processes in the brain and in the body that are different than those associated with *controllable* stress. A response to *controllable* stress is characterized by an increase in adrenalin and noradrenalin (Huether, 1998). These hormones increase "…heart rate and force of contraction, peripheral vasoconstriction, and energy mobilization" (Ulrich-Lai & Herman, 2009, p. 398). As the stress becomes perceived as *uncontrollable*, there is an increased release of cortisol in addition to the release of adrenaline and noradrenalin (Huether, 1998).

Cortisol levels are moderated in part by glucocorticoid receptors in the hippocampus. Research has found that childhood abuse (i.e., uncontrollable stress) negatively impacts the expression of glucocorticoid receptors, which contributes to sustained increases in cortisol levels (McGowan et al., 2009). Cortisol has been shown to have a neurotoxic effect on the prefrontal cortex (PFC) and hippocampus (Wolf, 2008) (Fig. 4.1; Box 7), which are two brain regions crucial for the down-regulation of stress reactions and negative emotions. Both human and animal research suggests that frequent and sustained increases in cortisol levels have long-lasting negative effects on these two areas of the brain (Lupien, McEwen, Gunnar, & Heim, 2009). Individuals who experience frequent and sustained increases in cortisol levels may end up with lasting negative effects on the brain's "hardware" crucial for emotion regulation (Graham, Heim, Goodman, Miller, & Nemeroff, 1999; Nemeroff, 2004; Fig. 4.1; Boxes 8 and 9).

4.2.3 Deficits in Parental Coaching and Modeling of Emotion Regulation

Children primarily learn emotion regulation skills through interactions with their parents or caregivers. For children with reactive temperaments, parents and caregivers play an especially crucial role in the development of a child's regulatory capacities. Unfortunately, parents and caregivers often fail to provide adequate support for a child's emotional development in the following ways:

(a) Insufficient emotional coaching (Fig. 4.1; Box 10)
(b) Insufficient modeling of effective emotion regulation skills (Fig. 4.1; Box 11)
(c) Criticism of the child when the child displays negative emotions (Fig. 4.1; Box 12)

The following section will address each of these three concepts in detail:

(a) **Insufficient emotional coaching** (Fig. 4.1; Box 10)
    Effective parenting includes being aware of and responding appropriately to the emotional signals of a child. When a child experiences positive emotions, the parent has an opportunity to encourage the emotion and the experience that facilitated it (e.g., "Look how proud you are of yourself! Although this was difficult, you kept trying, and you finally did it!"). When a child experiences negative emotions, the parent has an opportunity to coach the child in regulation

strategies. Coaching a child in emotion regulation can be thought of as a process that may contain the following elements:

- Attuning to the current inner experience of the child and his distress signals.
- Approaching the child in an accepting and nonjudgmental manner (e.g., *The caregiver kneels down next to the child with an empathic, friendly expression and puts a hand softly on the child's shoulder.*).
- Effectively communicating to the child that his distress signals have been perceived and the caregiver is there to help with his problem as well as his distress related to the problem (e.g., *"What's this? Are you crying?"*).
- Helping the child identify and label his emotions. The caregiver can accomplish this by proposing several names for the emotions the child is likely experiencing. This begins to build the child's emotional vocabulary. An ever-expanding emotional vocabulary will assist the developing child as he learns to accurately identify and then effectively manage his emotions (*"Why are you crying? Are you sad?"*).
- Asking the child questions about the cause of his distress (*"What happened? Did Tom take away your favorite car?"*).
- Empathically validating the child's reaction and providing an explanation of why the emotion occurred. This helps normalize negative emotions and provides insight into the causes of emotions (*"So, he took the car you were waiting a long time to play with? I can imagine that made you sad and angry, didn't it."*).
- Offering support and brainstorming effective strategies to help the child cope with his emotion (*"I am sorry you are feeling sad and angry. Shall we see what we can do about this? Would you feel better if we tried to talk to Tom about letting you play with the car?"*).
- Reinforcing effective strategies (*"See, now you got it back! It was a good idea to get somebody to help you with this."*).
- Encouraging the child to keep trying and look for other solutions if the first one does not work (*"Never fear! We will find a way. If this does not work, let's see what else we can do."*).
- Addressing ways of accepting the current situation if the situation (for the time being) cannot be changed (*"If it is really Tom's turn to play with the car and we cannot get it back right now, would you like to play with the fire engine instead? I don't know about you, but I like the fire engine better than the car anyway."*).

Through this kind of *emotional coaching*, in the context of a strong bond with the parent, a child can learn how to be aware of, identify, label, and accept his emotions, as well as learn ways to support himself in emotionally charged situations. With this foundation, the child is then able to experiment with various strategies for regulating and tolerating distressing emotions. In the absence of such emotional coaching due to neglect or a lack of parental skills, it will be very difficult for the child to develop effective emotion regulation strategies.

(b) **Insufficient modeling of effective emotion regulation skills** (Fig. 4.1; Box 11)
    In addition to the emotion regulation coaching provided by parents and caregivers, children also learn to manage their emotions by observing how others around them, especially their caregivers, manage their own emotions. For example, if a son sees his father cry without embarrassment about a significant loss, the son may also learn to accept and validate his own feelings of sadness, just as his father did. However, if the son sees his father get drunk after a loss to avoid experiencing sadness, the child may learn that painful feelings are too scary to feel and that alcohol use is an effective strategy to avoid feeling sad.

(c) **Criticism of the child when the child displays negative emotions** (Fig. 4.1; Box 12)
    Without effective emotion regulation skills, a child may display frequent and intense affective reactions (e.g., crying, screaming, or outbursts of rage) when in distress. These forms of behaviors may become a considerable source of stress for caregivers, especially if the caregivers themselves have difficulties regulating their own emotions. In this type of scenario, the chances are high that caregivers will respond to the child's intense signals of distress with anger.
    If the caregiver cannot effectively regulate his/her anger, it will likely turn into aggressive behavior toward the child such as criticism (e.g., *Stop whining, you little brat!*) or even physical abuse (e.g., hitting the child for crying). The criticism and abuse invalidates the child's emotions by inferring that the child should not feel the way she does (Linehan, 1993). When her emotional experience is invalidated, the child is prevented from exploring the underlying causes of her emotions. This results in severe deficits in the child's ability to accept and regulate her negative emotions.
    Through frequent pairing of the child's negative emotions with the parent's invalidating verbal or physical attacks, the child may develop a negative self-image that is strongly associated with the experience of negative emotions. Therefore, when the child experiences negative emotions in the future, the negative self-image (Fig. 4.1; Box 13) could be activated automatically. The negative self-image is likely to trigger additional distressing feelings (e.g., guilt, shame, or fear of others' reactions). These "secondary" emotions may further impair the regulation of distressing "primary" negative emotions and undermine the development of emotion-related self-efficacy (Fig. 4.1; Box 14).
    While it is important to understand the negative consequences that can occur if a parent does not nurture a child's emotional needs, it is also important to emphasize the positive impact that attuned and nurturing parenting has on a child's emotion regulation abilities (reviewed by Morris, Silk, Steinberg, Myers, & Robinson, 2007). Recently, neuroscience research has found evidence for the positive effects of nurturing parenting on the emotion regulation capacities of a child's brain. For example, in a longitudinal study nurturing parenting was found to significantly predict the future volume of a child's hippocampus, which is a brain region involved in effective emotion regulation (Luby et al., 2012). Further evidence for the positive impact of nurturing parenting comes from animal research which found that rats with nurturing mothers (mothers that licked

their pups and arched their backs while nursing) had increased hippocampal glucocorticoid receptor expression compared with rats whose mothers did not exhibit these nurturing behaviors. These nurtured rats were less fearful and had a decreased stress response compared to the rats which were not nurtured by their mothers (Weaver, 2007; Weaver et al., 2004). Therefore, research involving humans and animals proves that nurturing parenting has a powerful and positive effect on children's emotion regulation abilities.

4.2.4   Avoidance

Negative emotions are by definition aversive. Without effective emotion regulation skills, these aversive emotions will be perceived as uncontrollable. A perceived loss of control often cues fear and panic (Fig. 4.1; Box 15), which typically trigger avoidant strategies (Fig. 4.1; Box 16). The various types of avoidant strategies can arguably be classified into the following three categories:

1. **Situational avoidance** (Fig. 4.1; Box 17)
   One way to avoid unpleasant and uncontrollable affective states is to avoid the situations that trigger these states. For example, someone who experiences anxiety in social situations may simply choose to avoid interactions with others. This avoidant strategy is extremely effective in reducing anxiety. However, this strategy will also limit opportunities to attain personal goals. For instance, avoiding job interviews or social interactions would in fact reduce distress felt by a person with social anxiety, but these avoidant behaviors would also hinder fulfillment of personal goals such as financial stability and supportive friendships.

2. **Suppression** (Fig. 4.1; Box 18)
   Suppression is often used to avoid aversive and uncontrollable emotions. This strategy decreases the internal distress caused by an emotion by preventing it from entering conscious awareness where it would be felt and experienced. Although suppression may work under certain circumstances and for limited amounts of time (e.g., Bonanno, Papa, Lalande, Westphal, & Coifman, 2004), research suggests that suppression may also backfire and lead to the paradoxical effect of intensifying and maintaining painful emotions (e.g., Campbell-Sills, Barlow, Brown, & Hofmann, 2006; Feldner, Zvolensky, Eifert, & Spira, 2003; Feldner, Zvolensky, Stickle, Bonn-Miller, & Leen-Feldner, 2006; Hayes et al., 2004; Levitt, Brown, Orsillo, & Barlow, 2004; Liverant, Brown, Barlow, & Roemer, 2008).

3. **Short-term tension reduction through activities that (a) distract, (b) restore a sense of control, or (c) provide short-term mood improvement** (Fig. 4.1; Box 19):

   (a) **Activities that distract**
      Distraction (Fig. 4.1; Box 19a) involves various processes that shift attention away from painful emotions onto often-unrelated targets (Gross, 1998). Short, intermittent episodes of distraction (e.g., taking a break from a frustrating task)

are adaptive when they are intentionally used to reduce negative emotions while still being willing to accept and tolerate these emotions. Utilized in this manner, distraction can be a highly effective regulation technique.

However, distraction may become harmful when it becomes a chronic reaction to negative emotions that is motivated by an inflexible and fear-driven unwillingness to experience a negative emotion and involves maladaptive behaviors. For example, distraction from painful emotions can take the form of a pathological focus on body sensations, to the extent that even slight (and entirely natural) bodily changes or discomforts are misinterpreted as symptoms of physical health problems. Other forms of distraction may include a fixation on weight loss or over-involvement in work.

(b) **Activities that restore a sense of control**
People often engage in a variety of activities (Fig. 4.1; Box 19b) to avoid feeling out of control. For example, worry can be conceptualized as a strategy used to restore control. When a person worries, he is constantly thinking about all of the possible threats he could encounter and ways he could prepare himself for these threats. This process provides some reassurance that he is well prepared for any potential threat, which may, to some extent, restore his sense of control. Similarly, thoughts of self-blame, commonly found in mental disorders, such as depression and posttraumatic stress disorder, are also often utilized to avoid feeling out of control. When a person encounters challenging circumstances, it can feel unsettling if the cause of the negative situation cannot be easily assigned to someone or something. In these cases, relief may be sought by blaming oneself for the troubles. The self-blame is likely to cue other negative feelings, but for a person who feels out of control, the negative feelings from self-blame may seem a small price to pay for a semblance of control.

(c) **Activities that provide short-term mood improvement**
Individuals may also engage in mental activities, which temporarily provide mood improvement and/or reduce internal tension (Fig. 4.1; Box 19c) but result in long-term negative consequences. An example of one such activity is the use of hopelessness by an individual who is facing challenging life circumstances. When encountering difficult situations, most people will feel an internal pressure to fix their problems. The more intense people's problems are, the more pressure they are likely to place on themselves to resolve them. People often believe they "must" or "should" (Ellis, 1962) be able to find solutions, which only increases their sense of urgency for resolution. The intense pressure they place on themselves is hard to bear for very long.

Declaring the situation to be "uncontrollable" and giving in to feeling *hopeless* is often used to reduce the pressure of finding resolution by someone who has tried long and hard to resolve her problems without success. By resigning to feelings of hopelessness, she accepts the fact she is not able to change her current dilemma and the situation is unlikely to change any time soon. Hopelessness also gives her permission to finally rest from the disappointing and exhausting task of trying unsuccessfully to solve her problems.

While hopelessness may provide relief in some ways for a person who is unsuccessful in resolving negative circumstances, the "giving up" aspect of hopelessness could also lead to the development of depression (Teasdale & Barnard, 1993). In the same manner as depression, almost any mental disorder can be conceptualized as resulting from the use of activities that provide short-term reduction in negative affect (substance use, binge eating, self-induced vomiting, compulsive gambling/sex, self-harm behavior, etc.) but have long-lasting negative consequences for a person's mental health (e.g., see Chapman, Gratz, & Brown, 2006).

We have just presented three (sometimes overlapping) categories of avoidant strategies: (1) situation avoidance, (2) suppression of emotions, and (3) short-term tension reduction through activities that (a) distract, (b) restore a sense of control, and/or (c) provide short-term mood improvement. Avoidant strategies are commonly used for the simple reason that they can, at least temporarily, reduce negative emotions in the absence of other more adaptive strategies. In fact, avoidance often works so well that individuals tend to rely on it without developing other more adaptive regulatory strategies. Also, for adults who did not have adequate opportunities as children to learn effective emotion regulation skills, avoidance may be the only regulatory tool available to them. A vicious cycle then develops as the absence of adaptive strategies increases avoidance, which further decreases their use of adaptive strategies and so on. Thus, avoidance is likely to perpetuate the regulatory deficits that began in childhood into adulthood.

4.2.5   Exposure to Events Creating Incongruity: An Important Trigger Mechanism

The lack of adaptive emotion regulation strategies, maintained by avoidance, becomes problematic when individuals are suddenly faced with a challenging circumstance (Fig. 4.1; Box 20) in which there is a large discrepancy between what they *want to experience* and what *they actually experience*. As described before, we refer to this incongruity as "Motivation-Perception Discrepancy" (MPD) (Fig. 4.1; Box 21). MPD may refer to circumstances that are either internal (feeling fearful when they want to feel confident) or external (losing a job when they want secure employment), based on one event (death of a relative), or based on multiple events (marital conflict, financial problems, occupational problems, etc.). The consequences of acute MPD will be described in the following section.

4.2.6   Consequences of Motivation-Perception Discrepancy (MPD)

When individuals who commonly avoid negative emotions whenever possible encounter intense MPD, their routine avoidant strategies may become overloaded and cease to function adequately. For example, a business manager who has always successfully distracted himself from negative emotions by focusing on his work may not be able to do so anymore when he loses his job, his wife divorces him, and he is forced to sell his home. Such difficult circumstances will likely elicit a strong stress response that is associated with a high degree of physiological arousal and very strong negative emotions that are too strong to be successfully suppressed for an extended period of time (Fig. 4.1; Box 22).

As part of the stress response, the brain begins assessing whether the current circumstance that initiated the MPD can be controlled or not. There are two types of control a person can have to resolve MPD. The first type is what we call "primary control," which refers to the ability to resolve MPD by either fulfilling a goal related to the current situation (e.g., finding a new job after being laid off) or giving up on a goal related to the current situation (e.g., quit trying to find a new job).

The second type of control that a person can achieve to resolve MPD is what we call "secondary control," which refers to the ability to manage the negative consequences of the MPD. In psychotherapy, patients often seek help for problems over which they are unlikely to achieve primary control. For example, a bereaved widower will not be able to have his wife back in his life and may also not be able to give up the desire for her to return. Similarly, an unemployed person may find it very difficult (and not helpful in the long run) to give up the goal of finding a new job. In instances like these, where the present circumstances cannot be changed, the attainment of secondary control becomes crucial in resolving MPD. The widower, for example, could achieve secondary control by successfully managing the consequences of his bereavement (e.g., by accepting his sadness and constructively processing his grief), and the unemployed person could accept his fear of long-term unemployment and use it as motivation to actively look for a new job. However, without access to effective emotion regulation skills, secondary control is very difficult to achieve.

If a person is unable to attain either primary or secondary control (Fig. 4.1; Box 23), he will experience a highly aversive state, since his basic need of avoiding pain and his basic need for feeling in control have been violated (Epstein, 1990; Grawe, 2004). This will increase the pressure to end this seemingly uncontrollable anguish through the use of strategies that are effective in the short term although they have long-term negative consequences (e.g., reducing inner pressure through depresso-genic thinking, drinking alcohol to reduce anxiety, binging to reduce dysphoria; Tice, Bratslavsky, & Baumeister, 2001).

Biologically, the unresolved MPD they experience will trigger a strong stress response in the brain (Fig. 4.1; Box 24). This response will include elevated levels of stress hormones such as noradrenalin, dopamine, and cortisol. These hormones can impair functioning in the prefrontal cortex and in the hippocampus (Arnsten, 2009; McEwen, 1998); (Fig. 4.1; Box 25). Both the prefrontal cortex (Sapolsky, 2004) and the hippocampus (Grawe, 2007) play important roles in the regulation of cognitive, emotional, and behavioral responses. Here is a brief outline that describes how impairment in these brain regions can lead to emotion dysregulation:

Say, for example, one day a driver is speeding down the road when suddenly he hears a car horn and then immediately becomes involved in a car accident. Through the classical conditioning (Pavlov, 1927) that occurred during the accident, the sound of the horn (now a conditioned stimulus) is associated with a threatening situation by the amygdala, which generates a state of fear (conditioned response). According to LeDoux (2002), this conditioned response will never be extinguished from the amygdala, so the sound of a horn will always be associated with fear.

Thankfully, however, the driver in the accident will not be paralyzed with fear every time he hears a car horn, since the prefrontal cortex and hippocampus will be able to inhibit the state of fear generated by the amygdala. When in the future this person hears a car horn, his hippocampus will review the memory stored from the prior car accident and check to see if the car horn represents a threat to his *current* situation by comparing the context of the past and the present situations. The executive processes of the prefrontal cortex will also help to determine if the car horn is just another noise in the city or a signal of danger. If the hippocampus and the prefrontal cortex determine that the car horn, heard in the present, does not represent a current threat, these regions will inhibit the state of fear generated by the amygdala.[1]

Although we are not aware, the hippocampus and prefrontal cortex are continually checking the threat signals from the amygdala to see if they are justified and inhibiting them if they are not. Now, what would happen if the person in our scenario is frequently unable to achieve the "primary" or "secondary" control that we discussed earlier, resulting in sustained stress hormone levels? As you can guess, the stress hormones will limit the ability of these regions to inhibit amygdala activation while, at the same time, they will actually increase amygdala functioning (Arnsten, 2009), so the sound of a car horn may frequently cause this person to experience intense fear (Davidson, 2000).

The stress-induced reduction of prefrontal and hippocampal function will reduce an individual's self-management capacities. In particular, the individual will have greater difficulty resisting impulses to reduce aversive affective states by any means necessary, including dysfunctional ones that have unwanted, long-term consequences (Fig. 4.1; Box 26). Thus, the combination of unregulated anguish, a lack of perceived control, and the reduction of self-management capacities creates the "perfect storm" that initiates the use of dysfunctional ways to regulate emotions, including suppression, rumination, worry, self-blame, using drugs, self-harming behavior, focusing on body issues such as weight, avoiding feared situations, binging, purging, and avoiding feared stimuli. If the individual fails to replace these strategies with adaptive emotion regulation strategies, they will perpetuate and contribute to the development and maintenance of mental disorders (Fig. 4.1; Box 27).

---

[1] We realize that while it is scientifically inaccurate to anthropomorphize brain regions, we will occasionally do so as we found it to be a very effective way to get participants interested in how their emotions work and to provide them with a sense of understanding, which fosters their sense of control.

References

American Psychiatric Association. (2013). *Diagnostic and statistical manual of mental disorders* (5th ed.). Washington, DC: Author.

Arnsten, A. F. T. (2009). Stress signalling pathways that impair prefrontal cortex structure and function. *Nature Reviews. Neuroscience, 10*(6), 410–422.

Belsky, J., & Pluess, M. (2009). Beyond diathesis stress: Differential susceptibility to environmental influences. *Psychological Bulletin, 135*(6), 885–908.

Bonanno, G., Papa, A., Lalande, K., Westphal, M., & Coifman, K. (2004). The importance of being flexible: The ability to both enhance and suppress emotional expression predicts long-term adjustment. *Psychological Science, 15*(7), 482–487.

Campbell-Sills, L., Barlow, D. H., Brown, T. A., & Hofmann, S. G. (2006). Effects of suppression and acceptance on emotional responses of individuals with anxiety and mood disorders. *Behaviour Research and Therapy, 44*(9), 1251–1263.

Chapman, A. L., Gratz, K. L., & Brown, M. Z. (2006). Solving the puzzle of deliberate self-harm: The experiential avoidance model. *Behaviour Research and Therapy, 44*(3), 371–394.

Davidson, R. J. (2000). Affective style, psychopathology, and resilience: Brain mechanisms and plasticity. *American Psychologist, 55*(11), 1196–1214.

Ellis, A. (1962). *Reason and emotion in psychotherapy*. New York, NY: Stuart.

Ellis, B. J., Boyce, W. T., Belsky, J., Bakermans-Kranenburg, M. J., & Van Izendoorn, M. H. (2011). Differential susceptibility to the environment: An evolutionary-neurodevelopmental theory. *Development and Psychopathology, 23*(1), 7–28.

Epstein, S. (1990). Cognitive-experiential self-theory. In L. Pervin (Ed.), *Handbook of personality theory: Theory and research* (pp. 165–192). New York, NY: Guilford Press.

Feldner, M. T., Zvolensky, M. J., Eifert, G. H., & Spira, A. P. (2003). Emotional avoidance: An experimental test of individual differences and response suppression using biological challenge. *Behaviour Research and Therapy, 41*(4), 403–411.

Feldner, M. T., Zvolensky, M. J., Stickle, T. R., Bonn-Miller, M. O., & Leen-Feldner, E. (2006). Anxiety sensitivity—Physical concerns as moderator of the emotional consequences of emotion suppression during biological challenge: An experiential test using individual growth curve analysis. *Behaviour Research and Therapy, 44*(2), 249–272.

Graham, Y. P., Heim, C., Goodman, S. H., Miller, A. H., & Nemeroff, C. B. (1999). The effects of neonatal stress on brain development: Implications for psychopathology. *Development and Psychopathology, 11*(3), 545–565.

Grawe, K. (2004). *Psychological therapy*. Cambridge, MA: Hogrefe & Huber.

Grawe, K. (2007). *Neuropsychotherapy*. New York, NY: Psychology Press.

Gross, J. J. (1998). The emerging field of emotion regulation: An integrative review. *Review of General Psychology, 2*(3), 271–299.

Hayes, S. C., Strosahl, K., Wilson, K. G., Bissett, R. T., Pistorello, J., Toarmino, D., ... McCurry, S. M. (2004). Measuring experiential avoidance: A preliminary test of a working model. *Psychological Record, 54*(4), 553–578.

Hofer, M. A. (1984). Relationships as regulators: A psychobiologic perspective on bereavement. *Psychosomatic Medicine, 46*(3), 183–197.

Hofer, M. A. (1987). Early social relationships: A psychobiologist's view. *Child Development, 58*(3), 633–647.

Huether, G. (1998). Stress and the adaptive self-organization of neuronal connectivity during early childhood. *International Journal of Developmental Neuroscience, 16*(3), 297–306.

LeDoux, J. E. (2002). *Synaptic self: How our brains become who we are*. New York, NY: Penguin.

Levitt, J. T., Brown, T. A., Orsillo, S. M., & Barlow, D. H. (2004). The effects of acceptance versus suppression of emotion on subjective and psychophysiological response to carbon dioxide challenge in patients with panic disorder. *Behavior Therapy, 35*(4), 747–766.

Linehan, M. M. (1993). *Cognitive-behavioral treatment of borderline personality disorder*. New York, NY: Guilford Press.

Liverant, G. I., Brown, T. A., Barlow, D. H., & Roemer, L. (2008). Emotion regulation in unipolar depression: The effects of acceptance and suppression of subjective emotional experience on the intensity and duration of sadness and negative affect. *Behaviour Research and Therapy, 46*(11), 1201–1209.

Luby, J. L., Barch, D. M., Belden, A., Gaffrey, M. S., Tillman, R., Babb, C., … & Botteron, K. N. (2012). Maternal support in early childhood predicts larger hippocampal volumes at school age. *Proceedings of the National Academy of Sciences, 109*(8), 2854–2859.

Lupien, S. J., McEwen, B. S., Gunnar, M. R., & Heim, C. (2009). Effects of stress throughout the lifespan on the brain, behaviour and cognition. *Nature Reviews. Neuroscience, 10*(6), 434–445.

McEwen, B. S. (1998). Protective and damaging effects of stress mediators. *The New England Journal of Medicine, 338*(3), 171–179.

McGowan, P. O., Sasaki, A., D'Alessio, A. C., Dymov, S., Labonté, B., Szyf, M., … Meaney, M. (2009). Epigenetic regulation of the glucocorticoid receptor in human brain associates with childhood abuse. *Nature Neuroscience, 12*(3), 342–348.

Morris, A. S., Silk, J. S., Steinberg, L., Myers, S. S., & Robinson, L. R. (2007). The role of the family context in the development of emotion regulation. *Social Development, 16*(2), 361–368.

Nemeroff, C. B. (2004). Neurobiological consequences of childhood trauma. *Journal of Clinical Psychiatry, 65*(Suppl. 1), 18–28.

Ogawa, T., Mikuni, M., Kuroda, Y., Muneoka, K., Miori, K. J., & Takahashi, K. (1994). Periodic maternal deprivation alters stress response in adult offspring, potentiates the negative feedback regulation of restraint stress induced adrenocortical response and reduces the frequencies of open field-induced behaviors. *Pharmacology, Biochemistry, and Behavior, 49*(4), 961–967.

Pavlov, I. P. (1927). *Conditioned reflexes: An investigation of the physiological activity of the cerebral cortex* (G. V. Anrep, Ed. & Trans.). London: Oxford University Press.

Sapolsky, R. M. (2004). The frontal cortex and the criminal justice system. *Philosophical Transactions of the Royal Society of London. Series B, Biological Sciences, 359*(1451), 1787–1796.

Schore, J. R., & Schore, A. N. (2008). Modern attachment theory: The central role of affect regulation in development and treatment. *Journal of Clinical Social Work, 36*(1), 9–20.

Suomi, S. J. (1991). Up-tight and laid-back monkeys: Individual differences to social challenges. In S. Brauth, W. Hall, & R. Dooling (Eds.), *Plasticity of development* (pp. 27–56). Cambridge, MA: MIT Press.

Teasdale, J. D., & Barnard, P. J. (1993). *Affect, cognition and change: Re-modelling depressive thought*. Hove, UK: Lawrence Erlbaum Associates.

Thompson, P. M., Cannon, T. D., Narr, K. L., Van Erp, T., Poutanen, V. P., Huttunen, M., … & Toga, A. W. (2001). Genetic influences on brain structure. *Nature Neuroscience, 4*(12), 1253–1258.

Tice, D. M., Bratslavsky, E., & Baumeister, R. F. (2001). Emotional distress regulation takes precedence over impulse control: If you feel bad, do it! *Journal of Personality and Social Psychology, 80*(1), 53–67.

Ulrich-Lai, Y. M., & Herman, J. P. (2009). Neural regulation of endocrine and autonomic stress responses. *Nature Reviews. Neuroscience, 10*(6), 397–409.

van den Akker, A. L., Deković, M., Prinzie, P., & Asscher, J. J. (2010). Toddlers' temperament profiles: Stability and relations to negative and positive parenting. *Journal of Abnormal Child Psychology, 38*(4), 485–495.

Viltart, O., Mairesse, J., Darnaudery, M., Louvart, H., Vanbesien-Mailliot, C., Catalani, A., & Maccari, S. (2006). Prenatal stress alters Fos protein expression in hippocampus and locus coeruleus stress-related brain structures. *Psychoneuroendocrinology, 31*(6), 769–780.

Weaver, I. C. G. (2007). Epigenetic programming by maternal behavior and pharmacological intervention. Nature versus nurture: Let's call the whole thing off. *Epigenetics, 2*(1), 22–28.

Weaver, I. C. G., Cervoni, N., Champagne, F. A., D'Alessio, A. C., Sharma, S., Seckl, J. R., ... Meaney, M. J. (2004). Epigenetic program by maternal behavior. *Nature Neuroscience, 7*(8), 847–854.

Wolf, O. T. (2008). The influence of stress hormones on emotional memory: Relevance for psychopathology. *Acta Psychologica, 127*(3), 513–531.

Wurmser, H., Rieger, M., Domogalla, C., Kahnt, A., Buchwald, J., Kowatsch, M., ... von Voss, H. (2006). Association between life stress during pregnancy and infant crying in the first six months postpartum: A prospective longitudinal study. *Early Human Development, 82*(5), 341–349.

Chapter 5
Overview of Current Treatments that Enhance Emotion Regulation Skills

In the last chapter, we explored the origins of emotion regulation skills deficits and discussed the empirical and theoretical support for the ways in which these deficits contribute to the development of mental disorders. Therefore, it can be hypothesized that enhancing emotion regulation skills should be an important target in the treatment of mental health problems. In this chapter, we will provide an overview of the current state of psychological orientations and treatments that in various ways target emotion regulation skills.

Virtually all forms of psychotherapy implicitly or explicitly strive to improve affect regulation skills. In some therapies, such as person-centered or psychodynamic psychotherapy, affect regulation skills are not explicitly targeted but can be assumed to be enhanced through general techniques used in the process of therapy. For example, unconditional positive regard for the patient is a classic technique of person-centered therapy, while psychodynamic therapists help patients gain insight into unresolved family-of-origin issues. Through these two techniques, patients may learn to accept undesired emotions as they follow the therapist's example or find an explanation for their affective responses.

In other treatments, such as cognitive behavior therapy (CBT), therapists explicitly work to enhance emotion regulation skills. Consistently, such skills have been shown to improve during CBT (Berking et al., 2008). In CBT, a therapist mostly focuses on a patient's thoughts and behaviors in order to modify the affective state that is related to the patient's symptoms. This focus of CBT, in its traditional form, may limit the inclusion of other potentially effective techniques (e.g., the empty chair technique). Also, while CBT encourages patients to apply cognitive behavioral skills to other distressing emotions, the focus of treatment is primarily on the patient's presenting problem and not on enhancing the patient's *general* emotion regulation capabilities.

With increasing evidence that emotion regulation skills are important for mental health, several "third wave" (Hayes, 2004) cognitive and behavioral therapies have been developed that focus more on enhancing emotion regulation skills. For example, dialectical behavior therapy (DBT, Linehan, 1993) is arguably one of the first and most influential treatments to explicitly teach patients adaptive emotion regulation

M. Berking and B. Whitley, *Affect Regulation Training: A Practitioners' Manual*,
DOI 10.1007/978-1-4939-1022-9_5, © Springer Science+Business Media New York 2014

skills, such as identifying, accepting, and modifying emotions. Another such "third wave" therapy is acceptance and commitment therapy (ACT; Hayes, Strohsal, & Wilson, 1999), which focuses on reducing experiential avoidance of aversive experiences, such as undesired emotions, and facilitates the pursuit and attainment of important personal goals. A final example is mindfulness-based cognitive therapy (MBCT; Segal, Williams, & Teasdale, 2013). Originally designed as a group intervention to prevent relapses of depression, MBCT encourages patients to become more aware of mental phenomena, such as their feelings, and to view them as "… mental events rather than as aspects of the self or as necessarily accurate reflections of reality" (Teasdale et al., 2000, p. 616).

The stronger focus on emotion regulation that characterizes the development of psychotherapeutic interventions in the past decade is, however, not limited to the so-called third wave of CBT (e.g., DBT, ACT, MBCT). Even traditional CBT treatments are now more frequently targeting affect regulation skills in a very explicit and integrative fashion. For example, Keuthen and Sprich developed and investigated the efficacy of a CBT program that included "…instruction in skills to further enhance awareness and address problematic emotion regulation and distress tolerance" (Keuthen & Sprich, 2012, p. 373) as a treatment intervention for trichotillomania. As hypothesized, the authors found significant pre- to post-treatment improvement in emotion regulation occurred, and this improvement was correlated with reductions in hair pulling severity (Keuthen et al., 2010). Significant improvement from baseline at 3- and 6-month follow-up was also found on the measures of hair pulling severity and total scale scores for emotion regulation measures (Keuthen et al., 2011).

In another study of a CBT-based program with an explicit focus on affect regulation (Slee, Spinhoven, Garnefski, & Arensman, 2008), 90 people who exhibited deliberate self-harm behaviors were assigned to one of two treatment groups. One group consisted of any treatment desired by the participant such as CBT, interpersonal psychotherapy, or social skills training. The second treatment group involved CBT that was directed at "developing emotion regulation skills for coping with situations that interfere with effective emotion regulation" (p. 206). Those who received the emotion regulation-enhanced CBT treatment reported significantly lower measures for deliberate self-harm, emotion regulation difficulties, depression, anxiety, and suicidal cognitions. Mediation analysis showed that changes in deliberate self-harm behavior among the study participants were partially mediated by changes in emotion regulation difficulties. Since depression, anxiety, and suicidal cognitions were reduced in those who received the emotion regulation-enhanced CBT treatment, this study suggests treatment that targets emotion regulation difficulties can help reduce symptom severity as well as deliberate self-harm behaviors.

Emotion regulation therapy (ERT; Mennin & Fresco, 2014) is another example of CBT-based treatment that targets emotion regulation. ERT was originally developed for generalized anxiety disorder and conceptualizes this disorder as deficits in a variety of emotion regulation skills. This treatment therefore focuses on enhancing emotion regulation skills such as identifying emotions, accepting emotions, and managing emotions in adaptive ways without the use of avoidance (Mennin, 2006).

Emotion-focused CBT (ECBT) is yet another example of a CBT-based treatment modified to account for the recent research findings on the importance of affect regulation. ECBT (Kendall & Suveg, 2005) was specifically developed to strengthen emotion regulation skills in children with anxiety disorders. The program includes standard CBT content and adds emotion-specific components, such as exposure to emotion-evoking situations, as well as instruction regarding the recognition and management of emotions. While *standard* CBT treatment for anxiety tends to focus specifically on the treatment of anxious emotions, treatment of anxious children with ECBT addresses any emotions (e.g., guilt or anger) that pose difficulty for the child. In one study that evaluated ECBT, the majority of children showed improvements in both their anxious symptoms and their ability to understand and regulate emotions (Suveg, Kendall, Comer, & Robin, 2006).

The notable shift of focus onto emotion regulation has not only occurred in CBT-based treatments. Psychodynamic treatments, which have a long tradition of addressing affect and the management of it (Blagys & Hilsenroth, 2000), have also recently been developed to specifically target emotion regulation. One such treatment, developed by Fosha (2001), is accelerated experiential dynamic psychotherapy, which helps patients fully experience their emotions and use "… emotionally significant relationships to regulate affective experiences that are too intense or painful for the individual to manage alone" (Fosha, 2001, pp. 227–228). Furthermore, some newer humanistic approaches, such as emotion-focused therapy (EFT; Greenberg, 2004), have begun to emphasize emotion regulation. For example, in EFT, therapists operate as "emotional coaches" to help patients manage and utilize their emotions in helpful ways by increasing their emotional awareness and helping them make sense of their emotional experiences.

Finally, various clinicians not affiliated with a particular therapeutic tradition have developed programs aimed at enhancing affect regulation. For example, Izard and colleagues (2008) developed the emotion-based prevention (EBP) program. The goal of EBP is to "…increase young children's ability to understand and regulate emotions, utilize modulated emotions, and reduce maladaptive behavior" (p. 373). In an efficacy study, the authors compared this treatment with the standard Head Start program (a federal program that prepares children from low-income families to enter school) and found that children who received EBP had greater increases in knowledge of emotions and emotion regulation than children participating in the standard Head Start program. Interestingly, children receiving EBP also showed greater decreases in negative emotional expression, aggression, anxious and depressed behavior, and negative interactions with peers and adults.

Additionally, Gratz and Gunderson (2006) developed an acceptance-based emotion regulation therapy for borderline personality disorder (BPD). In a pilot study, women with BPD who also exhibited self-harming behaviors were treated with either their current outpatient group therapy or the same group therapy plus Gratz and Gunderson's acceptance-based emotion regulation group therapy. There were significant differences between the treatment groups. The women who received the adjunctive intervention showed significant improvement in emotion regulation and significant decreases in emotional avoidance, frequency of self-harm, BPD symptoms, depression, anxiety, and stress (Gratz & Gunderson, 2006). A mediation analysis of the data revealed that changes in self-harm were mediated by changes in emotion dysregulation and emotional avoidance (Gratz & Tull, 2010).

As demonstrated in this chapter, there are a variety of current theories and treatments that focus on emotion regulation skills. The available treatments, however, are not without limitations. For example, many of the types of treatment just described were designed for specific disorders such as borderline personality disorder or generalized anxiety disorder, and may not be appropriate across a broad spectrum of disorders. Additionally, many of the treatments just described do not focus exclusively on emotion regulation or do not focus on building a wide repertoire of emotion regulation skills. Instead, many of the existing treatment options aim to enhance a patient's emotion regulation capacity along with various other therapeutic goals, while other treatments only target limited aspects of emotion regulation. To address these limitations in available treatments, we will describe, in the next chapter, another intervention for enhancing emotion regulation.

References

Berking, M., Wupperman, P., Reichardt, A., Pejic, T., Dippel, A., & Znoj, H. (2008). Emotion-regulation skills as a treatment target in psychotherapy. *Behaviour Research and Therapy, 46*(11), 1230–1237.

Blagys, M. D., & Hilsenroth, M. J. (2000). Distinctive features of short-term psychodynamic-interpersonal psychotherapy: A review of the comparative psychotherapy process literature. *Clinical Psychology: Science and Practice, 7*(2), 167–188.

Fosha, D. (2001). The dyadic regulation of affect. *Journal of Clinical Psychology, 57*(2), 227–242.

Gratz, K. L., & Gunderson, J. G. (2006). Preliminary data on an acceptance-based emotion regulation group intervention for deliberate self-harm among women with borderline personality disorder. *Behavior Therapy, 37*(1), 25–35.

Gratz, K. L., & Tull, M. T. (2010). Emotion regulation as a mechanism of change in acceptance- and mindfulness-based treatments. In R. A. Bacr (Ed.), *Assessing mindfulness and acceptance: Illuminating the processes of change*. Oakland, CA: New Harbinger.

Greenberg, L. S. (2004). Emotion-focused therapy. *Clinical Psychology & Psychotherapy, 11*(1), 3–16.

Hayes, S. C. (2004). Acceptance and commitment therapy, relational frame theory, and the third wave of behavioral and cognitive therapies. *Behavior Therapy, 35*(4), 639–665.

Hayes, S. C., Strosahl, K. D., & Wilson, K. G. (1999). *Acceptance and commitment therapy. An experiential approach to behavior change*. New York, NY: Guilford.

Izard, C. E., King, K. A., Trentacosta, C. J., Morgan, J. K., Laurenceau, J. P., Krauthamer-Ewing, E. S., et al. (2008). Accelerating the development of emotion competence in head start children: Effects on adaptive and maladaptive behavior. *Development and Psychopathology, 20*(1), 369–397.

Kendall, P. C., & Suveg, C. (2005). Emotion-focused cognitive behavioral therapy for anxious children: Therapist manual. Unpublished manual.

Keuthen, N. J., Rothbaum, B. O., Falkenstein, M. J., Meunier, S., Timpano, K. R., Jenike, M. A., et al. (2011). DBT-enhanced habit reversal treatment for trichotillomania: 3-and 6-month follow-up results. *Depression and Anxiety, 28*(4), 310–313.

Keuthen, N. J., Rothbaum, B. O., Welch, S. S., Taylor, C., Falkenstein, M., Heekin, M., et al. (2010). Pilot trial of dialectical behavior therapy-enhanced habit reversal for trichotillomania. *Depression and Anxiety, 27*(10), 953–959.

Keuthen, N. J., & Sprich, S. E. (2012). Utilizing DBT skills to augment traditional CBT for trichotillomania: An adult case study. *Cognitive and Behavioral Practice, 19*(2), 372–380.

Linehan, M. M. (1993). *Cognitive-behavioral treatment of borderline personality disorder.* New York, NY: Guilford.

Mennin, D. S. (2006). Emotion regulation therapy: An integrative approach to treatment-resistant anxiety disorders. *Journal of Contemporary Psychotherapy, 36*(2), 95–105.

Mennin, D. S., & Fresco, D. M. (2014). Emotion regulation therapy. In J. J. Gross (Ed.), *Handbook of emotion regulation* (2nd ed., pp. 469–490). New York, NY: Guilford.

Segal, Z. V., Williams, J. M. G., & Teasdale, J. D. (2013). *Mindfulness-based cognitive therapy for depression* (2nd ed.). New York, NY: Guilford.

Slee, N., Spinhoven, P., Garnefski, N., & Arensman, E. (2008). Emotion regulation as mediator of treatment outcome in therapy for deliberate self-harm. *Clinical Psychology and Psychotherapy, 15*(4), 205–216.

Suveg, C., Kendall, P. C., Comer, J. S., & Robin, J. (2006). Emotion-focused cognitive-behavioral therapy for anxious youth: A multiple-baseline evaluation. *Journal of Contemporary Psychotherapy, 36*(2), 77–85.

Teasdale, J. D., Segal, Z. V., Mark, J., Williams, G., Ridgeway, V. A., Soulsby, J. M., et al. (2000). Prevention of relapse/recurrence in major depression by mindfulness-based cognitive therapy. *Journal of Consulting and Clinical Psychology, 68*(4), 615–623.

Chapter 6
Development of the "Affect Regulation Training" (ART) Program

In 2004, inspired by a lack of transdiagnostic interventions that specifically target a broad range of affect regulation capabilities, we began to develop the Affect Regulation Training (ART) program. Since then, the training has become quite popular in the German-speaking parts of Europe, where it is known as "Training Emotionaler Kompetenzen" (TEK, Berking, 2010; www.tekonline.info). The main difference between ART and the treatments reviewed in the last chapter is that ART has, from its very beginning, been focused on enhancing emotion regulation capabilities as a strategy to improve overall mental health and address emotion regulation skill deficits that are present across many disorders.

To improve regulation skills, ART systematically integrates techniques from various psychotherapeutic approaches such as CBT (e.g., Beck, 1995), compassion-based approaches (Gilbert, 2011; Weissman & Weissman, 1996), DBT (Neacsiu, Bohus, & Linehan, 2014), emotion-focused therapy (EFT, Greenberg, 2004), mindfulness-based interventions (Farb, Anderson, Irving, & Segal, 2014), neuro-psychotherapeutic translational approaches (Grawe, 2007), principles used in problem-solving therapies (D'Zurilla & Nezu, 2010), and strength-focused interventions (Duckworth, Steen, & Seligman, 2005; Grawe & Grawe-Gerber, 1999) into a highly standardized and transdiagnostic training program. Although ART certainly shares theoretical assumptions with many of these approaches and uses interventions related to these various approaches, we believe the uniqueness and advantage of ART lies with its transdiagnostic approach and comprehensive use of a wide variety of specific strategies, interventions, and exercises in a structured training program that explicitly and exclusively focuses on enhancing general affect regulation skills.

6.1 From Science to Practice: Overview of the ART Skills

Since our empirical research using the ERSQ validated the skills of the Adaptive Coping with Emotions (ACE) Model as important for mental health and well-being (see Sect. 3.3), we distilled these general skills from the model into

Fig. 6.1 ART skills and ART sequence

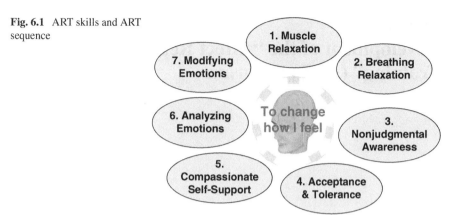

seven specific, teachable skills which we termed *ART Skills* (Fig. 6.1; see also Appendix B).

In the following section, we will describe each of the ART Skills using both a psychological and a neuroscience perspective. We have found that using neuroscience to explain emotion regulation and dysregulation is often more helpful for patients than exclusively providing psychological rationales. Many patients report feeling relieved to hear their emotions and behaviors have origins that can be understood in mechanistic terms instead of character flaws or rather abstract psychological concepts (e.g., unresolved family-of-origin issues). In our experience, this approach has helped to engage even patients who are only able to experience emotions somatically (e.g., stomach ache instead of nervousness). The ART Skills are presented to participants as techniques that can be used to interrupt neurological vicious cycles in the brain, which are involved in intensifying and maintaining negative emotions. The following section will describe these vicious cycles and the ART Skills that are presented as tools to effectively interrupt them.

ART Skills #1 & #2—Muscle Relaxation and Breathing Relaxation to effectively reduce psychophysiological arousal

In the first vicious cycle described to the participants, the amygdala initially becomes activated by a situation that is interpreted as a potential threat. The amygdala activation then initiates changes in the body, such as increased muscle tension and accelerated respiration. Because such physiological changes have occurred during threatening situations in the past, the increased muscle tension and respiration may be interpreted as danger signals by the amygdala, resulting in increased amygdala activation (classical conditioning Pavlov, 1927; somatic marker hypothesis Damasio, 2000), which could result in additional increases in muscle tension and respiration rate and a continuance of this vicious cycle. (For further information on how somatic processes are integrated into information processing related to emotion elicitation and maintenance, see Stemmler, 2004 or Teasdale & Barnard, 1993.)

When a person realizes that she is experiencing stress or negative emotions, she can stop this vicious cycle by applying the skills of consciously relaxing her muscles (ART Skill #1) and purposefully calming her breathing (ART Skill #2) to reduce the activation of the sympathetic system, the limbic system, and the brain stem (Lichstein, 1988; Porges, 2007). These skills are taught by introducing a technique based on *progressive muscle relaxation* (Jacobson, 1964) that is combined with a simple breathing relaxation method. Studies have consistently shown the effectiveness of muscle and breathing relaxation in the treatment of a variety of mental and physical disorders (e.g., Conrad & Roth, 2007; Gill, Kolt, & Keating, 2004; Öst, 1987). Additionally, with reduced limbic activity through breath and muscle relaxation, a shift can occur that changes the focus from primarily amygdala-driven limbic and brain stem-focused responses back to more prefrontal, cortical responses that are reflective instead of reactive (Arnsten, 2009). Thus, reducing psychophysiological arousal, with the help of muscle and breathing relaxation, facilitates the subsequent use of techniques that require significant cognitive resources.

ART Skill #3—Nonjudgmental Awareness

The next vicious cycle presented in the ART curriculum begins with amygdala activation in response to some type of a threat. The amygdala then alerts the prefrontal cortex which focuses attention and conscious thought on the threat (LeDoux 2007, 2012). This can be helpful in evaluating potential danger and in determining the most effective response. However, if this evaluation and brainstorming does not lead to resolving the threat, a continued focus on the potential danger can result in sustained amygdala activation. A vicious cycle is now set to occur as the sustained amygdala activation causes additional prefrontal cortex-driven analysis of the threat (Amaral, Price, Pitkänen, & Carmichael, 1992; Gray & McNaughton, 2000; Vuilleumier, Richardson, Armony, Driver, & Dolan, 2004), which may further increase amygdala activation.

Often, individuals try to rigidly suppress the negative thoughts (Ottenbreit & Dobson, 2004) and emotions (Campbell-Sills, Barlow, Brown, & Hofmann, 2006) that occur as the prefrontal cortex focuses thought and attention onto a threat. However, this strategy may actually have the paradoxical effect of increasing the intensity of negative thoughts and emotions instead of reducing them (Dalgleish, Yiend, Schweizer, & Dunn, 2009; Wegner, 2003). Thus, instead of fighting negative thoughts and emotions we encourage participants in the ART program to use ART Skill #3—Nonjudgmental Awareness in order to simply observe their situation, thoughts, and emotions without interpreting, judging, or reacting. This creates an opportunity to process what actually *is happening*, as opposed to automatically focusing on negative thoughts and evaluations of the situation.

When focusing on the nonjudgmental awareness of negative emotions, two important tasks (feeling and labeling) are involved:

1. *Feeling* consists of consciously experiencing one's emotions. This is important, since becoming aware of emotions is a critical first step in slowing run-

away limbic activation and reducing the process of automatic judgment and reaction. The idea of turning toward painful emotional experiences at first seems counterproductive. However, exposure therapy has been found to be effective and utilizes awareness of painful emotions in order to extinguish them (Hofmann, 2008).

2. *Labeling* utilizes words to create a mental representation of one's current internal experience. Evidence suggests that labeling emotions reduces their intensity by engaging the capacities of the prefrontal cortex to inhibit amygdala activation (Hariri, Brookheimer, & Mazziotta, 2000; Hariri, Mattay, Tessitore, Fera, & Weinberger, 2003; Lieberman et al., 2007). Once amygdala activation is decreased and prefrontal functioning is restored, cognitive resources such as planning, analyzing, and problem solving can be utilized to cope with the perceived emotion. In other words, with awareness that the churning feeling in my stomach is "anxiety," I can begin to calmly and thoughtfully figure out ways in which I could possibly change my emotion and my present situation.

Evidence supporting the value of *nonjudgmental awareness* comes from substantial research supporting the effectiveness of perception training (Papageorgiou & Wells, 2000; Wells, White, & Carter, 1997) and mindfulness-based approaches (Baer, 2003; Grossman, Niemann, Schmidt, & Walach, 2004; Hofmann, Sawyer, Witt, & Oh, 2010; Kabat-Zinn, 2003; Segal, Teasdale, & Williams, 2004), which view nonjudgmental awareness as an important mechanism of change (Baer, Smith, Hopkins, Krietemeyer, & Toney, 2006; Hölzel et al., 2011). Modinos, Ormel, and Aleman (2010) found that increases in dispositional mindfulness (observing emotions, describing emotional states, acting with awareness, and accepting emotional states; Baer, Smith, & Allen, 2004) were associated with increased activation in the dorsal medial prefrontal cortex when study participants responded to negative images with reappraisal. The increased activation in the dorsal medial prefrontal cortex (which has been associated with the downregulation of negative emotion) was inversely correlated in the study with amygdala activation.

ART Skill #4—Acceptance and Tolerance of Emotions

In the process of regulating limbic activation, the prefrontal cortex may activate in a more leftward or rightward lateralization. Left-lateralized activation has been associated with approach behavior and temperament, while right-lateralized activation has been associated with avoidance behavior and temperament (Berkman & Lieberman, 2010; Spielberg et al., 2011). Under the influence of a right-lateralization of prefrontal activation, people may attempt to escape from "threatening" limbic activation and negative emotions.

However, efforts to avoid experiencing negative emotions are unlikely to work, since we cannot simply turn off our emotions by sheer force of will. Emotions are primarily processed in the limbic system, and in the process of evolution, the limbic system has retained a degree of functional independence from the areas of our brain that initiate purposeful action (Amaral et al., 1992). Moreover, emotions initiate significant changes in the body, which often impede instant purposeful changes of emotions (Teasdale & Barnard, 1993). For example, it is difficult to get immediate relief from stress when all of the muscles in the body are tense and the body is flooded with stress hormones. Additionally, it is believed that areas in the brain that help regulate negative emotions, such as the ventromedial prefrontal cortex and the anterior cingulate cortex under the influence of dorsal or lateral regions of the pre-frontal cortex, may at times be "hijacked" by strong emotions. This can lead to decreased effectiveness of top-down regulation and increased rumination (Johnstone & Walter, 2014).

When a person is unsuccessful at attempts to instantly get rid of negative emotions, this failure will lead to increased amygdala activation and typically an increased sense of urgency to avoid the painful emotion (Martin, Tesser, & McIntosh, 1993; Rothermund, 2003). A vicious cycle may therefore ensue in which increasingly desperate attempts to get rid of a negative emotion only intensify the person's distress, while at the same time limiting the person's ability to effectively regulate negative emotions. *Acceptance and tolerance* (ART Skill #4) of negative emotions, instead of avoidance, can be used to interrupt or prevent this vicious cycle.

ART participants are encouraged to view negative emotions in a positive manner to facilitate acceptance and tolerance of them. This is accomplished by viewing emotions as "helpful allies that want to provide important information." (For additional information on adaptive conceptualizations of emotions, see Cosmides & Tooby, 2000.) Moreover, understanding the helpful functions of distressing emotions leads to more positive evaluations of one's feelings and thus cues positive emotions. For example, if I realize that my current feelings of anxiety are alerting me about a potential threat, I may perceive anxiety as helpful and experience positive feelings about my anxiety. Since positive emotions tend to inhibit negative ones, any such positive emotions help decrease negative ones.

ART Skill #4 also encourages a deeper understanding that emotions are both temporal and tolerable. This insight into the nature of emotions helps us more readily accept and tolerate negative emotions and resist the urge to avoid them. This skill becomes especially important during times when undesired emotions cannot be resolved quickly for various reasons. Evidence for the therapeutic potential of acceptance and tolerance comes from the previously mentioned research on the effectiveness of mindfulness-based approaches (Baer, 2003 Hofmann et al., 2010; Wupperman et al., 2012) and studies showing the effectiveness of Acceptance and Commitment Therapy, which involves acceptance of negative emotions and the willingness to experience unpleasant emotions in the interest of attaining important personal goals (Hayes, Luoma, Bond, Masuda, & Lillis, 2006). Additionally, support for the skill of acceptance and tolerance comes from studies that have shown its effectiveness in regulating emotions (e.g., Campbell-Sills, Barlow, Brown, & Hofmann, 2006; Gratz & Gunderson, 2006; Levitt, Brown, Orsillo, & Barlow, 2004).

ART Skill #5—Compassionate Self-Support

Many people criticize and devalue themselves for having negative emotional reactions such as stress, anxiety, anger, or sadness (e.g., "Why am I reacting this way? I must be going crazy! There must be something wrong with me! I am unable to stop feeling depressed, which shows how weak I really am"). However, when she criticizes her own emotional experience she threatens her basic *need for self-esteem* (Epstein, 1990; Grawe, 2004) and triggers additional negative emotions (e.g., anger, shame, guilt) that are associated with amygdala activation (Longe et al., 2010). The activation of the amygdala through self-criticism and additional negative feelings increases the stress response in the body and in the brain, likely leading to stronger negative emotions. These stronger negative emotions are responded to with even more intense self-criticism, resulting in a vicious cycle.

An effective strategy to interrupt this vicious cycle is to provide *Compassionate Self-Support* (ART Skill #5) that fosters empathy toward the suffering part of the self, takes active steps to encourage and soothe the suffering self, and lovingly coaches the suffering self through the steps necessary to alleviate one's suffering. Compassion, as used in this ART Skill, is a warm and powerful empathic feeling that is associated with the desire to help oneself cope with challenges (Gilbert, 2009, 2010, 2011; Weissman & Weissman, 1996) and should not be mistaken for self-pity, which is instead associated with passivity. Compassionate self-support not only inhibits self-criticism and self-blaming that generates negative emotions, such as shame and anger; it also results in positive emotions, such as feelings of safety and comfort.

Preliminary evidence has demonstrated the effectiveness of interventions that target compassionate self-support (Gilbert & Procter, 2006; Kuyken et al., 2010; Laithwaite et al., 2009; Lucre & Corten, 2013; MacBeth & Gumley, 2012; Mayhew & Gilbert, 2008; Neff & Germer, 2013). In a recent review of loving-kindness and compassion meditation, the authors conclude that these interventions "when combined with empirically supported treatments, such as cognitive-behavior therapy (…) may provide potentially useful strategies for targeting a variety of different psychological problems" (Hoffman, Grossman, & Hinton, 2011).

ART Skill #6—Analysis of Emotions

Unfortunately for many people, the origins of their own emotional reactions are a mystery, causing them to feel confused and out of control. This stress activates the amygdala, which leads to a release of stress hormones in the brain. These hormones have the capacity to strengthen amygdala functioning while impairing areas of the brain that are associated with cognitive processing (Huether, 1998; LeDoux, 2012). These brain regions, including the prefrontal cortex and the hippocampus (LeDoux, 2007), play important roles in the analysis of emotions. The capacity to analyze emotions facilitates a person's understanding of how and why the person feels the way she does, providing a sense of mastery and control over her emotions.

However, if through weakened prefrontal and hippocampal functioning, a person's capacity to analyze her emotions is impaired, she will likely feel confused and out of control. A vicious cycle now develops, since feeling confused and out of control triggers further amygdala activation. Now even more stress hormones are released in the brain, and the vicious cycle is repeated as stress hormones further weaken prefrontal and hippocampal functioning and increase amygdala activation.

For a person in this vicious cycle or to prevent the cycle from occurring in the first place, it is important to regain a sense of mastery and control over her emotions. This can be achieved through understanding how an emotion originally developed and how it is maintained. In ART Skill #6—*Analysis of Emotions*, participants are taught a method to systematically analyze the origins of an emotion by identifying a variety of specific factors that contribute to the development and maintenance of emotions. In addition to regaining a sense of control, analyzing an emotion also provides an important starting point to begin the subsequent process of modifying distressing emotions. Evidence for the skill of analyzing emotions comes from studies that demonstrate the effectiveness of insight-oriented psychological treatments. (For an overview of these treatments, refer to Gibbons, Crits-Christoph, Barber, & Schamberger, 2007.)

ART Skill #7—Modification of Emotions

Just as not understanding the causes of emotions can lead to feeling out of control, not knowing *how to modify* distressing emotions can also lead to feeling out of control. This can result in a vicious cycle similar to the one that was previously described, in which feeling out of control leads to amygdala activation and the release of stress hormones in the brain. As previously discussed, these hormones have the capacity to strengthen amygdala activation while impairing the cognitive processing capacities of regions in the brain that play important roles in the modification of emotions.

The ability to modify negative emotions provides a sense of control and mastery. If this ability is impaired by stress hormones, a vicious cycle may develop as out-of-control feelings lead to increased amygdala activation and further impairment in regions of the brain that are associated with the capacity for modifying emotions. In order to interrupt this vicious cycle, it is important to restore a sense of mastery and control. Just as control can be restored by analyzing emotions, control can also be achieved and enhanced by successfully modifying distressing emotions.

In ART Skill #7—*Modification of Emotions*, participants are taught an empowering step-by-step process, based on the general problem-solving model (D'Zurilla & Nezu, 2010), to actively modify the intensity and/or duration of an undesired emotion, thereby restoring a sense of control. In line with the general problem-solving model, the process begins with participants setting a goal for how they would rather feel. Then, a series of options are considered for how the goal could be achieved, and a plan for achieving the goal is created and implemented. Evidence for the efficacy of the problem-solving approach used in ART Skill #7 comes from research on problem-solving therapy (Bell & D'Zurilla, 2009; D'Zurilla & Nezu, 2007).

By acquiring the seven ART Skills just described, participants gain the ability to adaptively manage negative feelings. ART participants discover that negative emotions are only harmful if they become chronic or result in dysfunctional coping methods. They learn that negative emotions are temporal in nature and that they serve important positive functions in our lives. Participants also develop the ability to understand what has cued their emotions in a given moment and to modify undesired emotional states by working to change relevant maintaining factors. Finally, they learn how to cope with setbacks that arise in their efforts to regulate their emotions. These important benefits, which result from enhanced regulation skills, are coupled with improvements in how participants view themselves (e.g., with more compassion and acceptance), resulting in stronger motivation to pursue wellness. Ideally, a reinforcing cycle occurs in which an improved self-concept increases a participant's motivation to utilize the ART Skills, resulting in successful application of the skills, which enhances the participant's self-concept and continues the positive cycle.

6.2 "Chaining" ART Skills Together to Create the ART Sequence

In ART, the seven ART Skills are introduced individually, and time is allocated to discuss and practice each skill in detail. As participants become familiar with each skill and its application, the individual ART Skills are chained together to create the *ART Sequence*. The ART Sequence (Fig. 6.1) can be viewed as a highly structured self-management strategy, which can be used any time the individual suffers from significant undesired affective states. In such situations, the ART Sequence can be used as a regulation strategy, which provides a sense of control and guides effective coping behavior. Ideally, ART participants use the following instructions to initiate and successfully complete the ART Sequence:

In order to cope with this challenging feeling, I will now …

- *Take a few moments to relax my muscles (ART Skill #1).*
- *Calmly and consciously breathe in and out a few times (ART Skill # 2).*
- *Observe what is happening, without judgment. I try to label my emotions as specifically as possible (ART Skill #3).*
- *Accept my emotions as they are occurring in the moment. They provide me with valuable information. They inform me that ____. They will help me to ____. I am also aware that emotions are not permanent and that I can tolerate unpleasant emotions (ART Skill #4).*
- *Actively support myself in a compassionate and caring way (ART Skill #5).*
- *Constructively analyze why I feel the way I do (ART Skill #6).*
- *Use a step-by-step process to modify my emotions if I decide to change how I feel (ART Skill #7).*

As participants initially learn the seven ART Skills, it is important to remind them that they are not expected to master the skills immediately. The therapist should encourage participants to have compassion for themselves as they face the challenging task of learning and applying these new skills. Participants should also be instructed that while the skills in the ART Sequence are being introduced in this training, learning and applying these skills should continue long after the class is over as part of their lifelong pursuit of growth.

As participants gain proficiency in the ART Skills, they are free to modify the skills in the manner that will be personally most helpful. For example, some participants may decide to omit certain skills from the ART Sequence. Others may choose to modify the individual skills, and some may benefit from combining the ART Skills with additional strategies or techniques. However, we strongly encourage participants to practice the *complete* ART Sequence for at least six weeks before making any modifications in order to give themselves ample opportunity to thoroughly understand and assess each skill in the ART Sequence.

6.3 Practice and Repetition

Fostering adaptive emotion regulation involves strengthening synaptic networks in the brain that are responsible for effective emotion regulation. Strengthening these networks requires activating them frequently and intensely. To accomplish this, ART first helps participants identify specific emotion regulation goals that are personally important to them. Then, the ART Skills are explained from different angles, incorporating a variety of teaching methods including the use of group exercises, pictures, diagrams, and lectures. Finally, exercises designed to practice each skill are presented in the training sessions. These exercises constitute the core of the ART program. They should be practiced regularly, integrated into daily life, and continued after the training program has been completed.

In order to assist the participants in developing and maintaining a practice regimen, the ART program provides several tools. The first tool is the participant manual that includes the theory behind the ART Skills, descriptions of the ART Skills, and exercises the participant can utilize to practice the skills. The second tool is a set of guided audio exercises. These audio exercises either may be downloaded by the therapist (at www.AffectRegulationTraining.com—with access code: ART_Pcn2cfY) and provided directly to the participants or are available for purchase as prerecorded CDs. Information for ordering the CDs can be found at www.AffectRegulationTraining.com.

The third practice tool available for participants is a form of electronic or "e-coaching," in which several short exercises such as "Relax your shoulder muscles" or "Praise yourself for something you did well today" are sent to the participants daily during the course of the training via text messaging or email. Approximately 150 short exercises are sent between the delivery of the first and last

ART sessions. To activate the electronic coaching feature, ART therapists should refer to the instructions listed at www.AffectRegulationTraining.com.

The fourth practice tool is a training calendar document that contains the same short 150 exercises described above. ART therapists may download this training calendar document at www.AffectRegulationTraining.com—with access code: ART_Pcn2cfY. The therapist may then print and distribute the printed calendar to the participants.

References

Amaral, D. G., Price, J. L., Pitkanen, A., & Carmichael, S. T. (1992). Anatomical organization of the primate amygdaloid complex. In J. P. Aggleton (Ed.), *The amygdala: Neurobiological aspects of emotion, memory and mental dysfunction* (pp. 1–66). New York, NY: Wiley-Liss.

Arnsten, A. F. T. (2009). Stress signalling pathways that impair prefrontal cortex structure and function. *Nature Reviews Neuroscience, 10*(6), 410–422.

Baer, R. A. (2003). Mindfulness training as a clinical intervention: A conceptual and empirical review. *Clinical Psychology: Science and Practice, 10*(2), 125–143.

Baer, R. A., Smith, G. T., & Allen, K. B. (2004). Assessment of mindfulness by self-report: The kentucky inventory of mindfulness skills. *Assessment, 11*(3), 191–206.

Baer, R. A., Smith, G. T., Hopkins, J., Krietemeyer, J., & Toney, L. (2006). Using self-report assessment methods to explore facets of mindfulness. *Assessment, 13*(1), 27–45.

Beck, J. S. (1995). *Cognitive therapy: Basics and beyond.* New York, NY: Guilford.

Bell, A. C., & D'Zurilla, T. J. (2009). Problem-solving therapy for depression: A meta-analysis. *Clinical Psychology Review, 29*(4), 348–353.

Berking, M. (2010). *Training emotionaler kompetenzen* (ART-The Affect Regulation Training 2nd ed.). Heidelberg, Germany: Springer.

Berkman, E. T., & Lieberman, M. D. (2010). Approaching the bad and avoiding the good: Lateral prefrontal cortical asymmetry distinguishes between action and valence. *Journal of Cognitive Neuroscience, 22*(9), 1970–1979.

Campbell-Sills, L., Barlow, D. H., Brown, T. A., & Hofmann, S. G. (2006). Effects of suppression and acceptance on emotional responses of individuals with anxiety and mood disorders. *Behaviour Research and Therapy, 44*(9), 1251–1263.

Conrad, A., & Roth, W. T. (2007). Muscle relaxation therapy for anxiety disorders: It works but how? *Journal of Anxiety Disorders, 21*(3), 243–264.

Cosmides, L., & Tooby, J. (2000). Evolutionary psychology and the emotions. In M. Lewis & J. M. Haviland-Jones (Eds.), *Handbook of emotions* (2nd ed., pp. 91–115). New York, NY: Guilford.

D'Zurilla, T. J., & Nezu, A. M. (2007). *Problem-solving therapy: A positive approach to clinical intervention.* New York, NY: Springer.

D'Zurilla, T. J., & Nezu, A. M. (2010). Problem-solving therapy. In K. S. Dobson (Ed.), *Handbook of cognitive-behavioral therapies* (3rd ed., pp. 197–225). New York, NY: Guilford.

Dalgleish, T., Yiend, J., Schweizer, S., & Dunn, B. D. (2009). Ironic effects of emotion suppression when recounting distressing memories. *Emotion, 9*(5), 744–749.

Damasio, A. R. (2000). *The feeling of what happens: Body and emotion in the making of consciousness.* San Diego, CA: Harcourt.

Duckworth, A. L., Steen, T. A., & Seligman, M. E. P. (2005). Positive psychology in clinical practice. *Annual Review of Clinical Psychology, 1*, 629–651.

Epstein, S. (1990). Cognitive-experiential self-theory. In L. Pervin (Ed.), *Handbook of personality theory and research: Theory and research* (pp. 165–192). New York, NY: Guilford.

Farb, N. A. S., Anderson, A. K., Irving, J. A., & Segal, Z. V. (2014). Mindfulness interventions and emotion regulation. In J. J. Gross (Ed.), *Handbook of emotion regulation* (2nd ed., pp. 548–567). New York, NY: Guilford.

Gibbons, M. B. C., Crits-Christoph, P., Barber, J. P., & Schamberger, M. (2007). Insight in psychotherapy: A review of empirical literature. In L. G. Castonguay & C. E. Hill (Eds.), *Insight in psychotherapy* (pp. 143–165). Washington, DC: American Psychological Association.

Gilbert, P. (2009). Introducing compassion-focused therapy. *Advances in Psychiatric Treatment, 15*(3), 199–208.

Gilbert, P. (2010). *Compassion focused therapy: Distinctive features*. New York, NY: Routledge.

Gilbert, P. (2011). *Compassion focused therapy: The distinctive features*. London: Routledge.

Gilbert, P., & Procter, S. (2006). Compassionate mind training for people with high shame and self-criticism: Overview and pilot study of a group therapy approach. *Clinical Psychology and Psychotherapy, 13*(6), 353–379.

Gill, S., Kolt, G. S., & Keating, J. (2004). Examining the multi-process theory: An investigation of the effects of two relaxation techniques on state anxiety. *Journal of Bodywork and Movement Therapies, 8*(4), 288–296.

Gratz, K. L., & Gunderson, J. G. (2006). Preliminary data on an acceptance-based emotion regulation group intervention for deliberate self-harm among women with borderline personality disorder. *Behavior Therapy, 37*(1), 25–35.

Grawe, K. (2004). *Psychological therapy*. Cambridge, MA: Hogrefe & Huber.

Grawe, K. (2007). *Neuropsychotherapy*. New York, NY: Psychology.

Grawe, K., & Grawe-Gerber, M. (1999). Ressourcenaktivierung [Resource activation]. *Psychotherapeut, 44*(2), 63–73.

Gray, J. A., & McNaughton, N. (2000). *The neuropsychology of anxiety: An enquiry into the functions of the septo-hippocampal system* (2nd ed.). Oxford: Oxford Psychology Series.

Greenberg, L. S. (2004). Emotion-focused therapy. *Clinical Psychology & Psychotherapy, 11*(1), 3–16.

Grossman, P., Niemann, L., Schmidt, S., & Walach, H. (2004). Mindfulness-based stress reduction and health benefits: A meta-analysis. *Journal of Psychosomatic Research, 57*(1), 35–43.

Hariri, A. R., Bookheimer, S. Y., & Mazziotta, J. C. (2000). Modulating emotional responses: Effects of a neocortical network on the limbic system. *NeuroReport, 11*(1), 43–48.

Hariri, A. R., Mattay, V. S., Tessitore, A., Fera, F., & Weinberger, D. R. (2003). Neocortical modulation of the amygdala response to fearful stimuli. *Biological Psychiatry, 53*(6), 494–501.

Hayes, S. C., Luoma, J. B., Bond, F. W., Masuda, A., & Lillis, J. (2006). Acceptance and commitment therapy: Model, processes and outcomes. *Behaviour Research and Therapy, 44*(1), 1–25.

Hofmann, S. G. (2008). Cognitive process during fear acquisition and extinction in animals and humans. *Clinical Psychology Review, 28*(2), 199–210.

Hofmann, S. G., Grossman, P., & Hinton, D. E. (2011). Loving-kindness and compassion meditation: Potential for psychological interventions. *Clinical Psychology Review, 31*(7), 1126–1132.

Hofmann, S. G., Sawyer, A. T., Witt, A. A., & Oh, D. (2010). The effect of mindfulness-based therapy on anxiety and depression: A meta-analytic review. *Journal of Consulting and Clinical Psychology, 78*(2), 169–183.

Hölzel, B. K., Lazar, S. W., Gard, T., Schuman-Oliver, Z., Vago, D. R., & Ott, U. (2011). How does mindfulness meditation work? Proposing mechanisms of action from a conceptual and neural perspective. *Perspectives on Psychological Science, 6*(6), 537–559.

Huether, G. (1998). Stress and the adaptive self-organization of neuronal connectivity during early childhood. *International Journal of Developmental Neuroscience, 16*(3), 297–306.

Jacobson, E. (1964). *Anxiety and tension control: A physiologic approach*. Philadelphia, PA: J. B. Lippincott.

Johnstone, T., & Walter, H. (2014). The neural basis of emotion dysregulation. In J. J. Gross (Ed.), *Handbook of emotion regulation* (2nd ed., pp. 23–42). New York, NY: Guilford.

Kabat-Zinn, J. (2003). Mindfulness-based interventions in context: Past, present, and future. *Clinical Psychology: Science and Practice, 10*(2), 144–156.

Kuyken, W., Watkins, E., Holden, E., White, K., Taylor, R. S., Byford, S., et al. (2010). How does mindfulness-based cognitive therapy work? *Behaviour Research and Therapy, 48*(11), 1105–1112.

Laithwaite, H., O'Hanlon, M., Collins, P., Doyle, P., Abraham, L., Porter, S., et al. (2009). Recovery after psychosis (RAP): A compassion focused programme for individuals residing in high security settings. *Behavioural and Cognitive Psychotherapy, 37*(5), 511–526.

LeDoux, J. (2007). The amygdala. *Current Biology, 17*(20), R868–R874.

LeDoux, J. E. (2012). Evolution of human emotion: A view through fear. *Progress in Brain Research, 195*, 431–442.

Levitt, J. T., Brown, T. A., Orsillo, S. M., & Barlow, D. H. (2004). The effects of acceptance versus suppression of emotion on subjective and psychophysiological response to carbon dioxide challenge in patients with panic disorder. *Behavior Therapy, 35*(4), 747–766.

Lichstein, K. L. (1988). *Clinical relaxation strategies*. New York, NY: Wiley.

Lieberman, M. D., Eisenberger, N. I., Crockett, M. J., Tom, S. M., Pfeifer, J. H., & Way, B. M. (2007). Putting feelings into words: Affect labeling disrupts amygdala activity in response to affective stimuli. *Psychological Science, 18*(5), 421–428.

Longe, O., Maratos, F. A., Gilbert, P., Evans, G., Volker, F., Rockliff, H., et al. (2010). Having a word with yourself: Neural correlates of self-criticism and self-reassurance. *NeuroImage, 49*(2), 1849–1856.

Lucre, K. M., & Corten, N. (2013). An exploration of group compassion-focused therapy for personality disorder. *Psychology and Psychotherapy: Theory, Research and Practice, 86*(4), 387–400.

MacBeth, A., & Gumley, A. (2012). Exploring compassion: A meta-analysis of the association between self-compassion and psychopathology. *Clinical Psychology Review, 32*(6), 545–552.

Martin, L. L., Tesser, A., & McIntosh, W. D. (1993). Wanting but not having: The effects of unattained goals on thoughts and feelings. In D. M. Wegner & J. W. Pennebaker (Eds.), *Handbook of mental control* (pp. 552–572). Englewood Cliffs, NJ: Prentice-Hall.

Mayhew, S. L., & Gilbert, P. (2008). Compassionate mind training with people who hear malevolent voices: A case series report. *Clinical Psychology and Psychotherapy, 15*(2), 113–138.

Modinos, G., Ormel, J., & Aleman, A. (2010). Individual differences in dispositional mindfulness and brain activity involved in reappraisal of emotion. *Social Cognitive and Affective Neuroscience, 5*(4), 369–377.

Neacsiu, A. D., Bohus, M., & Linehan, M. M. (2014). Dialectical behavior therapy: An intervention for emotion dysregulation. In J. J. Gross (Ed.), *Handbook of emotion regulation* (2nd ed., pp. 491–507). New York, NY: Guilford.

Neff, K. D., & Germer, C. K. (2013). A pilot study and randomized controlled trial of the mindful self-compassion program. *Journal of Clinical Psychology, 69*(1), 28–44.

Öst, L. G. (1987). Applied relaxation: Description of a coping technique and review of controlled studies. *Behaviour Research and Therapy, 25*(5), 397–409.

Ottenbreit, N. D., & Dobson, K. S. (2004). Avoidance and depression: The construction of the cognitive–behavioral avoidance scale. *Behaviour Research and Therapy, 42*(3), 293–313.

Papageorgiou, C., & Wells, A. (2000). Treatment of recurrent major depression with attention training. *Cognitive and Behavioral Practice, 7*(4), 407–413.

Pavlov, I. P. (1927). *Conditioned reflexes: An investigation of the physiological activity of the cerebral cortex* (G. V. Anrep, Ed., Trans.). London: Oxford University Press.

Porges, S. W. (2007). The polyvagal perspective. *Biological Psychology, 74*(2), 116–143.

Rothermund, K. (2003). Automatic vigilance for task-related information: Perseverance after failure and inhibition after success. *Memory and Cognition, 31*(3), 343–352.

Segal, Z. V., Teasdale, J. D., & Williams, J. G. (2004). Mindfulness-based cognitive therapy: Theoretical rationale and empirical status. In V. M. Follette, M. Linehan, & S. C. Hayes (Eds.), *Mindfulness and acceptance: Expanding the cognitive behavioral tradition* (pp. 45–65). New York, NY: Guildford.

Spielberg, J. M., Miller, G. A., Engels, A. S., Herrington, J. D., Sutton, B. P., Banich, M. T., et al. (2011). Trait approach and avoidance motivation: Lateralized neural activity associated with executive function. *NeuroImage, 54*(1), 661–670.

Stemmler, G. (2004). Physiological processes during emotion. In P. Philippot & R. S. Feldman (Eds.), *The regulation of emotion* (pp. 35–72). Mahwah, NJ: Erlbaum.

Teasdale, J. D., & Barnard, P. J. (1993). *Affect, cognition and change: Re-modelling depressive thought*. Hove, UK: Lawrence Erlbaum Associates.

Vuilleumier, P., Richardson, M. P., Armony, J. L., Driver, J., & Dolan, R. J. (2004). Distant influences of amygdala lesion on visual cortical activation during emotional face processing. *Nature Neuroscience, 7*(11), 1271–1278.

Wegner, D. M. (2003). Thought suppression and mental control. In L. Nadel (Ed.), *Encyclopedia of cognitive science* (pp. 395–397). London: Macmillan.

Weissman, S., & Weissman, R. (1996). *Meditation, compassion & lovingkindness. An approach to vipassana practice*. York Beach, ME: Samuel Weiser.

Wells, A., White, J., & Carter, K. (1997). Attention training: Effects in anxiety and beliefs in panic and social phobia. *Clinical Psychology and Psychotherapy, 4*(4), 226–232.

Wupperman, P., Marlatt, G. A., Cunningham, A., Bown, S., Berking, M., Mulvihill-Rivera, N., et al. (2012). Mindfulness and modification therapy for behavior dysregulation: Results from a pilot study targeting alcohol use and aggression in women. *Journal of Clinical Psychology, 68*(1), 50–66.

Chapter 7
Guidelines for Effective Delivery of ART

The therapist plays an important role in teaching the ART Skills. The manner in which the therapist conducts the training sessions and interacts with the participants will, in large part, determine the participants' ability to engage in the learning process. The following sections provide guidelines to help therapists deliver ART more effectively.

7.1 Activating the Approach Orientation

A number of renowned researchers (e.g., Elliot, 2006; Grawe, 2007; Gray, 1996) distinguish between the approach and avoidance orientations, which guide a person's thoughts, emotions, and actions. The approach orientation is associated with the formation and pursuit of approach goals, which focus on attaining something important (e.g., *I want to buy this fantastic new mountain bike*.). The avoidance orientation, on the other hand, is associated with the formation and pursuit of avoidance goals, which focus on avoiding something unwanted (e.g., *I must avoid being criticized by my boss.*).

While the approach and avoidance orientations are not mutually exclusive to each other, they do have a mitigating effect on each other, since activation of one orientation diminishes the effect of the other. For many people, experiencing negative emotions creates a distressing, out-of-control feeling, which activates the avoidance orientation. Since ART encourages participants to experience and work through negative emotions, ART is likely to activate the avoidance orientation and result in behaviors that could impede treatment.

For example, a participant who experiences negative emotions evoked from the training may become cynical of the ART Skills and distrustful of the therapist, while refusing to engage during the training or practice the ART Skills outside of the training sessions. Such behavior would likely reduce the chance of benefitting from the training, thus reinforcing the participant's negative perceptions of ART. The training may ultimately be viewed by the participant as ineffective or even unsafe

M. Berking and B. Whitley, *Affect Regulation Training: A Practitioners' Manual*, 67
DOI 10.1007/978-1-4939-1022-9_7, © Springer Science+Business Media New York 2014

and cause the participant to drop out. The avoidance orientation, in this example, also simultaneously *limits* the approach orientation, which could otherwise lead the participant to actively participate in the training and explore new ways of dealing with challenging emotions.

Thus, it is important for the therapist to work toward reducing the participant's avoidance orientation and encouraging the approach orientation. The most effective way to do this is to foster positive experiences in the training. The question then becomes, "How is this done?" According to Grawe (2007), these positive experiences are achieved by the fulfillment of basic needs that we all share and the attainment of personally relevant goals related to these basic needs.

Based on Seymore Epstein's cognitive-experiential self-theory (CEST; Epstein, 1990, 1993a), Grawe (2004, 2007) claimed that the following four basic needs are most important in the context of psychotherapy:

1. *The need to maximize pleasure and minimize pain*
2. *The need to understand and control important aspects of one's life*
3. *The need for relatedness with others*
4. *The need for self-esteem* (also see Epstein 1993b)

Grawe believed that successful fulfillment of these four basic needs results in well-being and significantly helps to maintain or restore mental health. On the other hand, chronic unsuccessful need fulfillment or "Motivation Perception Discrepancy" (MPD; refer to Sect. 4.2.2) results in a state of inner tension, leading to negative emotions and the possible use of dysfunctional behavioral strategies to avoid these emotions.

Based on this conceptualization, ART therapists consciously work to activate the approach orientation by providing participants with experiences that help meet their basic needs. The following is a list of the basic needs and examples of how ART and the ART therapist can address these needs.

1. *The need to maximize pleasure and minimize pain*

   • The training setting should be comfortable and inviting.
   • The therapist should be positive, upbeat, and energetic and use humor when appropriate.
   • Real life examples and statements are utilized to clarify abstract or confusing concepts and techniques.

2. *The need to understand and control important aspects of one's life*

   • The ART format and goals are described at the beginning of the training, so participants know what to expect and what will be expected of them.
   • Psychoeducation regarding the neurological and physiological components of emotion is provided to help participants make sense of their emotional states.
   • Participants are encouraged to identify their personal motivation for learning the ART Skills.
   • Easier ART Skills are introduced in the beginning to foster a sense of mastery and accomplishment before more difficult skills are later added.

- The therapist should conduct the training sessions in a flexible manner by taking into account the participants' needs and concerns (e.g., more or less time spent on certain topics, timing of breaks, etc.).
- After going through all of the ART Skills and completing the ART Sequence, participants are free to modify the ART Skills and ART Sequence in ways that are personally helpful.

3. *The need for relatedness with others*

- The therapist should be empathic, compassionate and kind, and should create a strong therapeutic alliance with all participants.
- The therapist intentionally encourages positive interaction among the participants during the training sessions through facilitated discussions and group exercises.

4. *The need for self-esteem*

- The therapist should focus on the participants' strengths and model appreciation of these strengths to the participants.
- The therapist should acknowledge and praise the participants' efforts at making positive changes.
- The therapist should display optimism and confidence in the participants' abilities to successfully utilize the ART Skills.

While this conceptualization posits that all people share these four basic needs, the strength of each need varies individually for each person. The variation in how strongly a particular need resonates with each individual person is partly guided by temperament. For example, a person with an outgoing personality may more closely identify with *the need for relatedness with others* as compared to a person who has an introverted personality. In order to provide positive interpersonal experiences to individuals with both temperaments and thus foster the approach motivation, the ART therapist may want to be especially open and friendly towards a participant with an outgoing personality while being a bit more reserved and cautious (albeit kind and compassionate) with an introverted client.

Early experiences can also impact the significance of these four basic needs. Those who frequently experienced Motivation Perception Discrepancy (MPD) in childhood may value more highly one of the basic needs that were repeatedly violated during the MPD-inducing situations. An adult, for example, may have developed a strong *need to understand and control important aspects of one's life* in response to childhood abuse, since as a child he frequently felt out of control when he instead desired to feel safe and loved. An ART therapist who is working with this participant could encourage the approach orientation by facilitating experiences that fulfill the participant's basic *need to understand and control important aspects of his life*, by giving him as much control as clinically appropriate during the therapeutic process.

Just as the fulfillment of basic needs activates the approach orientation, so too does the fulfillment of personally important goals, which are stepping stones on the

Motivational Clarification:
The Importance of Wishes, Goals, and Intentions

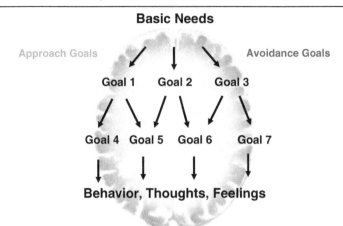

Fig. 7.1   The hierarchy of goals model

path to achieving basic needs. A child, for example, may observe that if his mother is around, he is fed, wearing soft clothes, and warm, fulfilling his *need to maximize pleasure and minimize pain*. He then develops the approach goal of ensuring that his mother stays around, so he continues to have his basic need (maximize pleasure and minimize pain) met. As he strives for his goal of keeping his mother close by, he may learn that his mother spends more time with him when he is affectionate with her.

In a hierarchical fashion, his basic *need to maximize pleasure and minimize pain* leads to his personal goal of keeping his mother around, which results in the boy showing affection toward his mother. This hierarchy of goals model (see Fig. 7.1) helps us better understand ART participants' thoughts, feelings, and behaviors, as we see how their thoughts, feelings, and behaviors are motivated by specific goals that have developed as a means to fulfill unmet needs.

Such a model also helps us gain insight into the ART participants' emotions by viewing the participants' emotions as appraisals of their current situation in the context of their goals and basic needs. Finally, the model helps us facilitate attainment of the participants' personal goals, which creates positive experiences that strengthen the approach orientation.

7.2   Strengthening the Therapeutic Alliance

By attuning to the participants' needs and goals, the ART therapist not only activates the approach orientation but also strengthens the therapeutic alliance (Caspar, 2007; Holtforth & Castonguay, 2005; Holtforth, Thomas, & Caspar, 2011). A strong working alliance is crucial for encouraging the participants to explore new ways of thinking and acting. Thus, ART therapists should routinely assess the status of the therapeutic relationship with the participants. Ruptures in the alliance often occur when a therapist is misaligned with a participant's needs and goals. Conceptualizing breaks in the relationship in this manner, the ART therapist is able to reassess the participant's needs and goals and help realign treatment with the participant's particular needs and goals in order to restore the therapeutic relationship.

However, while the therapeutic relationship is important, the ultimate goal of treatment is not to facilitate the therapeutic relationship; it is to facilitate change. Facilitating change often involves experiencing discomfort, such as during times when the ART therapist presents the participants with material or information they would rather avoid. So how can an ART therapist maintain a strong therapeutic alliance while at the same time encouraging change that may involve distress for the participant? The answer involves building the therapeutic relationship to a point where it is strong enough to withstand the distress a participant may feel when she is challenged.

A good way to conceptualize this is to think of the therapeutic alliance as a bank account. Deposits into the account are made when the therapist is aligned with the participant's needs and goals and helps the participant achieve them. After sufficient deposits have been made, the therapist is in a position to utilize a challenging intervention that, while important for facilitating change, will place a burden on the therapeutic relationship, causing a withdrawal on the account (e.g., "In what way did you contribute to the escalation of the situation?"). More goal and need satisfying deposits will now need to be made before making the next withdrawal during a challenging intervention.

In individual psychotherapy, a therapist has many opportunities to use a patient's needs and goals to tailor treatment to the particular patient. For example, treatment planning can be intentionally aimed at fulfilling specific unmet needs and goals and session material can be discussed with the patient in the context of his/her particular hierarchy of needs and goals. Although ART is more structured than individual psychotherapy, it is helpful for ART therapists to keep the concept of goal and need structures in mind while working with participants in the training sessions.

7.3   Creating Goals that Result in Effective Self-Management

Understanding the participants' basic needs and goals structure is also important in helping participants create goals for themselves, which drives them to engage in ART and use the skills they learn to manage themselves in new and more adaptive ways. Goals that facilitate effective self-management have the following characteristics:

1. Have a high degree of personal importance
2. Are attainable
3. Are measurable, specific, and concrete

We will now explore each of these characteristics in more detail.

1. *Have a high degree of personal importance*
   For a goal to facilitate self-management, it must involve something that a person deeply desires to achieve. In other words, the goal must be something that the person cares about. All too often, people try unsuccessfully to adopt the goals that others (e.g., parents, spouse, therapist, etc.) have for them. When a person is, however, working toward a personally important goal, the neurotransmitter dopamine is released in the brain. Successful behaviors that lead to the accomplishment of important goals are reinforced as the dopamine strengthens synaptic connections related to the successful behaviors. As the synaptic connections related to these behaviors are strengthened, there is a greater likelihood these successful behaviors will occur again in the future (Grawe, 2007; Hoebel, Rada, Mark, & Pothos, 1999).

2. *Attainable*
   Goals that are unrealistic and unattainable will not be achieved and therefore are incapable of facilitating self-management. People often create goals they are not likely to achieve (e.g., happy while in the middle of tragedy), which unfortunately sets them up for experiencing failure. Instead, goals should be created that are reasonable given a person's unique situation and abilities.

3. *Measurable, specific, and concrete*
   Goals are targets that should be measurable, specific, and concrete. Clearly defining a goal focuses a person's efforts on attaining it and provides a clear end point that will signal successful accomplishment. In addition, goals that are defined in detail are capable of being visualized. When we can imagine ourselves reaching an intended goal, positive emotions are often generated. This "taste" of what it would feel like to accomplish a goal provides motivation to stay committed to accomplishing it.

At the beginning of the ART program (see Sect. 9.1), participants are encouraged to form personal goals for their training, based on the three characteristics of successful goals that we just described. Throughout the training, ART therapists continue to help participants further refine their goals according to these three characteristics, so the participants' goals result in adaptive self-management.

7.4   Recommended Education and Training for Therapists

In the previous sections, we described a few general therapeutic strategies that are important for delivering ART effectively. In addition to these general strategies, there are several specific treatment approaches that are also helpful for an ART therapist to grasp in order to enhance participants' emotion regulation skills. One such important treatment approach is cognitive behavior therapy (CBT), since ART draws heavily from CBT techniques.

CBT proposes that psychological disorders are the result of dysfunctional thinking that influences a person's mood and behavior. In CBT, the therapist helps the patient change his/her thinking and beliefs in order to positively impact the patient's emotions and behaviors. Unfortunately, CBT is often falsely accused of focusing on cognitions and excluding emotions in the process of treatment. Effective CBT, however, artfully uses a patient's emotional experience to access and challenge the irrational thoughts and beliefs that lead to negative emotions. For additional reading on CBT, see Barlow (2008); Beck (1995); and Dobson & Dobson (2009).

Additionally, it is important for the ART therapist to have skills in the following clinical areas:

1. *Resource Activation*

   The term *resource activation* (Grawe, 2004, 2007) refers to a treatment approach in which the therapist focuses on the patient's strengths and abilities (i.e., resources) instead of problems and deficits. For example, a therapist utilizing resource activation would focus on an instance when a person *did not* engage in problematic behavior despite exposure to a high risk situation. The therapist would highlight this exception to problematic behavior and would explore the resources that enabled the patient to behave differently. Areas of potential resources include positive memories, positive emotions, physical abilities, monetary resources, supportive social relationships, as well as skills and abilities (Flückiger, Caspar, Holtforth, & Willutzki, 2009; Flückiger, Grosse-Holtforth, Del Re, & Lutz, 2013). For additional reading on resource activation, also see Flückiger, Wüsten, Zinbarg, & Wampold (2010).

2. *Motivational Interviewing*

   Motivational interviewing is a clinical method for *being* with patients in a manner that assists them in resolving their ambivalence to make positive changes. This method involves a collaborative process between the therapist and the patient that utilizes the patient's own resources for growth and change. For additional information on motivational interviewing, see Miller and Rollnick (2002).

3. *Empirically Validated Treatments*

   Therapists delivering ART should be well-versed in empirically supported treatments for a variety of disorders. Nathan and Gorman (2007) have written a third edition of their groundbreaking text, A Guide to Treatments that Work, which reviews empirically supported treatments for a variety of disorders. Also, Oxford University Press offers a book series called "Treatments that Work" that has numerous works describing various empirically supported treatments. Such treatments include cognitive behavioral therapy (CBT), mindfulness-based approaches (Kabat-Zinn, 2003; Segal, Williams, & Teasdale, 2013), emotion-focused therapy (Greenberg, 2002), dialectical behavior therapy (Linehan, 1993), schema therapy (Young, Klosko, & Weishaar, 2003), and short-term psychodynamic psychotherapy (Leichsenring, Rabung, & Leibing, 2004).

4. *Managing Difficult Clinical Situations*

   The process of change is complex and oftentimes involves difficulties including crises, impasses, and relapses. These challenges may tempt the therapist to knowingly or unknowingly collude with the patient's dysfunctional patterns. Therapists providing ART are encouraged to have a wide range of clinical tools at their disposal to enable these situations to serve as opportunities for growth and positive change. For a good resource on this topic, see Leiper & Kent (2001).

Finally, therapists are encouraged to participate in ART themselves prior to using ART to help others. We also encourage ART therapists to engage in the same exercise regimen as the participants any time they are running an ART group. This helps therapists be more empathic toward the participants working to acquire the ART Skills. Moreover, it will enable therapists to share with the participants the challenges and successes they have experienced during their own training. This often helps build rapport and encourages participants, who sometimes feel inadequate, as they struggle to understand and integrate the ART concepts.

References

Barlow, D. H. (Ed.). (2008). *Clinical handbook of psychological disorders: A step-by-step treatment manual* (4th ed.). New York, NY: Guilford.

Beck, J. S. (1995). *Cognitive therapy: Basics and beyond.* New York, NY: Guilford.

Caspar, F. (2007). Plan analysis. In T. D. Eells (Ed.), *Handbook of psychotherapy case formulation* (pp. 251–289). New York, NY: Guilford.

Dobson, D., & Dobson, K. S. (2009). *Evidence-based practice of cognitive-behavioral therapy.* New York, NY: Guilford.

Elliot, A. J. (2006). The hierarchical model of approach–avoidance motivation. *Motivation and Emotion, 30*(2), 111–116.

Epstein, S. (1990). Cognitive-experiential self-theory. In L. Pervin (Ed.), *Handbook of personality theory and research: Theory and research* (pp. 165–192). New York, NY: Guilford.

Epstein, S. (1993a). Emotion and self-theory. In M. Lewis & J. M. Haviland (Eds.), *Handbook of emotions* (pp. 313–326). New York, NY: Guilford.

Epstein, S. (1993b). Implications of cognitive-experiential self-theory for personality and developmental psychology. In D. C. Funder, R. D. Parke, C. A. Tomilinson-Keasey, & K. Widaman (Eds.), *Studying lives through time: Personality and development* (pp. 399–438). Washington, DC: American Psychological Association.

Flückiger, C., Caspar, F., Holtforth, M. G., & Willutzki, U. (2009). Working with patients' strengths: A microprocess approach. *Psychotherapy Research, 19*(2), 213–223.

Flückiger, C., Grosse-Holtforth, M., Del Re, A. C., & Lutz, W. (2013). Working along sudden gains: Responsiveness on small and subtle early changes and exceptions. *Psychotherapy, 50*(3), 292–297.

Flückiger, C., Wünsten, G., Zinbarg, R. E., & Wampold, B. E. (2010). *Resource activation.* Göttingen, Germany: Hogrefe.

Grawe, K. (2004). *Psychological therapy.* Cambridge, MA: Hogrefe & Huber.

Grawe, K. (2007). *Neuropsychotherapy.* New York, NY: Psychology.

Gray, J. A. (1996). The neuropsychology of anxiety: A reprise. In D. A. Hope (Ed.), *Nebraska symposium on motivation: Vol 43. Perspectives on anxiety, panic, and fear* (pp. 61–134). Lincoln: University of Nebraska Press.

Greenberg, L. S. (2002). *Emotion-focused therapy: Coaching clients to work through their feelings.* Washington, DC: American Psychological Association.

Hoebel, B. G., Rada, P. V., Mark, G. P., & Pothos, E. N. (1999). Neural systems for reinforcement and inhibition of behavior: Relevance to eating, addiction, and depression. In D. Kahneman, E. Diener, & N. Schwarz (Eds.), *Well-being: The foundations of hedonic psychology* (pp. 558–572). New York, NY: Russell Sage.

Holtforth, M. G., & Castonguay, L. G. (2005). Relationship and techniques in cognitive-behavioral therapy—A motivational approach. *Psychotherapy: Theory, Research, Practice, Training, 42*(4), 443–455.

Holtforth, M. G., Thomas, A., & Caspar, F. (2011). Interpersonal motivation. In L. M. Horowitz & S. Strack (Eds.), *Handbook of interpersonal psychology: Theory, research, assessment, and therapeutic interventions* (pp. 107–122). Hoboken, NJ: Wiley.

Kabat-Zinn, J. (2003). Mindfulness-based interventions in context: Past, present, and future. *Clinical Psychology: Science and Practice, 10*(2), 144–156.

Leichsenring, F., Rabung, S., & Leibing, E. (2004). The efficacy of short-term psychodynamic psychotherapy in specific psychiatric disorders: A meta-analysis. *Archives of General Psychiatry, 61*(12), 1208–1216.

Leiper, R., & Kent, R. (2001). *Working through setbacks in psychotherapy.* London: Sage.

Linehan, M. M. (1993). *Cognitive-behavioral treatment of borderline personality disorder.* New York, NY: Guilford.

Miller, W. R., & Rollnick, S. (2002). *Motivational interviewing: Preparing people for change.* New York, NY: Guilford.

Nathan, P. E., & Gorman, J. M. (Eds.). (2007). *A guide to treatments that work.* New York, NY: Oxford University Press.

Segal, Z. V., Williams, J. M. G., & Teasdale, J. D. (2013). *Mindfulness-based cognitive therapy for depression* (2nd ed.). New York, NY: Guilford.

Young, J. E., Klosko, J. S., & Weishaar, M. E. (2003). *Schema therapy: A practitioner's guide.* New York, NY: Guilford.

Part II
Delivery of Affect Regulation Training (ART)

Chapter 8
Training Format and Logistics

While part one of this manual described the theoretical conceptualizations and scientific research upon which ART is based, part two will slowly walk therapists through the specifics of the training procedures, format, and curriculum in order to provide all of the tools and information necessary to effectively deliver the ART program.

8.1 Intended Audience for ART

The range of application for ART is very broad. The training can be used:

- As an adjunct treatment to individual therapy with patients suffering from mental disorders
- As a stand-alone, first-step intervention for individuals suffering from mental health problems
- As preventative treatment for individuals at high risk for developing mental health problems
- As training for nonclinical populations who wish to foster their personal growth

ART was originally developed as a group intervention. When delivering ART to a psychiatric population, the participants should receive concurrent individual therapy to ensure that personal issues arising in the group training can be adequately processed. Although the ART program was designed for use with groups, it can be presented to individuals as well. As an individual modality, the entire curriculum or even parts of it can be utilized to assist patients to manage emotion regulation problems, which they may find difficult to discuss in a group setting.

While ART was developed as a transdiagnostic treatment, we certainly acknowledge the importance of addressing the unique characteristics of specific disorders. Thus, when delivering the ART program to participants in a group who all share the same diagnosis, ART should be supplemented with disorder-specific interventions as needed. The disorder-specific interventions could also be provided in concurrent individual therapy or in other group treatments that focus on the specific disorder or problem.

M. Berking and B. Whitley, *Affect Regulation Training: A Practitioners' Manual*,
DOI 10.1007/978-1-4939-1022-9_8, © Springer Science+Business Media New York 2014

It should be noted that the training requires a considerable amount of concentration and attention from the participants. Therefore, when evaluating whether ART is appropriate for a particular patient, one must consider the patient's ability to engage in the skill-building exercises used in ART. Additionally, the manner in which the ART groups are led should be matched to the participants' capabilities. ART can be successfully delivered to even severe psychiatric populations in appropriate settings if additional time is provided and if training content and exercises are simplified or shortened as needed. In psychiatric populations, it is usually more effective to offer ART in the later stages of treatment to help foster and solidify treatment gains instead of using ART as a first-line treatment.

Explicit contraindications include:

• An acute psychotic or manic state
• Acute intoxication or severe and active substance abuse problems
• Severe depression that prevents effective processing of the training concepts

Beyond these relatively clear exclusion criteria, the suitability of ART for potential participants should always be determined through clinical assessment by experienced and well-trained therapists. The therapist should estimate to what extent a potential participant is capable of integrating the training concepts. If the training is to be administered in its original group format, the therapist should ensure that the potential participants would be capable of working in a group setting and would not impair the therapeutic progress of other ART participants. Regarding the age of participants, the training has been found to be suitable for participants aged 16 and older. When used with younger participants, the materials and procedures should be adapted as necessary.

8.2 Clarifying the Format

Participants should be reminded at the beginning of the training that although ART is delivered in a group format it is *not* group psychotherapy; not all participants will have the opportunity to process their individual problems in depth. ART uses a systematic, didactic approach to explain skills and concepts, followed by guided collective discussions of the material and group exercises to practice the skills and concepts. While ART encourages participants to describe their individual experiences and concerns, in-depth exploration of these experiences and concerns goes beyond the scope of the training. Participants who would like to process personal issues more deeply are invited to consider supplementing ART with individual therapy.

Since ART was originally designed to be time limited, the ART therapist is challenged to teach the skills and encourage participants to apply the material to their personal situations while not permitting personal issues to be discussed at such a deep level that the training becomes derailed or the participants begin to discuss issues that cannot be adequately resolved. If the therapist discusses the scope of ART at the beginning of the training, participants are less likely to discuss in-depth, personal issues that cannot be adequately addressed during the sessions.

Additionally, they will be more understanding if they are redirected during a group discussion, since they were made aware of this boundary in the beginning. However, if the therapist is not limited to the eighteen hours needed to adequately cover the ART curriculum, ART can easily and effectively be incorporated into a group therapy format, as participants utilize other group members, the ART Skills, and the ART therapist to work in depth on their personal issues.

8.3   Teaching Style

Many of us have had the unfortunate opportunity of participating in training classes in which the instructor was dull and did not engage the participants. These classes are difficult to sit through and generally limit the amount of learning that can occur. In order to prevent this, we encourage therapists to actively engage the participants during ART. For some therapists, this comes naturally. Others, however, will need to intentionally focus on engaging the participants by displaying an energetic personality, asking questions of the participants, sharing appropriate personal experiences, and showing enthusiasm for the training material. Regardless of the therapist's teaching style, we suggest mindfully monitoring the participants' level of engagement and taking appropriate action if needed to ensure the success of the training.

8.4   Schedule for Training Sessions

The ART material is divided into nine training modules (Fig. 8.1). As previously mentioned, a minimum of 18 hours of classroom instruction is needed to sufficiently address the material in the nine ART modules. Clinical experience has shown that 3 weeks is the minimum amount of time in which the ART program should be delivered, while 6 weeks is preferable. The ART modules can be delivered using a variety of training schedule formats. Regardless of the schedule format, sufficient time must be allotted between training sessions for participants to practice and integrate the skills they have learned during the previous training session.

Examples of schedule formats include delivering the modules over 12 weekly, 1½-hour sessions. This schedule delivers the content in smaller and easier-to-process "portions," which can be practiced during the time before the next session when another ART Skill will be introduced. This training schedule is especially advantageous for participants with more severe mental health difficulties and/or attention problems. The 12-session version may also be more conducive to certain groups such as employees at a business who may be able to meet for only short periods at a time.

In situations when participants are not able to meet as frequently or when ART must be concluded in a shorter period of time, ART can also be delivered, for example, over the course of 3 days (each consisting of 6 training hours), with 2-week intervals between each training day (see Fig. 8.2). However, since the suggested

ART 9-Session Version:

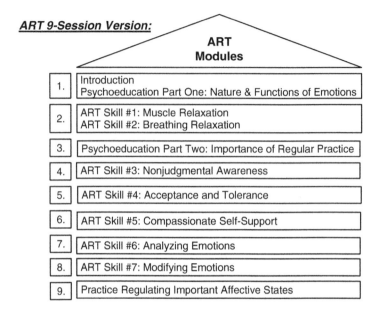

Fig. 8.1 Nine ART training modules

ART 3-Day Version:

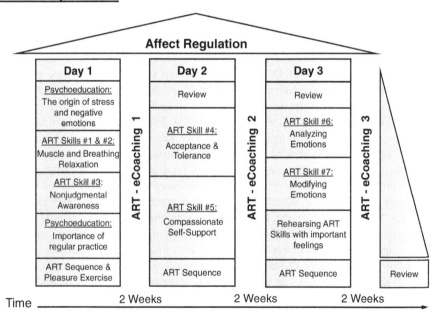

Fig. 8.2 3-Session ART schedule

interval between each training day is longer than the interval in the 12-session schedule, it becomes more difficult for ART therapists in this schedule to intervene in a timely fashion if participants abandon their daily skills practice regimen during the program.

It should be noted that any other scheduling variations beyond these two examples are also acceptable. In determining an appropriate training schedule, ART therapists are urged to consider the characteristics and needs of the intended audience. Additionally, it is important to remember that the nine individual training modules were not designed to be delivered in equal amounts of time. Some modules will take longer than others to deliver, due to the amount and type of information contained in the module. Also, some modules may take longer to present because of unique participant needs or issues that unexpectedly arise while presenting the material. In our experience, therapists become far more comfortable delivering ART when they resist the tendency to rigidly present a predetermined amount of training material in a given amount of time.

8.5   Size of Training Classes and the Co-therapist

If possible, the class size of ART training groups should be chosen in accordance with the needs and characteristics of the intended audience. Smaller class sizes are especially recommended for participants suffering from more severe disorders. In clinical populations, we recommend limiting class sizes to between four and eight participants per class. This class size allows for good interaction between the participants, as well as between the participants and the therapist. We have also had good experiences with clinical "groups" consisting of only two or three participants. There are, however, also situations where larger class sizes cannot be avoided. While larger class sizes may be appropriate for less severely impaired populations, usually there is less interaction and emotional disclosure. However, in some cases, such as in an occupational setting, this might even be preferred.

We recommend that two therapists co-facilitate the training sessions if possible. This allows one therapist to focus on instructing the course material, while the other therapist can focus on the individual participants and on the group dynamics. While one therapist could possibly do both, this would be challenging and could lead to frustrations for both the therapist and the participants.

8.6   Additional Training Materials

There are various materials that a therapist will need in order to present the training sessions, such as audio/visual equipment, flip-charts, writing instruments, etc. These training materials are described in the following sections as the curriculum is presented. The complete list of these materials is provided in Appendix C.

Chapter 9
ART Module One: Introduction and Psychoeducation

9.1 Introducing ART to the Participants

As people are generally more familiar with the concept of stress than with concepts such as "feelings" or "emotions," we describe ART in the beginning as a "stress-reduction program" (see Slide 1). As the training progresses and participants feel more secure in the group and with the training concepts, the focus gradually shifts from talking about general stress to talking about challenging "feelings" and "emotions."

The training curriculum will now be described in step-by-step detail. The presentation slides that are shown to the participants during the training sessions are listed in numerical sequence on the left side of the page. The slides can be downloaded as a computer presentation at www.AffectRegulationTraining.com with access code: ART_Pcn2cfY. The therapist narrative that corresponds to each presentation slide is listed on the right side of the page. The narrative is provided as an example which could, or rather should, be adapted to some extent in order to fit each therapist's personal style.

M. Berking and B. Whitley, *Affect Regulation Training: A Practitioners' Manual*,
DOI 10.1007/978-1-4939-1022-9_9, © Springer Science+Business Media New York 2014

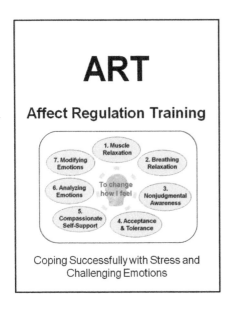

Slide 1: Welcome to Affect Regulation Training (ART)! I want to start today by congratulating all of you for deciding to learn new ways to manage stress and negative emotions! (*The therapist introduces themselves to the participants.*) We will begin today by discussing the reasons for participating in this training. I will also give you an overview of what to expect during this and the following sessions.

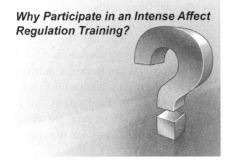

Slide 2: In this training, we will invite you to spend a lot of your time and energy on learning and practicing a number of exercises that are designed to enhance your mental fitness. Since your time and energy is a very precious resource that should not be wasted, let's start by answering the question, "Why should I spend my time and energy doing this?"

Slide 3: For me, one of the most important reasons to engage in such an intense training is that chronic stress, painful emotions, and negative moods that are left unchecked are likely to make us suffer!

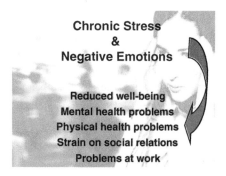

Slide 4: Chronic stress, painful emotions, and negative moods are all considered negative "affect." They reduce enjoyment in life and threaten our mental and physical health. They can also make us irritable and lower our energy level, which can cause problems in intimate relationships and with friends and coworkers.

Slide 5: All these problems (*point to problems in lower part of slide*) cause additional stress and negative feelings, which only further aggravates these problems. So eventually a vicious cycle develops in which problems just keep getting worse and worse, and the whole cycle of stress, negative emotions, and problems just seems more and more difficult to get rid of.

Note to the therapist:

When ART is provided to a homogeneous-disorder group, examples should be given to demonstrate how stress and negative emotions contribute to the maintenance of the relevant disorder. In such instances, the use of disorder-specific presentation slides and information should be considered. For example, when working exclusively with participants who have chronic pain, depression, anxiety, etc., the vicious cycle described in Slide 5 could show stress and negative emotions resulting from, as well as contributing to, the escalation and maintenance of chronic pain, depression, anxiety, etc.

The therapist continues speaking to the participants:

Slide 6: So to prevent this from happening, we need to interrupt this vicious cycle! Or even better, we need to prevent this vicious cycle from happening in the first place! But how do we do this?

Slide 7: By improving our abilities to cope with negative affect more effectively! Using more helpful ways of handling significant stress and challenging emotions will improve our mental health, physical health, and our relationships with others. Since effectively regulating our emotions can be very difficult, it is crucial to learn and practice the "ART" (*play on words*) of emotion regulation. This training was designed to provide you with some powerful tools—skills which have been shown to be very helpful when coping with stress and painful emotions.

Slide 8: What is ART?

ART Skills and ART Sequence

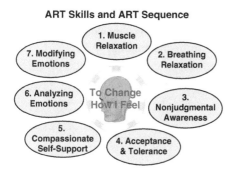

Slide 9: ART stands for Affect Regulation Training. It is an intense training program specifically designed to strengthen your abilities to regulate stress as well as challenging emotions and moods by teaching you seven specific emotion regulation skills called "ART Skills." Our goal is to help you master these skills so that you will eventually be able to use them automatically, without a lot of thought or effort. However, that won't happen overnight. You will first need to learn and practice each ART Skill **extensively**. If you do that, you will increasingly learn how to apply these skills quickly and effectively.

The ART curriculum is divided into nine modules, which we will go through during our training sessions. Our schedule for this program is … (*explain the schedule for the training sessions including session dates, times, and locations*). I want to give you an outline of the nine modules: First, we will talk about the scientific research that explains the development of stress and negative emotions. On the basis of this information, we will begin to discuss each of the seven ART Skills that can help us cope with negative affect more effectively. The first two of these are the skills of *muscle* and *breathing relaxation* that are used to calm the brain and body. The skill of *nonjudgmental awareness* is the third skill which enables us to take a mental "step back" when we are stressed and just observe what is happening.

The fourth skill is *accepting and tolerating* emotions. This skill is important because we often can't change stress reactions and feelings by sheer force of will. Often, the only alternative is to tolerate negative feelings as best we can, without engaging in a struggle to change them. This, of course, is a big challenge, and we will explain how we can meet this challenge with the fifth skill of *compassionately supporting ourselves* in difficult situations. The final two skills, *analyzing and modifying emotions*, help us understand what is causing our emotions and choose a plan of action to modify or change them. This is great news and what makes this training worthwhile! We can change how we feel!

As we learn each new skill, we will practice linking it to the skills we have already learned. This will result in a step-by-step process, called the ART Sequence. The ART Sequence can be practiced regularly at home, in order to strengthen your emotion regulation skills. With practice, the ART Sequence can then be applied in stressful situations as a powerful tool to help you cope with difficult stress reactions, emotions, and moods.

How would you like to benefit from this training?

Slide 10: Now we would like each of you to tell us how you would like to benefit from this training.

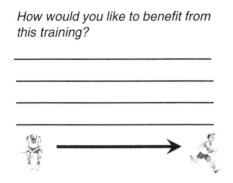

Note to the therapist:

The idea here is for the therapist to help each participant develop an "approach goal" (related to the approach orientation described in Sect. 7.1). An approach goal is focused on attaining something (e.g., I want to feel calm.), and it should reflect the previously described characteristics of successful goals: (1) have a high degree of importance, (2) be attainable, and (3) be measureable, specific, and concrete (see Sect. 7.3). Approach goals generate feelings of joy and contentment when they are attained and fill us with energy and vitality. Additionally, when an approach goal is accomplished, the behaviors that led to the accomplishment of the goal are reinforced.

It is often difficult, however, for people to form an approach goal, since people's goal structures are commonly dominated by avoidance goals (e.g., I don't want to feel anxious.), which strive to prevent something from happening. This results in constant pressure to avoid something undesired. Moreover, avoidance goals focus attention on negative concepts (e.g., "anxiety" in the goal "I don't want to feel anxious.") and are thus more likely to generate negative emotions. Finally, the only positive emotion that avoidance goals can provide is "relief" that the feared outcome did not occur. However, even this relief is often short lived as the feared outcome might still occur in the future. When compared with approach goals, research has frequently linked avoidance goals with more negative outcomes (e.g., Elliot & Church, 2002; Elliot, Sheldon, & Church, 1997; Impett, et al., 2010).

Forming an approach goal that is aligned with a person's hierarchy of goals and needs will beneficially activate the dopamine system. Dopamine releases will reinforce and strengthen behaviors that are successful in accomplishing the goal, increasing the likelihood that these helpful behaviors will occur again in the future. Now the question is, "How do we help participants develop approach goals for their problems that are aligned with their unique needs and goals structure?"

A method for developing approach goals includes the following general steps:

1. Explore and validate the person's stated problem.
2. Ask the person what she would rather have/experience instead.

3. Help her make this new positive goal as concrete as possible.
4. Encourage her to visualize a scene in which she has accomplished her goal.

These steps are used in ART by the therapist to help the participants develop approach goals by first asking the participants how they would like to benefit from ART. The therapist validates the participants' descriptions of their goals and helps them refine their goals if necessary. Following the rule of thumb that images cue emotions and emotions cue motivation, the therapist then asks the participants to describe an imagined scene of what their lives would look like if they accomplished their goals. The therapist asks the participants to elaborate on their imagined scene until it elicits positive affect (e.g., a smile) from the participants. Finally, the therapist helps the participants brainstorm a catchphrase that accurately describes the positive and realistic goals the participants would like to achieve through the ART program.

Example of turning an avoidance goal into an approach goal:

In order to show the application of this process in ART, let's assume that the therapist asks a participant in the group how they would like to benefit from ART, and the participant responds with an avoidance goal, "I do not want to be so anxious!" The therapist in this example would respond by first validating the participant's description of his/her goal.

Therapist: Feeling less anxious is a great goal. Let's try to refine this a little bit. What would happen if you weren't so anxious?
Participant: I would do more things outside of the house … like go to the mall.
Therapist: Just for a moment, would you please try to imagine or visualize in your head a scene in which you are enjoying yourself at the mall?
Participant: Yes. I see myself walking in the mall with shopping bags.
Therapist: And how do you feel in this scene?
Participant: I feel calm and happy. I am enjoying myself.
Therapist: If we were to find a short phrase to describe this scene, could we call it "mall joy"?
Participant: Yeah (smiling) … that sums it up.
Therapist: So it sounds like your reason for participating in ART (therapist points to Slide 10) is "getting back my mall joy."
Participant: Yeah, I think you're right (continuing to smile—signaling the approach orientation has been triggered).

After an approach goal has been articulated by each participant, the therapist then asks the participants if there is anything they <u>do not</u> want to experience during the training. Participants typically respond by saying they do not want to be put on the spot in front of others. This question is asked in order to address the participants' basic *need for control* and the *need to maximize pleasure and minimize pain*, by demonstrating to the participants that they will be well taken care of during the training and not recklessly or thoughtlessly put in situations in which they could feel unsafe or experience distress. This further reinforces the approach orientation.

After the participants have had an opportunity to develop an approach goal and to express what they do not want to occur during ART, the therapist addresses the participants as a whole again. The therapist reinforces the importance of holding onto the approach goals they developed throughout the training as a way to keep themselves motivated, especially during some of the more challenging parts of the training.

The following exercise is then conducted to lighten the mood and build rapport between participants. First, the therapist asks that everyone stand and form a circle. The therapist should participate as well. Everyone faces the middle of the circle. One of the participants is given a foam ball. The participant with the ball is asked to complete the following sentence, "My name is ..., and I feel stressed when ...." After the participant with the ball has completed the sentence, he/she passes the ball to another participant or to the therapist who also completes the sentence before passing the ball again to someone else.

After everyone has had a chance to complete the sentence, the last person with the ball then singles one person out and attempts to accurately state that participant's name and when he/she feels stressed. After doing so correctly or after being coached by other participants, the person passes the ball to someone else, who also attempts to accurately state another participant's name and when he/she feels stressed.

After everyone has attempted to correctly identify someone else's name and when he/she feels stressed, the person who ends up with the ball modifies the original sentence to, "My name is ... and I can tell when I am feeling stress because ... (e.g., my stomach is in knots or my shoulder muscles are tight)." This participant passes the ball to someone else who completes the sentence and passes the ball again until everyone has completed the sentence. The last person to complete the sentence then singles someone out and, just as before, attempts to state that participant's name and how that person can tell he/she is under stress. Once the participant has done this correctly or has been coached by other participants, he/she passes the ball to the person he/she singled out who then identifies someone else's name and how that person can tell he/she is under stress. In this manner, the ball is passed around again.

The last person holding the ball begins the third and final round of the exercise by completing the sentence, "My name is ... and one way I relax is by ...." This participant passes the ball to someone else who completes the sentence and passes the ball again until everyone has completed the sentence. The last person to complete the sentence then singles someone out and again as before attempts to state that participant's name and one way he/she relaxes. Once the participant with the ball has done this correctly or has been coached by other participants, the ball is passed to the person he/she singled out who identifies someone else's name and the way he/she relaxes. In this manner the ball is passed around again. After everyone has finished this round, the exercise is completed.

The therapist should provide examples of how to complete the sentences during this exercise, since even basic identification of feeling states may be very foreign to some participants. For example, participants may not know "how to tell they are feeling stress." Additionally, many participants will not be able to remember other participants' names or what they said to complete their sentences. These are excellent opportunities for the therapist to encourage and model compassion as the tendency for some participants may be to berate themselves for not being able to remember what was said.

After this exercise is concluded, the therapist begins in the next section to introduce the theoretical and empirical background for the ART Skills.

9.2 Psychoeducation: Theoretical and Empirical Background of the ART Skills

The following section is designed to educate the participants on the development and function of stress and negative emotions and how this information can be used to manage stress and negative emotions more effectively. In order to actively engage participants in the learning process, therapists can complement their energetic teaching style with the use of the Personal Insights Worksheet (Fig. 9.1; Appendix D) at some point during the psychoeducation presentation.

This worksheet asks participants to (1) choose a piece of information from the training they found most interesting so far and write it down in the column on the left-hand side of the worksheet and (2) decide how they will practically apply this information to make a positive change in their life and then write this practical application in the column on the right-hand side of the worksheet. A participant, for example, may write that it was helpful to learn that "trying hard *not* to experience an emotion

	What I learned	How I can apply it
1)		
2)		
3)		
4)		
5)		
6)		
7)		
8)		
9)		
10)		

Personal Insights

Fig. 9.1 Personal Insights Worksheet

can actually make it stronger." The practical application of this information could be that in the future they "will try not to automatically avoid or dismiss their negative emotions." The ART therapist may choose to have participants complete the worksheet, and then encourage the participants to share what they wrote with the group.

The therapist continues speaking to the participants:

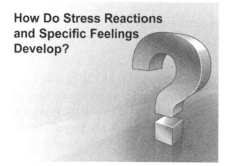

How Do Stress Reactions and Specific Feelings Develop?

Slide 11: Thank you for introducing yourselves. Are there any questions so far? Then let's get started. We are going to start by gaining a better understanding of stress and negative emotions. This understanding helps us develop and apply effective techniques to constructively deal with stress and negative emotions.

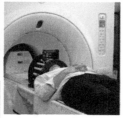

Functional Magnetic Resonance Imaging (fMRI) machine

Slide 12: In the past few years, our knowledge about stress and emotions has increased dramatically. This increase is due to enormous technical progress in this field. For example, research methods like functional magnetic resonance imaging (fMRI) allow us to practically look into the brain and watch it work. In fMRI studies, people are put into a magnetic tube while being exposed to different images or tasks, which trigger stress reactions or specific feelings.

The Amygdala: Anxiety and Stress Center

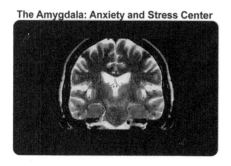

Slide 13: Here you can see that an area in the brain called the *amygdala* is being activated in response to stress.[1]

---

[1] It is important to remember that while amygdala activation occurs in response to negative stimuli, it also occurs in response to positive stimuli (Costafreda, Brammer, David, & Fu, 2008; Hamann, Ely, Hoffman, & Kilts, 2002; Herbert et al., 2009).

The Amygdala: Anxiety and Stress Center

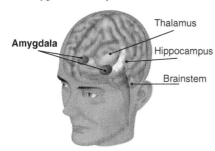

Slide 14: The amygdala constantly "scans" our environment and interprets whether or not our goals are potentially being threatened. If the amygdala thinks our needs and goals are threatened, it becomes active. Then the nerve cells in the amygdala fire and send electrical signals to other areas of the brain, for example, to the hypothalamus.[2]

Amygdala Activation → Changes Mind and Body

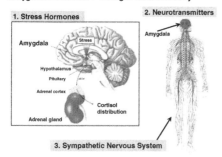

Slide 15: The hypothalamus causes the release of stress hormones like adrenaline, noradrenaline, and cortisol. These stress hormones then cause massive changes in the body. For example, they increase the muscles' energy, so the muscles become as efficient as possible in potentially dangerous situations. The amygdala also releases neurotransmitters, such as acetylcholine, in the brain that cause the mind to become attentive and alert. Finally, the amygdala sends electrical signals into the body, activating the sympathetic nervous system, which does things like increasing heart rate and respiration. (*Briefly refer to the areas of activation on the slide.*)

What is the Purpose of Stress Reactions and Emotions?

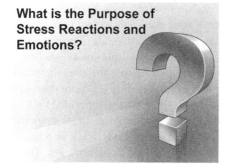

Slide 16: And all of these physical and mental changes have a specific purpose.

---

[2] We realize that it is scientifically inaccurate to anthropomorphize brain regions. However, since we have found it to be very helpful in explaining important complicated processes to our clients, we have decided to continue utilizing this approach in spite of appropriate concerns.

The Stress Response Prepares for Action

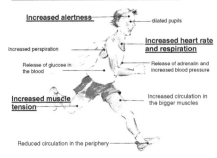

Slide 17: They prepare us for any action that is needed to ward off potential threats. The increased mental focus ensures that we are mentally wide awake, so we can be vigilant for any threats and respond quickly at even the slightest hint of danger. The increased muscle tension ensures we can flee or fight with speed, strength, and dexterity. Increased heart and breathing rates ensure that our muscles have more blood and oxygen to make them more efficient.

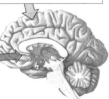

Stress is a rapidly triggered, nonspecific activation that prepares the body for actions to protect itself from potential threats

e.g., by fighting, escaping, or freezing

Slide 18: Thus, the stress reaction is the result of a rapidly triggered, nonspecific activation that prepares our body for actions to help protect us from possible threats by fighting, fleeing, or even freezing. Freezing is a state in which we are able to remain motionless to avoid detection, such as from a predator whose eyes are very sensitive to even the slightest amount of movement.

2 Steps in the Development of Emotions

2. Subsequent, slow and thorough **analysis in higher cortical areas (prefrontal cortex)** turns a general **stress response** into **specific emotions**

1. **Rapid activation of the Amygdala** when threatened causes a **stress response (i.e. non-specific activation,** which facilitates numerous coping responses)

Slide 19: As part of this stress response, the prefrontal cortex (PFC) (*show on the slide*) and the hippocampus (*show on the slide*) are also activated and begin another slower, more thorough evaluation than the evaluation initially conducted by the amygdala. Depending on the outcome of this more thorough (cognitive) analysis, the stress reaction is either inhibited (if the more thorough analysis shows that danger does not in fact exist) or turns the stress response into specific emotions, such as anxiety, anger, shame, guilt, sadness, etc. These emotions facilitate more specific responses to cope with the challenging circumstance.

Emotions: Primary Reaction Plus Cognitive Appraisal

If thorough analysis = "I'm weaker!" → stress becomes fear

Fear: Helps detect threats; facilitates escape & avoidance

Emotions: Primary Reaction Plus Cognitive Appraisal

If analysis = "I'm stronger!" → stress becomes anger

Anger: Facilitates assertiveness & fighting back

Slide 20: For example, a situation such as seeing a hungry dinosaur would cause the amygdala to trigger a stress response. The prefrontal cortex would then conduct a more thorough assessment of the situation. If the prefrontal cortex-based analysis determines that (1) "Yes, there is a real threat to my needs and goals because I am being attacked by a dinosaur!" and (2) "I can't handle the threat because he is much stronger than I am," then the feeling *anxiety or fear* will be activated. The feeling of fear will help us quickly turn around and flee, which is likely the most appropriate behavioral response to this situation.

Slide 21: On the other hand, if the analysis determines (1) "Yes, there is a real threat to my needs and goals because I am being attacked by a dinosaur!", **but** (2) "Because it is much smaller than me I can handle the threat; I have this big club to use; and how dare this thing disturb me while I am sleeping!" then the feeling *anger* will be triggered instead. The emotion "anger" helps prepare the body and mind for assertive actions like fighting. Fighting back in this situation is probably the most appropriate response for the caveman in our example, since it will allow him to kill the mean dinosaur before it has the chance to attack him as a full-grown dinosaur.

Emotions developed over the course of evolution to help us protect our needs and achieve our goals.

Slide 22: Over the course of human evolution, we developed the ability to constantly analyze situations and to react with specific emotions. As we've just demonstrated with the dinosaur and the caveman, emotional reactions developed over the course of evolution in order to help us protect our needs and reach our goals as efficiently as possible. The more emotional prehistoric humans were able to react better and faster to the demands of the environment than the less emotional. Therefore, the more emotional humans were better at raising and protecting their offspring, so their offspring were more likely to survive and pass down the genetic propensity to experience intense emotions. This advantage was very meaningful in the evolutionary process. Thus, through the "survival of the fittest," all human beings react with emotions to significant events.

But watch out !!!

Slide 23: In order to deal constructively with stress and negative feelings, it is important to keep in mind that the basic patterns of our emotional reactions are anachronistic remains from the Stone Age. During that time, it was usually very helpful and adaptive to react with muscle tension and maximum activation in threatening situations.

Problems with our Evolutionary Heritage

Slide 24: However, while tensing your muscles, raising your shoulders, and flashing your teeth might have helped to intimidate a prehistoric opponent, it is completely useless when trying to make your computer boot up faster (*wait for the joke to kick in*). In this situation (point to the slide), such a reaction is not helpful at all. Instead the smart thing to do in this situation is to relax and wait, right?

So we have carried this outdated emotional reaction system with us into our modern times. This system wants to help us and to protect us, but it may not assess situations accurately and the response it suggests may not always be the most appropriate one. Thus, while recognizing our emotions as well-intentioned friends, it is also important to critically decide whether the information included in an emotion is correct and whether its suggested action would indeed be helpful.

Today, emotions:

1. **Provide us with <u>valuable information</u>** on (perceived) descrepancies between our needs and goals and what we think we are getting.

2. **<u>Help us take action</u>** to reduce such discrepancies, achieve our goals, and satisfy our needs.

Slide 25: However, when we learn how to use our emotions effectively, they can become helpful allies, even now in modern times. They provide us with valuable information. For example, fear tells us that our needs and goals are being threatened. Anger tells us that someone is hindering our attempts to attain our goals. Sadness tells us that despite our current efforts, we will not be able reach an important goal.

Emotions such as these also help us to engage in *specific actions* in order to cope effectively with challenging situations. For example, fear encourages us to be vigilant and to respond quickly. Anger gives us energy to assert our legitimate rights, even if we have to fight for these rights. Finally, sadness helps us to let go of goals that we will not be able to attain and instead find other more attainable goals.

Short-term Stress and Negative Emotions are not Harmful

1. Our body is prepared for the changes associated with a stress response or negative emotions.
For example: Anxiety causes a rapid pulse, but the heart is built to endure an accelared heart rate (We do not die when climbing stairs!)

2. *Lethal stress reactions and emotions would never have prevailed in evolution!*

Slide 26: We also need to remember that intense, short-term stress reactions and negative feelings may not necessarily be helpful, but they are not dangerous for the healthy body. In fact, the body is designed to produce and tolerate negative affect. For example, our heart beats faster when we are scared, but it also beats faster when we work out or even walk up a flight of stairs. The heart is built to endure this type of activation. If emotions had deadly consequences, they would have never prevailed through evolution!

However ... the Long-Term Consequences Might Be!

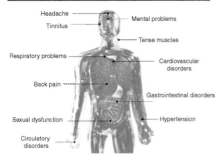

Slide 27: However, if we constantly experience high levels of stress or continually have intense negative feelings, the situation can look quite different. Long-term, intense stress can lead to a series of physical and mental problems. (*Ask for examples from participants.*) Physical difficulties can include muscle tension, chronic pain, tension headaches, migraines, sleep disturbances, heart attacks, skin problems, breathing problems, etc. Mental difficulties can include anxiety disorders, uncontrolled anger, social anxiety, burnout, low energy level, concentration difficulties, and symptoms of depression.

Automatic Down-Regulation of Stress and Negative Emotions

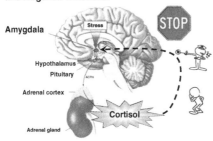

Slide 28: Stress reactions and negative feelings are *not* designed to last forever. Our body is equipped with mechanisms to ensure these reactions do not continue indefinitely. For example, there are unique cell structures in the brain that monitor levels of the stress hormone cortisol and are able to stop its release when high cortisol levels are sustained for extended periods of time. This can be viewed as the brain's own "self-defense system," since many areas of the brain, such as the prefrontal cortex, can be damaged by the neurotoxic effect of sustained high cortisol levels.

Typical Course of Feelings

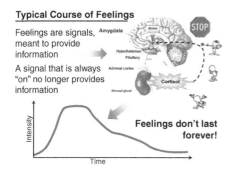

Feelings are signals,
meant to provide
information

A signal that is always
"on" no longer provides
information

Feelings don't last
forever!

Slide 29: In addition, emotional reactions are signals that are intended to communicate information to us such as when our needs or goals are being threatened. A signal that is always "on" is no longer communicating any information. That's another reason why reactions need to "shut down" after a while; otherwise, they lose their power to communicate. That is why the typical course of an emotion looks like this (*show on slide*). In other words, emotions are *not* permanent. They are temporary phenomena. If we do not avoid, fight, suppress, or in some way keep them going, the body will naturally regulate them, reducing their intensity.

References

Costafreda, S. G., Brammer, M. J., David, A. S., & Fu, C. H. Y. (2008). Predictors of amygdala activation during the processing of emotional stimuli: A meta-analysis of 385 PET and fMRI studies. *Brain Research Reviews, 58*(1), 57–70.

Elliot, A. J., & Church, M. A. (2002). Client-articulated avoidance goals in the therapy context. *Journal of Counseling Psychology, 49*(2), 243–254.

Elliot, A. J., Sheldon, K. M., & Church, M. A. (1997). Avoidance personal goals and subjective well-being. *Personality and Social Psychology Bulletin, 23*(9), 915–927.

Hamann, S. B., Ely, T. D., Hoffman, J. M., & Kilts, C. D. (2002). Ecstasy and agony: Activation of the human amygdala in positive and negative emotion. *Psychological Science, 13*(2), 135–141.

Herbert, C., Ethofer, T., Anders, S., Junghofer, M., Wildgruber, D., Grodd, W., et al. (2009). Amygdala activation during reading of emotional adjectives – an advantage for pleasant content. *Social Cognitive and Affective Neuroscience, 4*(1), 35–49.

Impett, E. A., Gordon, A. M., Kogan, A., Oveis, C., Gable, S. L., & Keltner, D. (2010). Moving toward more perfect unions: Daily and long-term consequences of approach and avoidance goals in romantic relationships. *Journal of Personality and Social Psychology, 99*(6), 948–963.

Chapter 10
ART Module Two: Muscle and Breathing Relaxation

10.1 Vicious Cycles #1 and #2: Amygdala Activation and Muscle Tension/Rapid Breathing

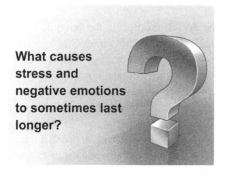

Slide 30: But sometimes stress and negative feelings remain intense for longer periods of time. How does this happen?

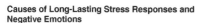
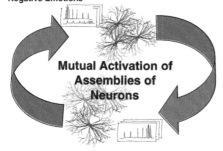

Slide 31: Stress responses and negative emotions last longer when different areas of the brain and body start to mutually activate each other. If this happens, these vicious cycles can override the natural regulation mechanisms in the brain and in the body.

M. Berking and B. Whitley, *Affect Regulation Training: A Practitioners' Manual*,
DOI 10.1007/978-1-4939-1022-9_10, © Springer Science+Business Media New York 2014

Vicious Cycle #1

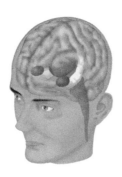

Slide 32: For example, when the amygdala is activated by a situation that is interpreted as potentially threatening, the amygdala facilitates an increase in muscle tension, which can be helpful in situations that require an immediate fight-or-flight response. Since we have normally experienced this muscle tension during threatening situations in which the amygdala was activated, the muscle tension itself becomes a danger signal to the amygdala. Thus, a vicious cycle develops: Activation of the amygdala causes increased muscle tension, and increased muscle tension causes further activation of the amygdala, which causes even more muscle tension.

Vicious Cycle #2

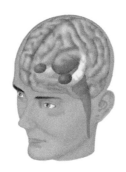

Slide 33: Similarly, the amygdala also facilitates rapid breathing. Since we have typically experienced this rapid breathing during threatening situations in which the amygdala was activated, rapid breathing itself, just like muscle tension, becomes a danger signal to the amygdala. This creates another vicious cycle: Activation of the amygdala causes rapid breathing, and rapid breathing causes further activation of the amygdala, which causes even more rapid breathing.

Vicious Cycles #1 & #2

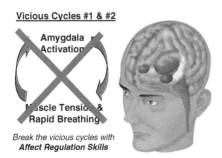

Break the vicious cycles with
Affect Regulation Skills

Slide 34: If we want to prevent stress and negative feelings from sticking around, we need to break the two vicious cycles we just talked about by using emotion regulation skills. Does anyone have an idea of what skills we would need in order to break these vicious cycles? (*Participants respond with ideas.*)

Breaking the Vicious Cycles

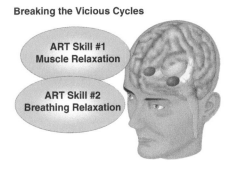

ART Skill #1
Muscle Relaxation

ART Skill #2
Breathing Relaxation

Slide 35: Whenever we realize that we are experiencing stress or negative emotions, we can break these vicious cycles by consciously relaxing our muscles and calming our breathing. By doing this we are telling the amygdala that it can go off "high alert" since the situation is really not so threatening. Relaxing our muscles and calming our breathing may not make the original stress or negative emotions go away, but it can keep them from spiraling out of control, intensifying, and lasting longer than they should. So let's take a look at ART Skills #1 and #2 that can help us break these vicious cycles by relaxing our muscles and calming our breathing.

10.2   ART Skills #1 and #2: Muscle and Breathing Relaxation

Note to the therapist:

At this point in the first module, the therapist begins the process of teaching ART Skills #1 and #2. The format for teaching all of the ART Skills is the same. The therapist first uses neuroscience to describe the rationale for the particular skill. Next, the therapist teaches the skill in detail through the use of a skill-building exercise. Finally, the skill is chained with previously learned skills to construct the *ART Sequence*, which at the end will be comprised of all seven ART Skills.

ART Skill #1 is based upon the well-established method of *progressive muscle relaxation* developed by Edmund Jacobson (1964), in which muscle groups in the body are sequentially tensed and then relaxed. ART Skill #2 consists of deep, controlled inhalations and long, slow exhalations, with a focus on the awareness of the breath during the exhalation. Skills #1 and #2 are combined in ART so that muscle relaxation begins with and is accompanied by long, calm breathing.

Muscle and breathing relaxation (ART Skills #1 and #2) are taught first using a longer version of muscle relaxation, which is later shortened in subsequent training modules. Participants are first taught to tense and relax four muscle groups separately, with relaxation occurring on the participants' exhalation. In a later training module, all four muscle groups are tensed together and relaxed together, with relaxation occurring during the participants' exhalation. By the end of the ART training, the participants are directed to relax all four muscle groups simultaneously, on the exhalation, without tensing the muscle groups prior.

The following is an overview of how ART Skills #1 and #2 are taught using progressively shorter versions of muscle relaxation:

Step One (long version):

Each muscle group below is first tensed and then relaxed during deliberately extended exhalations:

1. Muscles in the hands and arms (repeat once)
2. Muscles in the face (repeat once)
3. Muscles in the shoulders and back (repeat once)
4. Muscles in the stomach, buttocks, and legs (repeat once)

Step Two (short version):

All muscle groups are tensed simultaneously and then relaxed simultaneously during an extended exhalation. Repeat once.

Step Three (ultrashort version):

All muscle groups are simultaneously relaxed during an extended exhalation without tensing them first.

The following section includes specific instructions for teaching ART Skills #1 and #2:

The therapist continues speaking to the participants:

ART Skills and ART Sequence

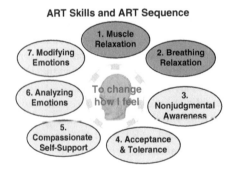

Slide 36: To give you a quick overview of ART Skills #1 and #2, we will be learning how, in these first two skills, to connect muscle relaxation with slow, calm breathing with a focus on long exhalations. Let's talk about how to do this. ART Skill #1 is based on something called progressive muscle relaxation. Do any of you have experience using progressive muscle relaxation? (*If yes:*) Would you mind telling us what it is? (*Supplement any responses from the group with the following information.*)

Progressive muscle relaxation, or PMR, is a form of relaxation training. In PMR, various muscle groups in the body are tensed for a short time and then deliberately relaxed … very slowly … and with focused attention. (*Demonstrate by clenching your fist and then slowly unclenching it. Ask the participants to do this all together.*) The goal of PMR is to create relaxation for the body and the mind. PMR is the most well-researched relaxation method, and many studies have shown that PMR can help decrease physical and mental discomfort.

In ART Skill #1 we use a modified version of PMR. In this modified version we will first learn to tense and relax muscles in large groups, in four different areas of the body. Once we have practiced tensing and relaxing each of the four muscle groups individually, we will learn to tense all four muscle groups simultaneously and then relax all four groups simultaneously. Finally, we will learn how to relax all of the muscle groups simultaneously, without tensing them beforehand.

Now as we talked about before, we are combining ART Skill #1 (muscle relaxation) with ART Skill #2 (breathing relaxation). So let's spend a little time now talking about breathing relaxation taught in ART Skill #2. Breathing relaxation consists of deliberately calming and slowing down our breathing. We'll pay particular attention to the exhalation or the out-breath, doing our best to exhale as slowly and calmly as possible. Let's try a short demonstration. When I say "now," I'd like everyone to breathe in … and exhale as long as possible … and then for three more seconds. Let's try it … Now. (*Model the exercise as the group participates.*) Breathe in … and exhale as long as possible and then for three more seconds. (*Pause.*) Good.

Since we are combining ART Skills #1 and #2, we begin muscle relaxation by focusing on deepening and calming our breathing. We will also relax our muscles only when we exhale, focusing on lengthening the exhalation as we intentionally allow the muscles to relax even more.

I'll now walk you through the instructions for the exercise we will use to practice ART Skills #1 and #2. I will be using the version of muscle relaxation that tenses and relaxes each of the four muscle groups individually. Don't worry about trying to remember what I say or the physical movements I make. Just follow along with me. When we later practice the exercise as a group I will provide all of the instructions. If you want, we will also give you a CD or audio files to download containing the exercise instructions, so you can practice later at home.

Let's first talk about our posture during this exercise. The goal of the training is to eventually be able to relax your muscles in any posture. However, we will start by using a sitting posture. We recommend placing both feet flat on the floor and shoulder width apart. Sit upright as much as is comfortable for you, and make sure your back is well supported. Your head should be balanced upright and be positioned in the middle of your shoulders. You can lay your hands on your thighs or on the armrests of the chair you are in. You can close your eyes or focus your gaze on a point in your lap or in the room.

Okay, everyone. Please follow along with me as I walk you through the muscle and breathing relaxation technique of ART Skills #1 and #2. First, take a slow, deep breath in and then exhale as long as possible and then for 3 s more. We will now focus on the first muscle group. Tense the muscles in your hands, forearms, and upper arms by clenching your fists, pointing your fists inwards toward your biceps, and pulling your fists toward your shoulders. Then, hold the tension, and after 3 s, with the next exhalation, relax your muscles slowly and very deliberately. Now that the muscles are relaxed again, lay your arms down. Let's repeat this process again. Remember that the focus in this exercise is on relaxation, not tension. (*Repeat the relaxation process for the first muscle group.*)

Next, we will focus on the second muscle group. Please follow along with me again. First, tense the face muscles by clenching your teeth, pulling the corners of your mouth outwards, and pressing your tongue on the roof of your mouth. At the same time, carefully squeeze your eyes shut and furrow your eyebrows. Tense your muscles as much as you can, but not so much that it hurts. Hold the tension for 3 s and then, when breathing out again, relax the muscles. Let's repeat the same procedure again. (*Repeat the relaxation process for the second muscle group.*)

Now we will work on the third muscle group. (*The group continues to follow along with the therapist throughout the remainder of the instructions.*) First, tense your neck and back by lifting your shoulders up high and pushing them back. At the same time, move your hips forward slightly and arch your back in order to tense the muscles in the lower back. Hold the tension for 3 s, and then release the tension with a long exhalation. Let's repeat this process one more time. (*Repeat the relaxation process for the third muscle group.*)

The fourth and final muscle group consists of the muscles in the stomach, buttocks, and legs. First, press your buttocks together while also straightening your legs in front of you and slightly lifting your feet off of the floor in order to tense the muscles in your stomach. Also, point your feet downward in order to tense the muscles in your thighs and hips. Continue tensing the muscles in your thighs and hips by pointing feet back toward your face. Hold the tension for 3 s, and then on the next exhalation relax the muscles. Let's finish by repeating this process one more time. (*Repeat the relaxation process for the fourth muscle group.*)

Does anyone have questions about the techniques we just discussed?

When doing this exercise, you will probably find that your attention will wander and you will start thinking about other things. This is very normal and completely fine. In fact, it's important for you to accept this as a natural process of your brain that happens to everyone. When you notice that your attention is wandering, just make a short mental note of what is happening by using words like "planning," "worrying," and "remembering" and then gently bring your attention back to the exercise. When your attention wanders again, simply make another mental note and then again gently bring your attention back to the training.

Just continue doing this any time you notice your attention is wandering, even if it happens 100 times during the exercise! If you become distracted during the exercise by something else, like noise or physical sensations, just make another mental note to yourself like "noise" and "ache" and then gently direct your attention back to the exercise. Does this process make sense? Are you ready for me to lead you in the exercise? Then let's go!

10.3   ART Sequence with ART Skills #1 and #2: Muscle and Breathing Relaxation

The therapist may guide the following ART Sequence Exercise using the "Exercise One" audio that can be downloaded from www.AffectRegulationTraining.com— with access code: ART_Pcn2cfY. All exercises described in this manual may be accessed via this same website and access code. The ART therapist may also guide this ART Sequence Exercise themselves using the following instructions:

We will start the exercise after the sound of the bell.

Sound of the bell

Find a comfortable posture in which you can sit for a while without difficulties. Make sure that your feet are flat on the ground and that your back is properly supported. You can put your hands on the armrests or on your thighs. Close your eyes or focus on a point in the room. Allow yourself permission to take this 15-min break in order to relax, build some strength, and recharge your batteries. Relax your muscles. Breathe in deeply (*deep audible inhalation*) and slowly and consciously exhale as long as possible and then for 3 s more (*audible long exhalation*), letting go of all the tension you have gathered during the day … as much as possible at this given moment. (*5 s pause*)

Then bring your attention to your hands and arms. Now tense the muscles in your hands and arms by clenching your hands into fists. Angle your fists inward. Angle the forearms toward your upper arms, and pull the fists toward your shoulders so that the shoulder muscles are tensed as well. Feel the tension in your hands and arms. Release all other muscles in your body. Keep on breathing. Pay attention to your muscle tension. Hold the tension (*3 s pause*), and then release the tension very slowly with the next long out-breath. Let the muscles relax. Release your arms back to a resting position, and be aware of the difference between the tension you felt before and the relaxation you feel now. Be aware of even the smallest changes you can perceive as you now release your muscles more and more. (*15 s pause*)

Now bring your attention to your hands and arms again. Tense these areas again by clenching your fists, angling them inward, angling your forearms toward your upper arms, and pulling the fists toward your shoulders so that the shoulders are tensed again. Feel the tension in your hands and arms. Release all other muscles in your body. Keep on breathing. Pay attention to your muscle tension again. Hold the tension (*3 s pause*), and release it very slowly with the next long out-breath. Let the muscles relax. Release your arms back to a resting position, and be aware of the difference between the tension you felt before and the relaxation you feel now. Be aware of even the smallest changes you can perceive as you now release your muscles more and more. (*15 s pause*) Breathe calmly and regularly, and feel how each muscle relaxes more and more with every out-breath … how the pleasant feeling of relaxation expands more and more. (*15 s pause*)

Continue by bringing your attention to your face. Now tense all the muscles in your face by clenching your teeth together, pulling the corners of your mouth outward, and pressing your tongue against the roof of your mouth. Carefully squeeze your eyes shut and furrow your eyebrows very slightly. Release all other muscles in your body. Keep on breathing. Feel the tension in your face. Hold the tension (*3 s pause*), and release it very slowly with the next long out-breath. Let the muscles in your face relax, and be aware of the difference between the tension you felt before and the relaxation you feel now. (*15 s pause*)

Then bring your attention back to your face. Again, tense all the muscles in your face by clenching your teeth, pulling the corners of your mouth outward, and pressing your tongue against the roof of your mouth. Carefully squeeze your eyes shut and furrow your eyebrows very slightly. Release all other muscles in your body. Keep on breathing. Feel the tension in your face. Hold the tension (*3 s pause*), and release it very slowly with the next long out-breath. Let the muscles in your face relax, and be aware of the difference between the tension you felt before and the relaxation you feel now. (*5 s pause*) Breathe calmly and regularly and feel how the muscles relax with every long and conscious out-breath ... more and more—how the pleasant feeling of relaxation expands more and more and becomes deeper and deeper. (*15 s pause*)

Continue by bringing your attention to your neck and back. Tense your neck by pulling your shoulders as near to your ears as possible. Then tense your upper and lower back by pulling your shoulders as far back as possible and simultaneously tilting your hips forward and slightly arching your back. Release all other muscles in your body. Keep on breathing. Feel the tension in your neck and back. Hold the tension (*3 s pause*), and then release it very slowly with the next long out-breath. Let the muscles relax, and be aware of the difference between the tension you felt before and the relaxation you feel now. (*15 s pause*)

Now return your attention again to your neck and back. Again, tense your neck by pulling your shoulders as near to your ears as possible. Then tense your upper and lower back by pulling your shoulders as far back as possible and simultaneously tilting your hips forward and slightly arching your back. Release all other muscles in your body. Keep on breathing. Feel the tension in your neck and back. Hold the tension (*3 s pause*), and then release it very slowly with the next long out-breath. Let the muscles relax, and be aware of the difference between the tension you felt before and the relaxation you feel now. (*15 s pause*) Breathe calmly and regularly, and feel how the muscles relax more and more with every long and conscious out-breath ... how the pleasant feeling of relaxation expands more and more.

Now bring your attention to your buttocks, your belly, and your legs. Tense these muscles by pressing your buttocks together while straightening your legs in front of you and slightly lifting your feet off of the floor. Also, point your feet downward. Feel the tension in your buttocks, your belly, and your legs. Release all other muscles in your body. Keep on breathing. Feel the tension. Hold the tension (*3 s pause*), and then release it very slowly with the next long out-breath. Release your legs back to a resting position. Let your muscles relax, and be aware of the difference between the tension you felt before and the relaxation you feel now. (*5 s pause*)

Now bring your attention back to your buttocks, your belly, and your legs. Tense the muscles again by pressing your buttocks together while straightening your legs in front of you and slightly lifting your feet off of the floor. This time, point your feet back toward your face. Feel the tension in your buttocks, your belly, and your legs. Release all other muscles in your body. Keep on breathing. Feel the tension. Hold the tension. (*3 s pause*) Then release it very slowly with the next long out-breath. Release your legs back to a resting position. Let your muscles relax, and be aware of the difference between the tension you felt before and the relaxation you feel now. (*5 s pause*) Breathe calmly and regularly, and feel how the muscles relax more and more with every out-breath ... how the pleasant feeling of relaxation becomes deeper and deeper. (*15 s pause*)

Now take some time to enjoy the feeling of relaxation ... to rest ... and to gain new strength. (*30 s pause*)

And now, when you are ready … slowly … at your own pace … bring your attention back from the relaxation exercise by breathing in deeply (*audibly inhale*), stretching and flexing your body (*demonstrate*), opening your eyes, and lightly tapping on your thighs a few times so that you become fully awake again.

Sound of the bell
Note to the therapist:

After the exercise, the participants are encouraged to discuss their experiences during the exercise. Therapists should start with an open-ended question such as "What was that like for you?" As the discussion progresses, the therapist may need to ask specific questions, so participants elaborate on their answers. Here are some questions and comments that may be helpful to facilitate discussion:

"Did you find your mind wandering a lot?" "If so, that's normal." "What did you do when you noticed your mind wandering?" If they say they brought their attention back to the exercise, offer reinforcement. If they say they got frustrated, normalize the feeling while also encouraging them to continue to practice being aware of distractions and then bringing their attention back to the exercise.

"Were you able to tense the specific muscle groups that we asked you to tense?" "What was it like to tense your muscles on purpose and then to relax them?" "What did it feel like?" "Did your muscles feel different after you did it?" (*It's okay if they did not notice a difference.*)

It is extremely important that the participants experience a feeling of success in this first exercise. Thus, any difficulties should be normalized, and successes should be highlighted. One success could be that participants were able to sit still throughout most of the practice, even if they had urges to move around. This can be quite difficult. If needed, the therapist may work in more detail with the participants to brainstorm strategies in order to manage difficulties encountered during the exercise.

If the conclusion of the ART Sequence Exercise corresponds with the end of the training session for the day, the following applies: (If not, skip forward to Module Three.) Prior to concluding for the day, participants should be given the audio CD containing Exercise #1. The participants should be encouraged to practice ART Skills #1 and #2 during the time before the next scheduled training session by using the audio CD containing ART Sequence Exercise #1 and by following along with the short exercises, using either the printed training calendar or messages sent via email or text messaging. Each day, the participants should ideally practice ART Sequence Exercise #1 from the audio CD and follow along with the short exercises from the training calendar, text messages, or emails. The audio CDs containing the ART Sequence Exercises and the short exercises in printed form, text, and email are described in further detail in Chap. 11 starting with Slide 50.

Reference

Jacobson, E. (1964). *Anxiety and tension control: A physiologic approach*. Philadelphia, PA: J. B. Lippincott Co.

Chapter 11
Module Three: Psychoeducation Part II (The Importance of Regular Practice)

Successful acquisition and utilization of the ART Skills depends on regular practice of the skills by the participants during the intervals between training sessions and also after the sessions have concluded. For many participants, however, regularly taking time out of their busy day to practice the skills is a challenging task. To encourage and motivate participants to engage in daily practice of the skills, the ART therapist should facilitate a structured discussion on the need for regular training. The following slides and instructions provide an example of this discussion for ART therapists.

The therapist continues speaking to the participants:

Why is practice so important?

Slide 37: Now that we've spent time learning ART Skills #1 and #2, we want to spend some time talking about the importance of practicing the ART Skills daily between our training sessions. Besides just telling you that regular practice is important, we will explain how regular practice affects the brain in ways that help us make positive changes in our lives.

M. Berking and B. Whitley, *Affect Regulation Training: A Practitioners' Manual*,
DOI 10.1007/978-1-4939-1022-9_11, © Springer Science+Business Media New York 2014

Electron Microscope

Slide 38: It goes without saying that it takes practice to master difficult skills. However, we've only recently begun to understand the reasons why practice is so important. As already mentioned, developments in modern technology over the last few years have enabled us to look straight into the brain, such as by using an electron microscope as shown here.

Neuron

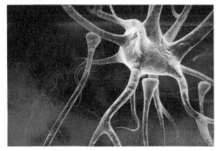

© *Jeff Johnson, Hybrid Medical Animation, mod. by M. Berking*

Slide 39: The brain is comprised of approximately 100 billion nerve cells called neurons. This slide shows a microscopic view of an individual neuron. Each neuron receives information from a multitude of other neurons through electrical and chemical signals. These signals either inhibit or activate the neuron. When a neuron is activated to a certain threshold, it sends a signal on to other neurons.[1]

---

[1] For those interested in learning more about neurons, refer to the Wikipedia article at http://en.wikipedia.org/wiki/Neuron. Also, the website www.BrainU.org has short educational videos about neurons at http://brainu.org/movies.

Neuron

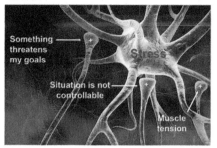

© *Jeff Johnson, Hybrid Medical Animation, mod. by M. Berking*

Slide 40: Earlier, we talked about the role that the amygdala plays in the stress response. The amygdala consists of a large number of neurons, which tend to react together. For the moment, let's focus on just one neuron in the amygdala. If neurons from other regions in the brain report that my goals are threatened and that I may not be able to handle the threat, these neurons send activating signals to this amygdala neuron. If my muscles are tense, this amygdala neuron could also receive activating signals coming from the tense muscles. The multiple activating signals eventually reach the threshold level causing the amygdala neuron to send a signal to other neural layers in the body, such as the muscles, the respiratory center, or to the prefrontal cortex, leading to the overall stress reaction.

Neuron

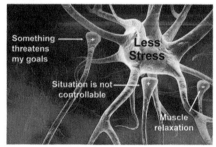

© *Jeff Johnson, Hybrid Medical Animation, mod. by M. Berking*

Slide 41: However, if the muscles in the body are relaxed, this same amygdala neuron could receive inhibitory signals from the relaxed muscles (*point to relevant area of slide*). Since the amygdala neuron is receiving inhibitory signals from the relaxed muscles, it will now be more difficult for the amygdala neuron to reach its activation threshold even though the amygdala neuron is still receiving activating signals from the perceived threat (*point to slide*). The significance of this is that the inhibiting signals from the relaxed muscles decrease the chance that this amygdala neuron will send activating signals to other neural layers in the body, which also decreases the overall stress reaction. This shows us the importance of strengthening neurons that inhibit the stress response, such as the neurons responsible for relaxation, in order to help us reduce negative emotions while increasing positive ones. So the big question is, "How do we do this?" The answer is … practice, practice, practice the skills offered in this training!

Neuron

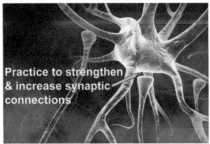

© *Jeff Johnson, Hybrid Medical Animation, mod. by M. Berking*

Slide 42: Through frequent practice, we activate the neurons and the connections between them, called synapses. This activation through practice causes the synapses to become stronger and even creates additional synapses. The strengthened and additional synapses allow neurons to activate more easily, including the neurons that are responsible for relaxation. An influential neuroscience researcher Donald Hebb (1949) is often paraphrased as saying "neurons that fire together, wire together."[2] Practicing relaxation, just like practicing anything else, changes the structure of the brain, so that relaxation can occur more easily in the future.

Motivation

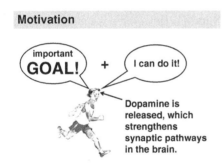

Slide 43: The processes that strengthen and increase the number of synapses tend to be even more effective when certain substances are released in the brain. One of these substances is called dopamine. Dopamine is released when we believe that our current behavior will help us eventually achieve the personal goals that we have set for ourselves. Here is what this means to you: To activate dopamine, you need to practice frequently and be aware of why you are practicing. What are your goals for the training? Why do you want to improve your emotion regulation skills? What makes this goal important enough to justify the effort and practice necessary for improving these skills? Finding your personal motivation and then being aware of your motivation (i.e., by imagining the fulfillment of your goal) while you practice is critical to fostering dopamine releases, which can lead to helpful changes in your brain.

---

[2] Carla Shatz, Ph.D. (director of the Shatz Lab and professor at Stanford University) is credited with this paraphrase of Hebbian theory, although the precise phrase she coined was "cells that fire together, wire together."

Neurons are like muscles...

They get stronger with training!

Slide 44: To summarize, neurons function like muscles. The more you train them, especially when you are working toward an important personal goal, the stronger they become.

Well-Developed Neurons in the Brain

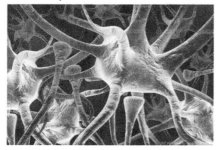

© *P. Fürstenberg, mod. by M. Berking*

Slide 45: We want areas in the brain that are responsible for relaxation, facilitating positive emotions, or inhibiting negative emotions to look like this … (*point to slide*)

Atrophy of Neurons Through Lack of Use

© *A. Vester*

Slide 46: … instead of like this (*point to slide*), in which a lack of use has caused neurons to atrophy. If we rarely use certain neurons, these neurons and their connections will become weaker. The connections between the neurons will disintegrate, and the neurons themselves will deteriorate. Ultimately, these areas in the brain will become smaller. If you study the brains of people suffering from depression, you will find that the areas in the brain responsible for positive emotions are often smaller and the areas responsible for negative emotions and stress reactions are often larger.

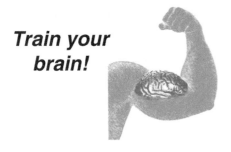

Train your brain!

Slide 47: Instead we want the areas in the brain related to stress and negative emotions to atrophy and the areas related to positive emotions and relaxation to strengthen. This can be accomplished by training with the ART Skills. We are teaching you how to "train your brain."

Problem

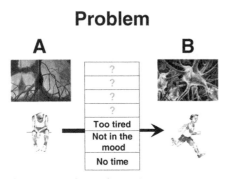

See image credits on the previous page

Slide 48: We have talked about the importance of practicing the ART Skills. But even if people make a commitment to practice, actually taking the time out of their busy schedules to practice regularly can be hard to do. Common obstacles include feeling too tired, not wanting to practice at the moment, or feeling like you just do not have the time. Could any of you see these obstacles possibly getting in your way as you try to practice the ART Skills? (*participants respond*) Can you think of any other obstacles that might make it difficult to practice? (*participants respond*)

Solution

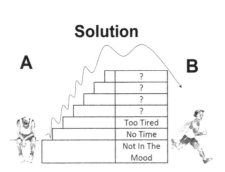

Slide 49: So how do we overcome these obstacles? Let's brainstorm ideas for how we can do this. (*The therapist solicits ideas from the participants for overcoming the obstacles they just listed. It may be helpful for the therapist to write down the participants' suggestions on a flip chart or dry erase board.*)

Slide 50: Since we all know how hard it can be to get ourselves motivated, we have thought a long time about ways we can help you develop a successful practice routine. In the end we came up with several tools that you may find helpful. These tools include (1) a participant manual, (2) an audio training program, (3) an e-coaching program, and (4) a printed training calendar.

Let's talk more about each of these tools. The participant manual describes in detail the skills we are working on in the training, explains why they are important, and provides you with exercises that can be used to build these skills.

The audio training program consists of CDs containing the same ART Sequence Exercises that we practice during the training sessions. The audio training guides you through the ART Sequence Exercises with step-by-step instructions. We ask that you set aside 20 min each day to practice one of the ART Sequence Exercises using the audio training program. We know that finding 20 min each day can be difficult. However, we strongly encourage you to make the choice to take this time each day to practice the skills that can help you make positive changes in your life.

E-Coaching

A few short messages are sent to you by text or email describing a quick exercise. For example, at 11:15 one day you may receive a message that looks like this:

"Relax your lower jaw for a moment..."

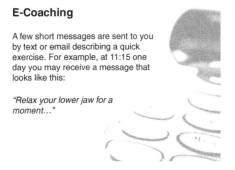

Slide 51: In addition to the audio training program, we encourage you to utilize the ART e-coaching program as well. The e-coaching program will send you a few short exercises each day either by text message or by email. Each exercise will only take a few minutes of your time. For example, at 11:15, you might receive a text message or email saying, "Relax your lower jaw for a moment." You can focus on relaxing your jaw for about 3 s and then continue going about your day.

ART Printed Training Calendar:

Slide 52: The same short exercises that can be received via text message or email are also available in a printed version in the training calendar.

Whether you use the printed training calendar or the e-coaching tool, practicing these short exercises just a few times a day will help you resist falling into old vicious cycles, especially when the short exercises are practiced alongside the ART Sequence Exercises contained in the audio training program.

What is the positive goal you want to attain through intense training of the ART Skills?

_____

_____

_____

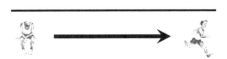

Slide 53: However, regardless of how many helpful tools we provide you with, the training will still require substantial time and effort. Ultimately, it depends on you deciding whether this effort is worthwhile and whether you want to invest your time and energy strengthening your emotion regulation skills. We spent some time in the beginning of the training thinking about the goals each of you have for yourselves. So we invite you to think again about what goals you hope to achieve by participating in this training. *The therapist passes out copies of the Personal ART Goal Worksheet* (Appendix E). Take a few minutes to think about your goals and then write some of them down on the worksheet.

Note to the therapist:

Provide a few minutes for the participants to remember and write down their goals. The therapist then reminds the participants that they could simply choose to only attend the sessions and not practice at home. However, should they in fact choose this option, they will not get the full benefits of the program. If they instead want to get the full benefits and maximize their chances to accomplish their personal goals, they should consider committing to the suggested daily practice consisting of the ART Sequence Exercise for 20–30 min using the audio training program and two to six short exercises, each taking only 10–30 s, using the e-coaching program or the printed training calendar.

The therapist then asks the participants if they are willing to create a personalized training schedule for themselves that lists the days and times they will commit to practice the ART Sequence Exercises. Asking this question does create a chance that the participants will decide *not* to develop a training schedule. However, from experience with thousands of participants, this rarely occurs. This does not mean, though, that all participants actually adhere to the plan they create for themselves.

For the participants who are willing to schedule time to practice the ART Sequence Exercises, the therapist provides them with a copy of the participant manual (rewarding those who want to practice) and the audio training program CD that contains the ART Sequence Exercises. These participants are also given a copy of the Personal Training Schedule (Appendix F) to record the days and times they intend to practice the ART Sequence Exercises.

Next, the therapist asks the participants if they would be willing to practice a series of short exercises over the course of each day during the training program. Those who wish to practice these short exercises are given an option to receive the exercises by text message, by email, or on a printed training calendar.

For the participants who would like to receive the short exercises by email or text message, they should be reminded that it may be "overwhelming" to receive up to four exercises each day, so they should first "carefully decide" if they are willing to participate in this intense training method before committing to it. The participants are also told that only those who wish to "participate in an advanced level of training" should receive the short exercises by text or email. By discouraging the participants from this practice method which is "too difficult" and possibly even "overwhelming," the therapist artfully utilizes paradoxical intent to encourage participants to use this practice tool.

In our experience, most participants choose to receive the short exercises by text or email. The therapist records the cell phone numbers and email addresses for the participants who wish to receive messages by text or email. After the session, the therapist initiates the system to deliver the text messages and emails through the ART website at www.AffectRegulationTraining.com—with access code: ART_Pcn2cfY. For those participants who wish to practice the short exercises, but do not want to receive the exercises via text or email, the therapist may give them a printed daily calendar that lists the short exercises to be performed each day. The daily calendar may be downloaded from the ART website using the access code: ART_Pcn2cfY.

The challenge for ART therapists at this point is to present the various training tools in a way that communicates to the participants that they are completely free to practice or not practice if they choose, but at the same time providing strong arguments (e.g., no pain—no gain) to encourage them to use the tools. Ideally, all participants would ultimately decide to practice using the available tools.

Reference

Hebb, D. O. (1949). *The organization of behavior: A neuropsychological theory*. New York, NY: Bantam Books.

Chapter 12
Module Four: Nonjudgmental Awareness

12.1 Vicious Cycle #3: Amygdala Activation and Negative Thinking

Vicious Cycles #1 & #2

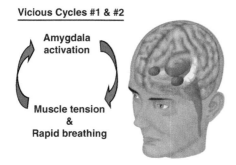

Slide 54: We talked earlier about Vicious Cycles #1 and #2 in which the amygdala in the brain activates muscle tension and rapid breathing in the body, both of which further activate the amygdala, causing even more muscle tension and rapid breathing and so on. Now we are going to talk about another vicious cycle that can occur, and later we will talk about a skill that we can use to break it.

Vicious Cycle #3

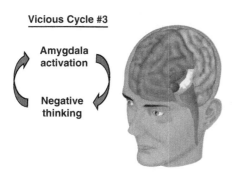

Slide 55: As a review, the amygdala detects potential threats. It can be thought of as a smoke detector. If it senses danger, it alerts the prefrontal cortex area in the brain. The prefrontal cortex focuses attention and thought onto this threat. This is very helpful in evaluating potential threats and determining the most effective action. However, if the focus by the prefrontal cortex on the problematic aspects of the situation does not lead to a solution to the problem, this problem-focused thinking will further activate the amygdala and could result in another type of vicious cycle.

In this vicious cycle, the negative thinking generated by the prefrontal cortex causes the amygdala to sound the alarm more loudly, resulting in negative emotions. This may cause the prefrontal cortex to focus even more attention on the problem, resulting in even more negative thinking and even stronger negative emotions and so forth. In other words, negative thinking likely leads to negative emotions which then reinforce our negative thinking. Have you ever experienced something like this yourself? Would you be willing to share this experience?

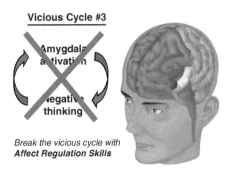

Vicious Cycle #3

Amygdala activation

Negative thinking

Break the vicious cycle with
Affect Regulation Skills

Slide 56: So, if negative thinking and negative emotions can cause each other, what can we do to break this vicious cycle? Yes, we could try to *not think* negative thoughts. (*typical answer*) Do you believe this strategy would work? (*The participants will likely have ambivalence about the potential success of this strategy.*)

So, let's test this strategy by not thinking about something for a few minutes. Please close your eyes. For 1 min, you may think about anything that you would like, except for a pink elephant. Remember you are free to think about anything you wish, but keep your mind completely free of pink elephants. (*1 min pause*) So how many were successful in their attempts to keep pink elephants out of their mind? It looks like this was not successful for all/most of you. So let's look at why trying not to think of something doesn't work very well.

When you remind yourself not to think of something, like a pink elephant, you create an intentional thought of the very thing you do not want to think about. Also, by intending not to think about the pink elephant, you are setting up a monitoring process to constantly watch out for thoughts of a pink elephant. As you monitor for any thoughts about a pink elephant (e.g., *Am I thinking of a pink elephant?*), even more thoughts about a pink elephant are created (e.g., *Oh no! I am having thoughts about a pink elephant!*). This is how attempts at avoiding or suppressing thoughts can keep them going and even make the thoughts stronger.

So if avoiding and suppressing thoughts is not helpful, what could be helpful instead? What about trying to think positively? It does make sense because positive thoughts can be a signal of safety for the amygdala. But there's a problem with this strategy. It's often very difficult to think positively when negative emotions are activated. Even more importantly, it's often impossible to actually *believe* these positive thoughts when our emotions are signaling something completely different to us, and if we have trouble believing these thoughts, they will not affect our emotions. Have you ever had this experience? (*Pause*)

Fortunately, there is another helpful way to cope with this vicious cycle of negative thoughts and negative emotions. You can take a moment to draw your attention away from the worries about potential threats and instead allow yourself to be aware of what's happening at that very moment. Now, we are not asking you to *not think* the thoughts you have because that usually backfires. Instead we are encouraging you to take the first step in breaking this vicious cycle by taking a "mental step back" in these situations and objectively observe the situation and your own emotions without interpreting, judging, or reacting.

12.2 ART Skill #3: Nonjudgmental Awareness

Breaking the vicious cycle

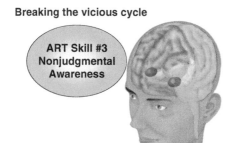

Slide 57: We call this skill *nonjudgmental awareness*. This skill, which is ART Skill #3, involves different areas of the brain than the areas in the brain related to automatic thought. We can, metaphorically speaking, "take cover in the back part of the cortex" (*point to the area on the slide*) in distressing situations, breaking out of thinking and ruminating and into simply feeling and perceiving. This involves taking a mental step back and allowing ourselves to view a situation and our emotions in a nonevaluative way by simply noticing what is happening. Let me explain how we can use the skill of nonjudgmental awareness to help us manage negative emotions.

Breaking the vicious cycle

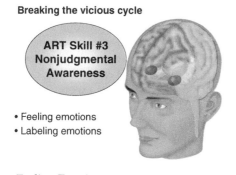

• Feeling emotions
• Labeling emotions

Slide 58: The skill of *nonjudgmental awareness* of emotions involves neutrally *feeling* and *labeling* emotions.

Feeling Emotions

"Feeling an emotion" involves neutrally and nonjudgmentally exploring what it is like to experience the particular emotion. Negative emotions can, however, trigger the tendency to automatically judge and react, especially when those negative emotions are intense.

Labeling Emotions

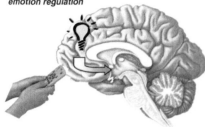

Consciously labeling emotions presses the "on-button" for rational thinking and effective emotion regulation

Slide 59: "Labeling emotions" is the process of using words to name the feelings we are experiencing. Labeling our emotions may seem unnatural at first, but it is extraordinarily important because of this reason; when we label feelings, we activate connections between the areas in the brain where these feelings develop and the areas in the brain that are responsible for our thoughts and awareness. By actively recruiting our thinking abilities, we can start to understand the emotion we are experiencing, discover the information it is trying to communicate, and make decisions about what we could do to accept or modify the emotion.

One method to nonjudgmentally explore an emotion by *feeling* and *labeling* is to:

1. Focus your attention on the most intense emotion you are experiencing at the time.
2. Label the emotion as best you can (anxiety, happiness, sadness, boredom, etc.).
3. Rate the intensity of the feeling on a scale from 0 to 10 (with 0 being the least intense and 10 being the most intense).
4. Identify where you feel the emotion in your body.

The process may then be repeated with other emotions that are experienced less intensely.

In order to work through this process of *feeling* and *labeling* emotions, it can be helpful for people to have an inner-conversation that sounds something like this, "Okay, this is anxiety. On a scale from 0 to 10, it's about a 9. I feel it in my body as muscle tension in my back. I also notice that my heart is pounding." Then after a while, you can start the process all over again with another emotion you are experiencing.

This process of neutrally *feeling* and *labeling emotions* avoids making judgments about the emotions or our experience of them. For example, when we feel fear, we try to focus our awareness on the fear, noticing how and where we experience this feeling in our body. We then say to ourselves "There is fear." We do not say, "Oh how awful! This fear is back again. It will never end! My body probably can't take it any longer!" Instead, we try to describe emotions neutrally, without judgment—"There is fear," and become aware of what fear feels like in the moment.

Let's take a few minutes now to try an exercise that will help us explore the concept of nonjudgmental awareness.

Note to the therapist:

In this introductory exercise into nonjudgmental awareness, participants are invited to sit in pairs opposite each other. If the group consists of an odd number of participants, the co-therapist can work with one of the participants. Each pair is given a

dowel rod that is 5/8 in. in diameter by 20 in. long. Once each pair has received a
dowel rod, the exercise begins.

Participants are first asked to close their eyes. With the help of short relaxation
instructions given by the therapist, the participants relax their muscles and calm
their breathing. Next, the therapist guides the participants on a brief mental journey
through the body, during which their attention is focused on their breathing, then on
the soles of their feet, then on their entire body from their feet to their head, and then
back down through their arms.

At the end of this brief body scan, the participants are asked to open their eyes
and concentrate their attention on the tip of their right index finger. The participant
who currently has the dowel rod holds it up, while the participant's partner places
the tip of his right index finger on one end of the dowel rod and applies slight pressure. This allows the participants sitting opposite each other to hold the dowel rod
by applying pressure from their index fingers on the opposite ends of the dowel rod.
The therapist should demonstrate this while explaining the instructions.

At this time, the participants close their eyes again. The participant who first held
the dowel rod begins to very slowly move his finger in whatever way he pleases:
small movements, big movements, circles, angles, or freestyle. The other participant must follow and mirror these movements, so they do not drop the dowel rod.
The pair will, however, frequently drop it, especially at first, until they become more
successful at holding the dowel rod between them for longer periods of time. After
about 2 min, the roles are switched. After two more minutes, the dowel rod is set
down, and the participants are asked to look inside themselves and be aware of how
they feel at the moment.

During the debriefing that follows, participants are asked to comment on their
experience. Participants usually describe the experience as calming, relaxing, soothing, and fun. The participants may also report that while they felt relaxed during the
exercise, they also felt alert. The therapist may then suggest that, based on their
positive comments, they probably engaged in nonjudgmental awareness by focusing their attention on the dowel rod during the exercise.

If, however, a participant describes feeling emotions such as anxiety during the
exercise, the therapist can inquire further about the participant's experience during
the exercise. As the therapist inquires, the participant will usually describe having
thoughts during the exercise that were judgmental or critical of himself ("I can't do
this right!"), his partner ("Why is he making this exercise so difficult?"), or the
exercise ("This is a stupid exercise!"). The therapist is able to use this situation as
an example to show how these analytical and judgmental thoughts tend to lower our
enjoyment and our mood. The therapist then begins to describe a method to encourage nonjudgmental awareness.

The therapist continues speaking to the participants:

By focusing on the dowel rod in this exercise, we were observing our experience
instead of what we normally do, which is to evaluate and judge our experiences.
From this exercise we can see that intensely focusing our attention on something
allows us to enter an observing mode, which can have a peaceful and calming effect.

I will now begin to explain the steps of a process that can help build the skill of nonjudgmental awareness. I will explain each of the steps, and then we will combine the steps in an ART Sequence Exercise. The first step in the process begins by focusing attention onto something. It might be difficult to use the dowel rod exercise most times when we are feeling stressed, since we might not have a partner handy, people in the office might stare, etc. So, what could we use to help us focus our attention that would not attract unwanted attention? What do we always have with us until our very last…? Right! Our breath! This has been used as a focus of attention by millions of people in various cultures for thousands of years in order to help engage in nonjudgmental awareness and to regulate emotions.

In ART, we direct our focus on our breath by observing the physical sensation of our breath, such as the rise and fall of our chest and belly as our lungs expand and contract or how the air feels as it flows in and out of our nostrils. We simply notice our breathing without trying to control it. We merely pay attention to the calm and steady inhalation and exhalation of the breath. We just focus on how it feels when we breathe in … and out again … flowing … without doing anything. Please close your eyes and let's all try this together.

In order to make it easier to focus your attention on your breathing, it may be helpful to say to yourself the word "in" when inhaling and "out" when exhaling. You will notice that maintaining focus on your breath even when saying these words to yourself is not easy to do. Our brain tends to almost immediately begin to divert our focus away from our breath and onto thoughts such as "I wonder what traffic will be like going home today."

When we realize that our attention has wandered to our thoughts, we make a short "mental note" of the distraction. We can say to ourselves something like "thinking," "planning," or "worrying" and then gently draw our attention back to our breathing. If we start to feel angry with ourselves because we "can't focus on our breathing for even 1 minute" (or sometimes even for 10 seconds), it can be helpful to simply allow ourselves to be aware of this anger and make a neutral mental note of it, "There is anger."—and then gently draw our attention back to our breathing.

You can do the same thing if you find yourself becoming anxious or discouraged by the fact that your mind wanders. You may need to repeat this process multiple times, which is absolutely fine and very normal. Actually, the process of becoming aware that our minds have wandered and then gently and lovingly leading our attention back to the sensation of our breathing is the core of this exercise!

After focusing our attention onto our breath, the next step in our practice of nonjudgmental awareness is to expand attention to anything we can perceive in the moment. For example, what bodily sensations (e.g., hunger, pain, etc.) do you currently feel? What sounds do you hear? What smells do you notice? What is the next thought that crosses your mind? … and what's the next thought after that … and after that? Now, imagine what you would do if anything was possible. Where would you be? What would you be doing? (*pause*) Based on what you see in these images, what is it that you are longing for? Maybe it is some time to yourself without pressure to get something done. What impulses to act (stand up, lay down, run out of the room, etc.) are present right now? Also, attention is directed to noticing and labeling any emotions you are experiencing. What emotions are you feeling right now? While you are labeling your emotions, rate their intensity. For example, "My anger is at an 8." In addition, notice any bodily sensations that correspond with the emotions. How do you feel your emotions in your body right now? (e.g., tense shoulders).

Now, does anyone have questions about this exercise before we incorporate it into the next ART Sequence Exercise? Okay, so as you remember, in the previous ART Sequence Exercise, we intentionally slowed our breathing by exhaling completely and then 3 s longer. Starting with this next ART Sequence Exercise, we will now let go of our attempts to control our breathing and simply observe it as we have just practiced.

Once the ART therapist believes the participants are ready, the therapist proceeds with the ART Sequence Exercise that links ART Skills #1–3 together. Remember that each ART Sequence Exercise connects the most recently learned ART Skill with the ART Skills that have already been learned.

12.3   ART Sequence with ART Skills #1–3

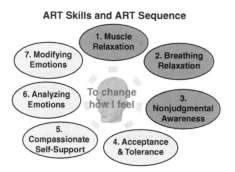

ART Skills and ART Sequence

Slide 60: Now we will go through the ART Sequence Exercise that links ART Skills #1–3 together. Just as before, I will provide the instructions as we go through the exercise together.

The therapist may guide the exercise using the "Exercise Two" audio that can be downloaded from the ART website, or the therapist may guide the exercise using the following instructions:

We will start the exercise after the sound of the bell.

Sound of the bell

Find a comfortable posture in which you can sit for a while without difficulties. Make sure your feet are flat on the ground and that your back is properly supported. You can put your hands on the armrests or on your thighs. Close your eyes or focus on a point in the room. Allow yourself to take a break right now in order to relax, build some strength, and recharge your batteries. Relax your muscles. Breathe in deeply (*deep audible inhalation*) and slowly and consciously breathe out (*audible long exhalation*), and let go of all the tension you have gathered during the day … as much as possible at this given moment. (*5 s pause*)

Now bring your attention to your hands and arms. Tense the muscles in your hands and arms … clench your hands into fists … angle your fists inward … angle the forearms toward your upper arms … and pull your fists toward your shoulders, so that the shoulder muscles are tensed as well. Feel the tension in your hands and arms. Release all other muscles in your body. Keep on breathing. Pay attention to your muscle tension. Hold the tension (*3 s pause*), and now release it very slowly with the next long out-breath. Let the muscles relax. Release your arms back to a resting position, and be aware of the difference between the tension you felt before and the relaxation you feel now. Be aware of even the smallest changes you can perceive as you release your muscles more and more. (*15 s pause*)

Now bring your attention to your hands and arms again. Tense these areas again by clenching your fists, angling them inward, angling your forearms toward your upper arms … and pull your fists toward your shoulders, so the shoulders are tensed. Feel the tension in your hands and arms. Release all other muscles in your body. Keep on breathing. Pay attention to your muscle tension again. Hold the tension (*3 s pause*), and now release it very slowly with the next long out-breath. Let the muscles relax. Release your arms back to a resting position, and be aware of the difference between the tension you felt before and the relaxation you feel now. Be aware of even the smallest changes that you can perceive as you now release your muscles more and more. (*15 s pause*) Breathe calmly and regularly, and feel how each muscle relaxes more and more with every out-breath … how the pleasant feeling of relaxation expands more and more. (*15 s pause*)

Continue by bringing your attention to your face. Now tense all the muscles in your face by clenching your teeth, pulling the corners of your mouth outward, and pressing your tongue against the roof of your mouth. Carefully squeeze your eyes shut and furrow your eyebrows very slightly. Release all other muscles in your body. Keep on breathing. Feel the tension in your face. Hold the tension (*3 s pause*), and now release it very slowly with the next long out-breath. Let the muscles in your face relax, and be aware of the difference between the tension you felt before and the relaxation you feel now. (*15 s pause*)

Then bring your attention back to your face. Again, tense all the muscles in your face by clenching your teeth, pulling the corners of your mouth outward, and pressing your tongue against the roof of your mouth. Carefully squeeze your eyes shut and furrow your eyebrows very slightly. Release all other muscles in your body. Keep on breathing. Feel the tension in your face. Hold the tension (*3 s pause*), and now release it very slowly with the next long out-breath. Let the muscles in your face relax, and be aware of the difference between the tension you felt before and the relaxation you feel now. (*5 s pause*)

Breathe calmly and regularly and feel how the muscles relax more and more with each long, conscious out-breath—how the pleasant feeling of relaxation expands more and more and becomes deeper and deeper. (*15 s pause*)

Continue by bringing your attention to your neck and back. Tense your neck by pulling your shoulders as near to your ears as possible. Then tense your upper and lower back by pulling your shoulders as far back as possible and simultaneously tilting your hips forward and arching your back. Release all other muscles in your body. Keep on breathing. Feel the tension in your neck and back. Hold the tension (*3 s pause*), and now release it very slowly with the next long out-breath. Let the muscles relax, and be aware of the difference between the tension you felt before and the relaxation you feel now. (*15 s pause*)

Now return your attention again to your neck and back. Tense your neck again by pulling your shoulders as near to your ears as possible. Then tense your upper and lower back by pulling your shoulders as far back as possible and simultaneously tilting your hips forward and arching your back. Release all other muscles in your body. Keep on breathing. Feel the tension in your neck and back. Hold the tension (*3 s pause*), and now release it very slowly with the next long out-breath. Let the muscles relax, and be aware of the difference between the tension you felt before and the relaxation you feel now. (*15 s pause*) Breathe calmly and regularly, and feel how the muscles relax more and more with each long and conscious out-breath … how the pleasant feeling of relaxation expands more and more.

Now bring your attention to your buttocks, your belly, and your legs. Tense the muscles there by pressing your buttocks together, while straightening your legs in front of you and slightly lifting your feet off of the floor. Also, point your feet downward. Feel the tension in your buttocks, your belly, and your legs. Release all other muscles in your body. Keep on breathing. Feel the tension. Hold the tension (*3 s pause*), and now release it very slowly with the next long out-breath. Release your legs back to a resting position. Let your muscles relax, and be aware of the difference between the tension you felt before and the relaxation you feel now. (*5 s pause*)

Now bring your attention back to your buttocks, your belly, and your legs one more time. Tense the muscles again by pressing your buttocks together, while straightening your legs in front of you and slightly lifting your feet off of the floor. This time, point your feet back toward your face. Feel the tension in your buttocks, your belly, and your legs. Release all other muscles in your body. Keep on breathing. Feel the tension. Hold the tension (*3 s pause*), and now release it very slowly with the next long out-breath. Release your legs back to a resting position. Let your muscles relax, and be aware of the difference between the tension you felt before and the relaxation you feel now. (*5 s pause*) Breathe calmly and regularly, and feel how the muscles relax more and more with each out-breath … how the pleasant feeling of relaxation becomes deeper and deeper. (*15 s pause*)

Now allow yourself to switch into the mode of nonjudgmental awareness. Focus your attention on the sensation of your breathing in your lower abdomen. Do not try to control your breathing; simply observe it. If it is shallow, it is shallow. If it is deep, it is deep. That's fine—just observe it. In order to help you focus on your breathing, you may mentally say "in" when breathing in, and "out" when breathing out. However, try to concentrate on the sensation of breathing with at least 80 % of your awareness. (*20 s pause*) If you realize that you get distracted or that other thoughts cross your mind, make a short mental note, such as "thinking" or "planning" and compassionately bring your attention back to your breathing. If you start to get angry at yourself for constantly getting distracted, again just make a short mental note, such as "Ah, there is anger" or simply "anger," and gently return to the observation of your breathing. Also, when you hear noises or feel distracting body sensations, just allow yourself to be aware of them, make a mental note such as "noises" or "sensations," and then return your attention to the sensation of your breathing. Bringing your attention back to the physical sensation of your breathing, while compassionately supporting yourself as you do this over and over again, is the very core of the exercise. Try practicing this now for the next 3 min. (*3 min pause*)

Now release your attention from your breathing. Broaden your awareness and focus on what body sensations you can feel in this given moment. Make a short mental note of what you can feel in your body. For example, "There is warmth in my hands. There is tension in my forehead," and so on. Just observe your sensations and briefly describe them without evaluating them. (*15 s pause*) Now allow yourself to focus on the sounds you can hear. What sounds can you hear coming from your left side? (*5 s pause*) What sounds can you hear coming from your right side? (*5 s pause*) What sounds can you hear behind you? (*5 s pause*) What sounds can you hear in front of you? (*5 s pause*) Now focus on what you can smell. If you can't smell anything, just focus on the sensation of your breathing in the inner parts of your nose. (*5 s pause*) Now do your best to become aware of what thoughts are crossing your mind at this given moment. You might find yourself thinking "Oh no, my mind is blank. I'm not thinking any thoughts," but that *itself* is a thought. Just allow yourself to be aware. What is the next thought that crosses your mind? (*2 s pause*) ... and what's the next thought after that ... and after that? (*10 s pause*)

Now, imagine what you would do if anything was possible. Where would you be? What would you be doing? (*pause*) Based on what you see in these images, what is it that you are longing for? Maybe it is some time to yourself without pressure to get something done. (*10 s pause*) Next, notice any impulses to act that may be present ... maybe it's an urge to stand up or laugh. Try to put a label on these impulses. (*10 s pause*)

Now please shift your focus to the emotions you are experiencing right now. How do you feel in this given moment? (*5 s pause*) Which emotions feel the strongest right now? Which ones are less intense but are still present in the background? Try to label your feelings with short mental notes without evaluating them. Just name your emotions as accurately as possible in this moment. (*10 s pause*) Maybe you can also estimate the intensity of these feelings on a scale from 0 to 10. For example, "There is anxiety, and its intensity is about 8." Take a moment to do this now. (*10 s pause*) Maybe you can also identify which bodily sensations go along with this feeling. For example, "There is anxiety. Its intensity is about 8, and I feel it as tension in my forehead." Please take a moment to label your emotions, rate their intensity, and notice any bodily sensations that go along with the emotions. Please try this with all of the emotions you are currently experiencing. (*30 s pause*)

Now slowly bring your attention back from the mode of nonjudgmental awareness into this room at your own pace by breathing in deeply (*audible inhale*), stretching and flexing your body (*demonstrate*), opening your eyes, and lightly tapping on your thighs a few times, so that you become fully alert again.

Sound of the bell
Note to the therapist:

After the exercise, the participants are encouraged to discuss their experiences during the exercise. Therapists should start with an open-ended question such as "What was that like for you?" As the discussion progresses, the therapist may need to ask specific questions, so the participants elaborate on their answers. Copies of the Feeling Faces handout (Appendix G) can be given at this time to the participants to help broaden their emotional vocabulary. Therapists can invite the participants to review the handout and to identify any of the feelings depicted on the handout that they experienced during the exercise. When participants identify a specific emotion, the therapist can ask them how they recognized they felt this particular emotion.

The therapist continues speaking to the participants:

I want to praise you all for your attention and hard work during this session. Today we discussed the benefits of nonjudgmental awareness as we focus our attention on our perception of the present moment without engaging in analytical thinking. We can also use nonjudgmental awareness to intentionally experience pleasure. As a reward for all of your hard work, I will lead you in an exercise that utilizes nonjudgmental awareness but goes one step further by using a strong neutral focus on sensations to trigger positive emotions.

Now, many of us are doing things all day long that could be pleasurable if we would take the time to notice. Instead of wolfing down a cookie, we could really savor the pleasurable experience of eating the cookie. While drinking our morning cup of coffee, we could focus on the pleasure that comes from feeling the warmth of the cup in our hands and the smell of freshly brewed coffee. These are pleasurable experiences that we can use to reward ourselves: savoring a cookie for working hard all morning or really enjoying a cup of coffee for getting to work on time.

Since many of us do not focus on these experiences of pleasure, I will explain and then guide you in an exercise as a reward for a job well done in today's session. In this exercise, which we will call a "pleasure exercise," we do our best to focus on things that we perceive as positive. Then as much as possible, we will do our best to use these perceptions to jumpstart or strengthen positive feelings within us.

(*For more information on the use of pleasure exercises as a treatment intervention, see Kaluza, 2004; Koppenhöfer, 2004; or Lutz, 2000.*)

Pleasure exercise:

We will start by briefly practicing muscle and breathing relaxation and nonjudgmental awareness. Next we will use a few, small, everyday objects in the exercise. I will ask you to close your eyes, and then I will place one of the objects into your hand. The idea is to thoroughly explore the object with your senses, other than sight. Allow yourself to focus all of your awareness on this object. You may take all the time you need. I will prompt you with a couple of instructions to deepen your experience of the object. Once you have finished exploring the object, just hold it at an arm's length in front of you, and I will exchange it for another object. Does this make sense?

Note to the therapist:

The therapist first gives a variety of objects with an interesting shape (such as shells, stones, or feathers). After a few minutes (or when participants hold out the object indicating they want another one), the objects are replaced by various objects with a pleasant or interesting smell (such as candles, incense sticks, or play dough). Finally, the objects are replaced with food items with a pleasant or interesting taste (such as orange slices, dried fruit, and, maybe toward the end of the exercise, chocolate). Be sure to ask the participants about any food allergies they may have before the exercise.

The therapist continues speaking to the participants:

Okay, let's begin. Find a comfortable sitting position. Close your eyes. Allow your muscles to relax. Breathe calmly and evenly. Focus your attention on your breathing and on your body. When you're ready, hold out your hand to receive an object. *The therapist distributes the first round of objects (items with an interesting shape). Pause briefly after each question throughout this exercise.* Begin exploring this object thoroughly by using your sense of touch. Can you feel its shape? What does its surface feel like? Do you notice any parts of the object that are smooth or rough? Does the object feel warm or cool? What does the outside edge of the object feel like? Visualize this object with your mind's eye.

Once you feel you have finished thoroughly exploring this object, extend it in front of you, and you will receive a new object (*another object with an interesting shape*). I am going to give you a few minutes on your own to explore this object before I give you a new set of objects. (*pause for several minutes*)

After 3–5 min, the therapist asks the participants to hold the objects out in their hands so the therapist can exchange their objects. The therapist retrieves the objects from the participants and replaces them with ones that have an interesting or pleasant smell.

This object can also be explored by touch. Can you feel its shape? What does its surface feel like? Do you notice any parts of the object that are smooth or rough? Does the object feel warm or cool? What does the outside edge of the object feel like? Visualize this object with your mind's eye.

When you have finished exploring this object by touch, you can also smell it. What does it smell like? Is the smell strong or weak? Does the smell change if the object is further or closer to your nose? What does the smell remind you of? Once you have finished thoroughly exploring this object, hold it out in front of you and you will receive a new one (*another object with an interesting or pleasant smell*). I am going to give you a few minutes on your own to explore this object before I give you a new one. (*pause for several minutes*)

After 3–5 min, the therapist asks the participants to hold the objects out in their hands so the therapist can exchange their objects. The therapist retrieves the objects and replaces them with food items that have an interesting or pleasant taste.

Hold the piece of food to your lips. Concentrate on just this initial contact. What does it feel like against your lips? Then, place the food on your tongue. Don't bite into it yet! First, allow yourself to experience what this feels like. (*pause*) Discover the food with your tongue. What does it taste like before you start chewing? Now you can begin to chew the piece of food very slowly—without swallowing it yet. Be aware of how the taste and consistency changes with every bite. Continue chewing slowly. If you now want to swallow tiny pieces of it, swallow with your full awareness. (*pause*) When you're ready, you may swallow the entire bite of food—being aware of what it feels like as it goes all the way down your throat.

If you'd like to receive a new food item, just hold out your hand. We're going to give you a few minutes to explore the food on your own. (*Pause for several minutes.*)

Now let's slowly begin to close this exercise. Allow yourself a few moments to consciously explore how you feel in this given moment. (*1 min pause*) Now, in your own time, allow your awareness to return to the room.

Note to the therapist:

In the ensuing group discussion of the exercise, the therapist reminds the participants that focusing on everyday pleasurable experiences is a relatively easy way to increase positive feelings. The therapist can also talk about a few things to remember when intentionally trying to increase pleasure:

- Pleasure takes time.
- Pleasure should be *allowed* to occur instead of forced to occur.
- We should not wait for pleasure to happen "accidentally." We should plan opportunities to increase pleasure.
- Pleasure is a matter of personal preference. Everybody has their own opinions about what is pleasurable.
- Focused concentration on a pleasurable experience can increase the amount of pleasure gained from the experience.
- "Less can be more" when focusing on a potentially pleasant experience (e.g., focusing on a small bite of cookie and chewing it carefully instead of wolfing down the whole cookie at once).
- The ability to experience pleasure is a learned skill that needs to be practiced. Practice leads to mastery.
- It is important to integrate pleasure into everyday life. What type of "pleasure exercise" could you do today?

References

Kaluza, G. (2004). *Stressbewältigung*. Berlin: Springer.
Koppenhöfer, E. (2004). *Kleine Schule des Genießens*. Lengerich: Papst.
Lutz, R. (2000). Euthyme Therapie. In J. Margraf (Hrsg.). *Lehrbuch der Verhaltenstherapie* (2. Aufl., S. 447–465). Heidelberg: Springer.

Chapter 13
Module Five: Acceptance and Tolerance

13.1 Vicious Cycle #4: Amygdala Activation and Avoidance Reactions

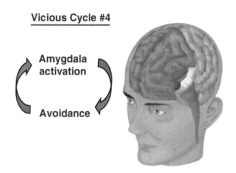

Vicious Cycle #4

Amygdala activation

Avoidance

Slide 61: So far in our training, we have talked about three examples of vicious cycles that can cause negative emotions to increase in their intensity and duration. Now, let's talk about another vicious cycle that can also develop. In the process of regulating amygdala activation, the prefrontal cortex may activate more on the left or on the right. Leftward activation has been associated with approach behavior, while rightward activation has been associated with avoidance behavior (Berkman & Lieberman, 2010; Spielberg et al., 2011), such as forming a goal "to not feel emotions."

This goal of not feeling emotions, however, is hard to attain. Emotions cannot be controlled by sheer force of will. They are usually beyond the realm of direct conscious control. The reason for this is that the amygdala and other parts of the limbic system act largely autonomously from the areas of the brain that initiate willfully controlled behavior. This functional autonomy of the limbic system was a significant evolutionary advantage to our ancestors. If those prehistoric men had been able to consciously control their feelings, they would have likely given in to the temptation to simply shut down unpleasant emotions. By doing so, they would not have received the important benefits of negative emotions such as "anger," which prepared our ancestors' bodies and minds for assertive action such as self-defense.

M. Berking and B. Whitley, *Affect Regulation Training: A Practitioners' Manual*,
DOI 10.1007/978-1-4939-1022-9_13, © Springer Science+Business Media New York 2014

Another reason why it is difficult to control emotions is that emotional reactions often cause significant changes in the body. These changes take time to dissipate, and as long as they are present, they impede the ability to make emotional changes. For example, it is difficult to quickly stop being angry when the body is flooded with stress hormones. Since emotions cannot be controlled by will alone, and since changes in the body make it difficult to control emotions, we see why the goal of getting rid of an emotion instantly and completely is often unattainable.

When a person is unsuccessful at their attempts to instantly rid themselves of a negative emotion, their failure will consequently lead to increased amygdala activation. The goal of getting rid of these negative emotions now becomes even stronger and more important, since the person is also experiencing increased distress due to the additional amygdala activation. However, the goal of avoiding the emotions is even more difficult at this point because of the heightened negative arousal. This leads to an even greater likelihood of failure to avoid the negative emotions, which causes more amygdala activation and so on. Thus, in this vicious cycle, the more the person attempts to get rid of the negative emotions, the stronger the emotions become.

13.2   ART Skill #4: Acceptance and Tolerance of Emotions

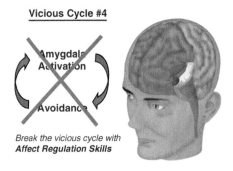

Slide 62: So if fighting to avoid our negative emotions is likely to make them stronger through the vicious cycle we described, what can we do instead?

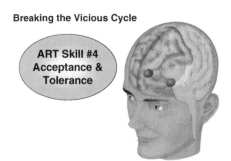

Slide 63: The opposite—accept and tolerate our emotions. But what does it mean to *accept* and *tolerate* our emotions? Let's talk about what acceptance and tolerance **does** and **does not** mean. (*The therapist may choose to pass out copies of Appendix H—Understanding Acceptance and Tolerance to the participants.*)

| Understanding Acceptance | **Slide 64:** Acceptance and tolerance … |

Acceptance & Tolerance <u>does not</u> mean...

• you have to like or enjoy the emotion you are trying to accept
• you have to accept everything always
• you accept the situation that triggered the negative emotion
• you give up and stop fighting to improve the situation

Acceptance and Tolerance <u>does</u> mean...

• intentionally permitting negative emotions to be present for the amount of time necessary for them to change, since fighting against emotions is likely to make them even stronger

• Does not mean you have to like or enjoy the emotion you are trying to accept
• Does not mean you have to accept everything always
• Does not mean you accept the *situation* that triggered the negative emotion (only the emotions cued by the situation)

• Does not mean you give up and stop fighting to improve the situation

Instead, acceptance and tolerance does mean …

• I intentionally permit negative emotions to be present, at least for the amount of time necessary for them to change. This is helpful because fighting against emotions is likely to make them even stronger.

Emotions exist to convey information to us. Once emotions have delivered their information, they will naturally change or subside unless we maintain them through avoidance. Accepting and tolerating, and hence openness to experiencing an emotion, is paradoxically an effective way of eventually changing the emotion. The concept of how acceptance and tolerance can change a negative emotion can be understood with the following metaphor:

Since the purpose of emotions is to convey important information, emotions can be thought of as a highly motivated mailman who wants to deliver a letter to us. Since he is conscientious, he will knock on your door and try to deliver it to you in person instead of just leaving it in your mailbox.

Now, say you are at home and you hear the mailman knocking at your front door. You look out of the window and see him. However, you decide not to open the door and receive the letter because you feel that it contains unpleasant information. The good mailman leaves, but he returns later in the day and knocks on your door again to deliver the letter. If you keep ignoring the mailman, he will continue to come back, since his/her sole purpose of existence is to deliver important letters. Thus, regardless of whether you barricade the door, put land mines in your front yard, and get a nasty watchdog, this highly dedicated mailman will keep trying to deliver the letter.

The most effective way to make the mailman stop bothering you is to simply accept the letter. You don't have to follow the advice written in the letter, but you need to accept it and find out what it says. Emotions function in much the same way as the mailman in this story. Your emotions will keep bothering you unless you experience them and consciously process the information your emotions want you to have.

For example, if you feel anxious, you could choose to allow yourself to focus on your anxiety and experience it without fighting against it. You could say to yourself,

"This is anxiety," and then begin to explore what this emotion is trying to tell you. For example, the anxiety may be telling you there is a really important exam coming up, and you should study hard in order get a good grade on it. You could then determine if this information is correct. Regardless of whether or not the information is correct, the first step is to simply allow the emotion tell you the information it wants to tell you. Once the emotion has done its job, it is far more likely that the body's regulatory functions will naturally kick in and reduce or change the emotion.

So we see how avoidance maintains our negative emotions, while acceptance and tolerance can begin the process to change them. I'd like to hear some of your ideas of how we could encourage acceptance and tolerance of our emotions. I will write your ideas on the flip chart. (*The therapist writes the participants' ideas to foster acceptance and tolerance on the flip chart.*)

5-Step Acceptance & Tolerance Plan

1) Set acceptance and tolerance as a goal
2) Give reasons for focusing on acceptance and tolerance
3) View your emotions as allies
4) Remind yourself how tough and resilient you are
5) Remind yourself that emotions are temporary

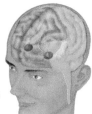

Slide 65: Thanks for all of the great feedback! Many of the ideas that you came up with are part of a specific method I am going to describe that we can use to help us accept and tolerate our negative emotions. In ART, this method is summarized in the 5-Step Acceptance and Tolerance Plan. (*Therapist hands out copies of Appendix I.*)

Let's review the plan together.

Step 1. Set acceptance and tolerance as a goal
Since accepting and tolerating negative emotions can be challenging, we will probably not do so without intentional effort. So first we must intentionally decide to make acceptance and tolerance of our emotions our goal. For example, you could say to yourself, "I will work to accept and tolerate my current emotion, even if it is difficult for me at the moment."

Step 2. Give reasons for focusing on acceptance and tolerance
Since the brain prefers changing things instead of accepting and tolerating them, we need to give our brain good reasons for engaging in this "second-rate" strategy. One of the most convincing reasons is that fighting against negative emotions often makes them stronger. Thus, it is smart to use acceptance and tolerance as a tool to calm down the system. This will significantly increase our ability to eventually change the emotion. For example, you could say to yourself, "I can't just turn off my feelings. If I try to fight them, I will only make them stronger, so I will accept and tolerate them at least for a certain period of time. This can bring me a sense of peace and calm that will help me eventually change my emotions."

Step 3. View your emotions as helpful

Viewing your emotions (especially challenging ones) in a more positive light can help you be more accepting and tolerating of them. One way to view emotions more positively is to see them as your allies, which are trying to give you important information and facilitate helpful behaviors.

So what are our emotions telling us? Positive emotions tell us that our needs and goals are generally being met, and because they feel good, they reinforce the behaviors that helped us meet our needs and goals. Since our needs and goals are being met, positive emotions are generally signals that we do not need to change anything or that we have attained a goal and can now rest and allow the positive emotions to recharge our "mental batteries."

Negative emotions, on the other hand, signal that our needs and goals are not being met. When we experience negative emotions, we can remind ourselves that our emotions are trying to let us know that our needs and goals are in some way not being met, and the *specific kinds of emotions* we experience provide us with important clues about what specific goals and needs are not being met. For example, you could say to yourself, "Although painful, these emotions are providing me with valuable information. They are helping me protect my needs and goals." You could also ask yourself, "What needs and goals are they telling me are not being met? What are they telling me I should do about these unmet needs and goals? What beneficial behaviors are facilitated by these feelings?" Say you are experiencing anger. You may find that anger is telling you that somebody or something is purposefully hindering your efforts to attain a certain important goal and that it might be helpful to prepare to fight and assert your rights, so you do not continue to be exploited by others. Think of what happens to individuals who are unable to get angry and use the anger to assert themselves. Right! They get exploited at work, end up with selfish partners, are unable to meet their needs, and eventually get severely depressed. So anger in this situation is providing you with really important information.

Note to the therapist:

Initially, it is often very challenging for the participants to positively reframe their negative emotions. In order to help the participants successfully reframe their negative emotions (e.g., by providing examples or using guided discovery techniques), therapists should have knowledge of the positive aspects of a broad range of emotions that are relevant to well-being and mental health. For additional information, refer to the Challenging Emotions chart (Appendix J), the Positive Emotions chart (Appendix K), as well as the following section that describes the positive and helpful aspects of various emotions:

Stress and Tension: Stress and tension informs us that the attainment of personally relevant goals may be threatened and that currently available resources may be insufficient to cope with these threats (conservation of resources theory; Hobfoll, 2001). Stress enhances the awareness of these threats and helps mobilize mental and physical energy to deal with them. For example, in a physically dangerous situation, stress focuses our thoughts on resolving the threat while causing increased respiration and muscle tension in order to flee (if the stress response turns into fear) or fight (if the stress response turns into anger).

Anxiety and Fear: Similar to stress, anxiety and fear promotes alertness for identifying and coping with potential threats. The more a *potential* threat turns into an *actual* threat (from the perspective of the individual), and the less it is believed that the threat can be managed successfully, the greater the likelihood that "stress" will turn into "anxiety and fear." The anxiety and fear response facilitates *flight responses* (getting out of the way of the threat) and sometimes *freezing* (not responding at all).

The flight response helps us get out of the danger zone as quickly as possible, such as when someone jumps out of the way of an oncoming car. Freezing probably developed originally as a successful protective evolutionary adaptation. When you stop moving and freeze, predators, including humans, have a more difficult time seeing you, since it is easier to detect moving objects instead of stationary ones. In modern times, it can be argued that freezing helps us to avoid doing something that may cause even greater harm. For example, a person may freeze when getting yelled at by their boss, since reacting could cause them to be fired.

Anger (also Annoyance and Irritation): Anger provides information that someone or something is impeding our goals and there is no valid excuse for the impediment. Believing that someone or some circumstance does not constitute a valid impediment of our goals is an important element in the development of anger, since we tend to feel angry only when we cannot justify what is happening to us. Anger facilitates the *fight response*, which fosters assertive action that helps us attain our goals, even when others object, and prevents us from being exploited by others.

Guilt, Shame, and Embarrassment: Guilt, shame, and embarrassment are often called the "self-conscious emotions" (Tangney & Tracy, 2012, p. 446). Although the terms have overlapping features, there are distinctions between them including their adaptive qualities. Guilt is experienced when a person breaks an important (moral) rule they have set for themselves (e.g., "I should not have acted cruelly toward that person."). Shame usually involves a rather global, negative self-evaluation that can occur in the context of a particular situation (e.g., "I am a bad person because I acted that way.") or in response to a generalized self-perception (e.g., "I am a bad person.") (Lewis, 2008). Embarrassment is experienced when a person believes some aspect of their identity and/or behavior is being judged negatively by others (e.g., "When I tripped up the stairs, I felt like such a klutz!") (Tangney & Tracy, 2012).

Social interaction is vitally important for health and survival. Guilt, shame, and embarrassment warn us that we are acting in a way that could cause us to be excluded by others and encourage us to take corrective actions. Therefore, these emotions can be regarded as very helpful for maintaining social connections (Tangney, Miller, Flicker, & Barlow, 1996). Specifically, guilt facilitates actions that make amends for misdeeds. The reparative actions that guilt facilitates, such as asking for forgiveness or compensating for damages, can serve to rebuild important social bonds.

The tendency to withdraw when feeling shame and hiding out until the problem blows over may at times be the most appropriate way to remain socially connected when we have violated a serious social norm. Withdrawal also strongly communicates an admission of wrongdoing, which can reassure others of our desire when we feel shamed to stop the social offense and our desire to remain socially connected. Feelings of embarrassment encourage us to take action to fix whatever we perceive is being judged by others in the moment (Tangney & Tracy, 2012), which could increase our standing in the group. Outward displays of embarrassment (i.e., blushing) maintain social inclusion by communicating to others we realize we have committed a faux pas and reassures others that it was not done on purpose (Leary, Landel, & Patton, 1996).

Sadness and Disappointment: Whereas stress and anxiety signal that goals are being threatened, sadness signals that important *goals* will not be achieved and disappointment signals that certain *expectations* will not be met. Both sadness and disappointment help us disengage from goals and expectations and cause us to reflect on why our goals will not be achieved or our expectations will not be met. As a result, sadness and disappointment allow us to eventually set new (and hopefully more attainable) goals and expectations.

Those who do not allow themselves to experience sadness and disappointment have difficulty letting go of unattainable goals and expectations. Since they do not let go of their unattainable goals and expectations, they continue to feel miserable, which may eventually turn into a mental disorder. By continuing to hang on to unattainable goals and expectations, they also reduce their opportunities to identify and achieve more realistic ones.

Depressed Mood: Whereas sadness refers to a specific event, a depressed mood signals to a person that (1) all their important goals have not been attained, (2) they do not possess the means to attain these goals, and (3) the impediments to attaining their goals are likely to persist. A depressed mood leads to withdrawal, inactivity, and rumination about the upsetting aspects of the situation. This is a very painful state, but depression can also be helpful. The distress that is experienced in a depressed mood encourages an individual to finally let go of all unattainable goals. The withdrawal feature in depression can provide a person with the critical time and space necessary to ponder a complete reorientation of his/her goals and the ways to best attain them.

Since a depressed mood is related to many or even all of a person's unattained goals, a reorientation of their goal structure does not occur quickly. Longer periods of time are often needed to work this through, and this important process does not happen without suffering. This is why depressed moods tend to last longer and be more upsetting than other emotional reactions. (For additional reading on adaptive conceptualizations of depression, see Nesse, 2000; Sharpley & Bitsika, 2010; Teasdale & Barnard, 1993.)

With this knowledge on the positive aspects of negative emotions, the therapist now facilitates an exercise in order to reinforce the idea that emotions are helpful allies. The therapist continues speaking to the participants:

Now let's go through an exercise to help us better understand the idea that challenging emotions give us important information and encourage helpful behaviors.

I am going to give three index cards to each participant. I would like each person to write the name of an emotion (negative or positive) they have experienced during the past week on one side of each of the three cards. Then on the back of each card write down (1) what information was being communicated by this emotion and (2) the helpful behavior that this information facilitated.

As an example using a negative emotion, the "anxiety" you experienced during this past week may have communicated that any errors in the business report you were preparing could have threatened your goal of receiving a promotion. The feeling of anxiety could have encouraged you to double-check your report before you gave it to your boss. As an example using a positive emotion, the "contentment" you experienced during this past week may have communicated that you have reached your goal of getting a certain type of position at the business where you work. In this case, contentment reinforced the hard work that went into getting that last promotion, which encouraged you to continue to be diligent at work.

Note to the therapist:

To help the participants with this exercise, the therapist may choose to pass out copies of the Challenging Emotions chart (Appendix J) and the Positive Emotions chart (Appendix K) that describes the positive function of various emotions. After spending 5–10 min to fill out the index cards, the participants take turns placing their cards on the floor (emotion name face up) in the center of the group and state for each card (1) the emotion they are referring to, (2) when this emotion occurred, (3) what important information the emotion communicated, and (4) what helpful behaviors the emotion facilitated. This exercise is often challenging, so the therapist should be ready to help coach the participants on the helpful aspects of emotions. To illustrate the value of aversive emotions, the therapist could pose the question, "What happens when people are unable to experience and utilize … (anger, anxiety, depression, etc.)?" It can also be helpful to explain that these emotions need to be unpleasant in order to motivate us to do something that is unpleasant but necessary. After everyone has discussed what they wrote on their cards and laid their cards on the floor, the therapist should check to see if any of the common negative emotions were not discussed. If some of the common negative emotions were not brought up by the participants, the therapist should take this opportunity to provide psychoeducation on the helpful aspects of these negative emotions as well.

The ART therapist may choose to implement a variation of this group exercise. In this variation, each participant writes the name of an emotion on an index card. The index cards are collected and shuffled. One of the index cards is then taped to each participant's back with the name of the emotion facing forward, without allowing the participant to see what is written on the card. The participants then move around the room and say to each other, "I am the emotion written on my back. What could I be trying to say?" (e.g., Anger—"My rights have been violated.") The participant also asks, "How could I be helpful?" (e.g., Anger—"I help you stand up for yourself.") Based on the responses, the participant with the card taped to his/her back tries to guess which emotion is listed on the card.

After the exercise, the therapist continues explaining the 5-Step Acceptance and Tolerance Plan:

Step 4. Remind yourself how tough and resilient you really are

Let's continue with the 5-Step Acceptance and Tolerance Plan. In Step 4, you take steps to remind yourself how tough and resilient you really are. Difficulties with accepting negative emotions are often caused by underestimating your ability to tolerate them. The influential psychologist Albert Ellis jokingly called this "syndrome" *I-can't-stand-it-itis*. It can be helpful to remind yourself that you may be underestimating your ability to endure negative emotions. To strengthen this argument, it is often helpful to remember that you have been able to endure negative feelings in the past on numerous occasions. Given such evidence of your resilience, you could say to yourself, "I have frequently proven that I can endure negative feelings, so I can do it again. I can tolerate these feelings even though they are painful!"

Note to the therapist:

Therapists should be aware that the idea of accepting negative emotions can be frightening to some participants based on their catastrophic assumptions about what would happen if they allowed themselves to accept and experience negative emotions. Common beliefs include, "If I allow my emotions to surface, they will overwhelm me, and I will become completely crazy, depressed, anxious, etc.," or "If I accept my feelings of depression, I will stop fighting them, and I will never be able to get rid of them." These beliefs are often the result of painful emotional experiences that have occurred in the past.

In such cases, therapists should first attempt to understand and validate the individual participant's avoidant reaction toward negative emotions that is based on her past experiences. For example, the therapist may validate her reaction by saying, "I can understand how you would feel that way, since emotions have felt so painful in the past. Avoiding your feelings in the past was probably very helpful during previous times in your life when you didn't have the ability to regulate your emotions, but now you have an opportunity to ask yourself if avoidance is still a helpful strategy for you."

After the therapist has gained an understanding of the participant's avoidant patterns and then validated these patterns, the therapist should gently and empathically confront her beliefs that underestimate her own ability to endure negative emotions. Confronting these beliefs involves showing the participant that despite experiencing many distressing emotions in the past, her darkest fears have not yet proven true (e.g., she did not die, go completely "crazy," etc.). In fact, the participant has managed to endure all of her prior negative emotions, since she is alive in the ART session with you this day.

For participants who have particular difficulties believing in their own ability to tolerate negative emotions, the *"Good Times—Bad Times"* exercise can be used (Fig. 13.1). Due to time constraints, this exercise would most likely be used when working on specific emotion regulation issues in adjunctive individual therapy. In this exercise, the participant is asked to plot the major past events of her life on a timeline, curving upward in good times and downward in unhappy times.

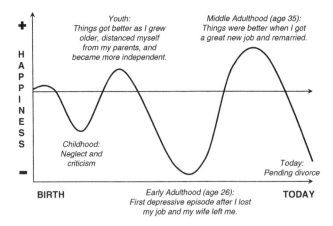

Fig. 13.1 Good times—Bad times

The timeline can then be analyzed from various perspectives. For example, to identify change-related skills, therapists can focus on sudden gains in happiness and analyze what the participant did to bring about these positive changes. However, when using this exercise to identify tolerance abilities, the therapist instead focuses on extended periods of unhappiness and asks the participant how she was able to endure such difficult times for so long.

The rationale behind this exercise is that (1) the participant almost certainly has had to deal with some painful situation in her past that she could not change and (2) she did obviously somehow survive the negative emotions during the painful situation, since she is alive and participating in ART. The exercise challenges the therapist to be both empathic and at the same time confront the participant's faulty beliefs in her own supposedly insufficient tolerance capacities.

While the timeline will help some participants gain insight into their ability to tolerate emotions, others will interpret the timeline as additional evidence that they do in fact lack the ability to tolerate their emotions. For example, a participant may make statements such as, "I did try to kill myself, but they found and rescued me. This proves that I cannot tolerate my emotions." It may be helpful in this situation to clarify how often the participant attempted suicide and mark those incidents with an "x" on the timeline. The therapist could then (very empathically and seemingly naively) point out all of the low points on her timeline without an "x," showing that there were in fact periods when she suffered but did *not* attempt suicide. The therapist could ask the participant to account for these times. Through this dialogue, the therapist leads the participant to the point where she does not so strongly oppose the hypothesis that "she may be more resilient than she thinks."

It should be noted that the focus in this exercise is not to quickly convince the participant that she is resilient, but rather to gently question the "evidence" that she is not resilient and to point out that just maybe … she has underestimated herself. It is important not to get stuck in an argument with the participant regarding whether she is resilient or not. Instead, the participant should be presented with the *option* of challenging her belief that she lacks resilience. The therapist could, for example, say, "If you decide that you want to foster your ability to accept and tolerate your emotions, it can be helpful to remind yourself of the many times you have successfully tolerated aversive emotions in the past and allow yourself to see that this means that you do, in fact, have the ability to tolerate negative emotions."

The therapist continues discussing the 5-Step Acceptance and Tolerance Plan:

Step 5. Remind yourself that emotions are temporary
In the final step of the plan, you remind yourself that an emotion does not last forever. Emotions communicate information. So, if you give the emotion an opportunity to convey its information, it will fade away sooner or later. Reminding yourself that no emotion lasts forever can help you better accept a negative emotion, since you will only need to tolerate it for a limited period of time. You may find it helpful to tell yourself something like, "This emotion is only temporary. I will not have to endure it forever."

Note to the therapist:

After the 5-Step Acceptance and Tolerance Plan has been discussed, participants are invited to pick an emotion that has been difficult for them to accept and tolerate in the past. The participants are then asked to utilize the 5-Step Acceptance and Tolerance Plan Worksheet (Appendix L) to increase their acceptance and tolerance of this challenging emotion.

At the end of the worksheet each participant is directed to develop a personal *Acceptance and Tolerance Statement*. This should be a summary of the phrases that were developed in the individualized 5-Step Acceptance and Tolerance Plan. An example of this personal Acceptance and Tolerance Statement is, "It's okay that I feel the way I do. This emotion is helping me see how I can get my needs met. I can tolerate these feelings for a while if necessary, and I know that they won't last forever."

The participants may work in teams of two to help each other complete the worksheet and develop a meaningful Acceptance and Tolerance Statement. While the participants are completing the worksheet, the therapist answers any questions that arise and proactively ensures that the participants understand how to complete the steps in the worksheet.

Later, the participants take turns presenting their Acceptance and Tolerance Statement. As the participants share their Acceptance and Tolerance Statements, the therapist encourages the participants to repeat their statements several times, aloud, to the group. This is done to ensure that the Acceptance and Tolerance Statement feels authentic to each participant. If necessary, the therapist gently helps participants modify their statement until they say it feels right to them.

When all of the participants have formulated an Acceptance and Tolerance Statement they feel comfortable with, the therapist explains to the group that it takes time and practice for the statement to actually trigger acceptance and tolerance of a challenging emotion. The participants are then encouraged to close their eyes and silently repeat their Acceptance and Tolerance Statements to themselves, until they begin to feel more accepting and tolerant of an emotion they may be experiencing at the time.

The participants are then encouraged to share their experiences of going through the 5-Step Acceptance and Tolerance Plan and creating an Acceptance and Tolerance Statement. The therapist answers any questions and addresses any problems they encountered prior to including ART Skill #4 into the ART Sequence.

13.3   ART Sequence with ART Skills #1–4

The therapist continues speaking to the participants:

So far, in the ART Sequence Exercises, we have tensed and relaxed our muscles in groups of specific muscles. However, starting with this next ART Sequence Exercise, we will tense and release all of these muscles at once. Let's try this together. Okay, now clench your fists. Angle your fists inward. Angle your forearms toward your upper arms. Pull your fists to your shoulders. Clench your teeth. Turn the corners of your mouth outward. Press your tongue against the roof of your mouth. Carefully squeeze your eyes shut. Furrow your eyebrows. Pull your shoulders up and then back. Tilt your hips forward, and arch your back. Press your buttocks together. Straighten and slightly lift your legs in front of you, and point your feet downward. Now hold the tension for a moment. (*Slight pause*) Continue breathing as calmly and deeply as possible. (*Slight pause*) And now, with the next out-breath … relax your muscles. Pay attention to the difference between the tension you felt before and the relaxation you feel right now. Keep breathing calmly and regularly, and let your muscles become more and more relaxed with each out-breath. (*15 s pause*)

Okay, one more time. Clench your fists. Angle your fists inward. Angle your forearms toward your upper arms. Pull your fists to your shoulders. Clench your teeth. Turn the corners of your mouth outward. Press your tongue against the roof of your mouth. Carefully squeeze your eyes shut. Furrow your eyebrows. Pull your shoulders up and then back. Tilt your hips forward and arch your back. Press your buttocks together. Straighten and slightly lift your legs in front of you, and this time point your feet back toward your face. Now hold the tension for a moment. (*Slight pause*) Continue breathing as calmly and deeply as possible. (*Slight pause*) Now, with the next out-breath … relax your muscles. Pay attention to the difference between the tension you felt before and the relaxation you feel right now. Keep breathing calmly and regularly, and let your muscles become more and more relaxed with each out-breath. (*15 s pause*)

Does anyone have questions about this shortened version of muscle relaxation?

ART Skills and ART Sequence

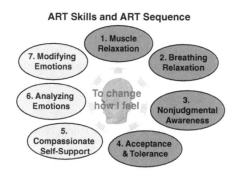

Slide 66: At this point in the training we have learned the first four ART Skills: Muscle Relaxation, Breathing Relaxation, Nonjudgmental Awareness, and Acceptance and Tolerance of Emotions. (*Acceptance and Tolerance of Emotions—ART Skill #4 is achieved through the completion of the 5-Step Acceptance and Tolerance Plan. The steps of this plan are now combined with ART Skills #1 through #3 that have already been added to the ART Sequence.*)

We will now practice linking these four ART Skills together in the ART Sequence. We will use the shortened version of muscle relaxation during this ART Sequence Exercise.

The therapist leads the participants in the ART Sequence with ART Skills #1–4:

Just as before, I will provide the instructions as we go through the exercise together. *The therapist may guide the ART Sequence Exercise using the "Exercise Three" audio that can be downloaded from the ART website, or the therapist may guide the exercise using the following instructions*:

We will start the exercise after the sound of the bell.

Sound of the bell

Find a comfortable sitting position. Close your eyes. Exhale slowly. Relax your body, and bring your attention to your muscles. In a moment, we will begin tensing and then relaxing our muscles. (*3 s pause*) Now, tense the muscles in your body by doing the following: Clench your fists. Angle your fists inward. Angle your forearms toward your upper arms. Pull your fists to your shoulders. Clench your teeth. Pull the corners of your mouth outward. Press your tongue against the roof of your mouth. Carefully squeeze your eyes shut. Furrow your eyebrows. Pull your shoulders up and then back. Tilt your hips forward and arch your back. Press your buttocks together. Straighten and slightly lift your legs in front of you, and point your feet downward. Now hold the tension for a moment. (*Slight pause*) Continue breathing as calmly and deeply as possible. (*Slight pause*)

Now, with the next out-breath … relax your muscles. Pay attention to the difference between the tension you felt before and the relaxation you feel right now. Keep breathing calmly and regularly, and let your muscles become more and more relaxed with each out-breath. (*5 s pause*)

Now, we will tense the muscles again, just like last time. Clench your fists. Angle your fists inward. Angle your forearms toward your upper arms. Pull your fists to your shoulders. Clench your teeth. Pull the corners of your mouth outward. Press your tongue against the roof of your mouth. Carefully squeeze your eyes shut.

Furrow your eyebrows. Pull your shoulders up and then back. Tilt your hips forward
and arch your back. Press your buttocks together. Straighten and slightly lift your
legs in front of you, and this time point your feet back toward your face. Now hold
the tension for a moment. (*Slight pause*) Continue breathing as calmly and deeply
as possible. (*Slight pause*)

With the next out-breath … relax your muscles. Pay attention to the difference
between the tension you felt before and the relaxation you feel right now. Keep
breathing calmly and regularly, and let your muscles become more and more relaxed
with each out-breath. (*5 s pause*)

Now, we will start to practice nonjudgmental awareness. Focus your attention on
the sensations of your breath—the way it flows … in … and out again … without
trying to control it. Say to yourself "in" when breathing in and "out" when breathing
out, and do your best to focus on the sensation of your breathing in your abdomen.
When you realize that you're getting distracted or that other thoughts are crossing
your mind, use a word to label what is happening, such as "planning," "worrying,"
or "remembering," and gently bring your attention back to your breathing. Every
time you become aware that you are distracted, praise yourself for noticing it, and
then focus on your breathing again. We'll now spend a minute simply focusing on
our breathing. Remember to say to yourself, "in" … and … "out." When you become
distracted, use a word to label what is happening such as "planning," "worrying," or
"remembering," and gently bring your attention back to your breathing. (*40 s pause*)

Now we are going to practice shifting our focus and awareness onto other things.
First, gently shift your attention from your breathing onto any sensations you are
feeling in your body at the moment. (*20 s pause*) Now pay attention to what you
are hearing at the moment. (*20 s pause*) Next, notice any smells you are aware of.
(*20 s pause*) Now see what thoughts are crossing your mind. (*20 s pause*) Notice any
desires you have right now. (*20 s pause*) Be aware of any emotions you are experiencing right now. Label each emotion. (*5 s pause*) Which of these emotions do you
feel more strongly? (*20 s pause*) What other emotions are maybe more subdued but
are still present in the background? (*20 s pause*) Estimate the intensity of each emotion you have labeled on a scale from 0 to 10, and become aware of how you feel
these emotions in your body. (*20 s pause*)

Now I will guide you through the 5-Step Acceptance and Tolerance Plan to specifically address either a negative feeling that you have become aware of presently
or a negative feeling that has been challenging for you in the past. Select which
emotion you would like to work with. First, set a goal to accept your present emotion as much as possible, and strengthen this goal with a reason. For example, you
might tell yourself, "I will work on accepting my feeling because I need to experience my emotion before I can regulate it," or "If I fight against my feeling, I will
only make it stronger." Take some time now to set a goal for yourself to accept your
emotion. Also decide for yourself why this goal is important to you. (*20 s pause*)

Now do your best to create a positive attitude toward your feeling. For example,
complete the following sentences in your head, "This feeling is helpful; it is telling
me that… ." (*15 s pause*) "It is trying to help me to… ." (*15 s pause*)

Next, remind yourself that you can tolerate challenging emotions, at least for a period of time. Think of ways you have been able to endure intense negative feelings in the past. Perhaps say to yourself, "I can tolerate this feeling. I have already endured difficult feelings in the past, so I am able to tolerate my present feelings." Take some time now to create a sentence you can believe in that reminds you why you are able to tolerate your present feelings. (*10 s pause*)

Now continue by reminding yourself that feelings are not permanent. Maybe you say to yourself, "Feelings come and go, and even difficult and distressing feelings will not last forever." Keep experimenting with this sentence until you believe it. (*10 s pause*)

Finally, take the most helpful ideas from the 5-Step Acceptance and Tolerance Plan and summarize them to create an Acceptance and Tolerance Statement. For example, you may say, "It's okay that I feel this way. These feelings are an important part of me, and they are trying to help me by providing me with valuable information. I can tolerate them for a period of time if I have to because I know they won't last forever." Take some time to create this Acceptance and Tolerance Statement for yourself, and then repeat this statement several times in your head. (*15 s pause*)

Now relax all the muscles in your body: hands, forearms, upper arms, face, neck, back, stomach, buttocks, and legs. Breathe calmly and regularly, and let your muscles become more relaxed with each out-breath. (*5 s pause*)

Now slowly bring your attention back into the room at your own pace by breathing in deeply (*audible inhale*), stretching and flexing your body (*demonstrate*), opening your eyes, and lightly tapping on your thighs a few times, so that you become fully alert again.

Sound of the bell
Note to the therapist:

As usual, a debriefing occurs at the end of the exercise. If the training setting and schedule permit, therapists may integrate additional exercises that focus on acceptance and tolerance. Here are a few examples of such exercises:

In the "tree-in-the-storm-exercise," a participant stands with his legs locked straight and together in the middle of a small circle made by the other participants who face the participant in the center. The surrounding participants lock hands tightly. The participant in the center allows himself to fall slightly sideways, forwards, and backwards, while the other participants catch him with their arms and gently push him back toward the middle of the circle. The participant in the middle is stiff like a board and is being moved according to the participants who encircle him.

In another variation of this exercise, the ends of a long rope are tied together to form a circle. The participants stand in a circle inside of the circle of rope. The participants hold the rope at waist level behind them, so the rope runs along the backs of the participants. The participants then all lean back at the same time against the rope, so the group does not fall. Sometimes, however, the group does fall, which gives the therapist the opportunity to discuss the idea that even if our fears do in fact come true, they will probably not be as horrible as we imagine.

Mindfulness meditation can also be used by the therapist as another tool to train the participants in the skills of acceptance and tolerance. All of these types of experiential exercises can be a helpful counterweight to the didactic portions of ART.

References

Berkman, E. T., & Lieberman, M. D. (2010). Approaching the bad and avoiding the good: Lateral prefrontal cortical asymmetry distinguishes between action and valence. *Journal of Cognitive Neuroscience, 22*(9), 1970–1979.

Hobfoll, S. E. (2001). The influence of culture, community, and the nested-self in the stress process: Advancing conservation of resources theory. *Applied Psychology, 50*(3), 337–421.

Leary, M. R., Landel, J. L., & Patton, K. M. (1996). The motivated expression of embarrassment following a self-presentational predicament. *Journal of Personality, 64*(3), 619–636.

Lewis, M. (2008). Self-conscious emotions: Embarrassment, pride, shame, and guilt. In M. Lewis, J. M. Haviland-Jones, & L. F. Barrett (Eds.), *Handbook of emotions* (3rd ed., pp. 742–756). New York, NY: Springer.

Nesse, R. M. (2000). Is depression an adaptation? *Archives of General Psychiatry, 57*(1), 14–20.

Sharpley, C. F., & Bitsika, V. (2010). Is depression "evolutionary" or just "adaptive"? A comment. *Depression Research and Treatment, 2010*, 1–7.

Spielberg, J. M., Miller, G. A., Engels, A. S., Herrington, J. D., Sutton, B. P., Banich, M. T., & Heller, W. (2011). Trait approach and avoidance motivation: Lateralized neural activity associated with executive function. *NeuroImage, 54*(1), 661–670.

Tangney, J. P., Miller, R. S., Flicker, L., & Barlow, D. H. (1996). Are shame, guilt, and embarrassment distinct emotions? *Journal of Personality and Social Psychology, 70*(6), 1256–1269.

Tangney, J. P., & Tracy, J. L. (2012). Self-conscious emotions. In M. Leary & J. P. Tangney (Eds.), *Handbook of self and identity* (2nd ed., pp. 446–478). New York, NY: Guilford.

Teasdale, J. D., & Barnard, P. J. (1993). *Affect, cognition and change: Re-modelling depressive thought*. Hove, UK: Lawrence Erlbaum Associates.

Chapter 14
Module Six: Compassionate Self-Support

14.1 Vicious Cycle #5: Amygdala Activation and Self-Criticism/Negative Secondary Emotions

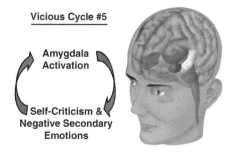

Slide 67: We have previously talked about four vicious cycles that can cause negative emotions to increase in their intensity and duration. Now we are going to focus on another vicious cycle that can develop. This vicious cycle begins when someone who feels stressed or upset starts to blame or criticizes themselves. They may say to themselves, "I can't do anything right. My reaction to this situation proves that I am weak. I am a complete a failure. Something is wrong with me." Some people believe these self-statements are necessary to keep themselves motivated by "whipping" themselves into shape.

These statements, however, are self-inflicted attacks that threaten the need to feel valued as a person. The amygdala then activates, sounding the alarm that the need to feel valued and worthwhile is under attack. The amygdala activation increases the stress response in the body and in the brain. At the same time, self-criticism leads to additional negative emotions such as anger, shame, and guilt.

The vicious cycle then plays out like this: Self-criticism leads to a threatened sense of self-worth that activates the amygdala and increases the current stress response. At the same time, self-criticism triggers negative emotions that lead to additional amygdala activation. This dual activation of the amygdala increases the stress response in the body and in the brain, leading to more negative feelings, which leads the person to be even more self-critical. Tragically, additional criticism only continues to fuel this vicious cycle.

M. Berking and B. Whitley, *Affect Regulation Training: A Practitioners' Manual*,
DOI 10.1007/978-1-4939-1022-9_14, © Springer Science+Business Media New York 2014

14.2   ART Skill #5: Compassionate Self-Support

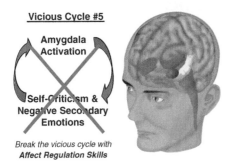

Slide 68: So if self-criticism fuels this vicious cycle and does not help us regulate our negative emotions, what could we do instead to help us regulate our emotions?

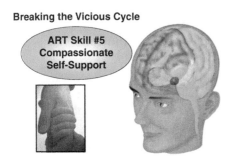

Slide 69: The answer is that we could compassionately support ourselves instead of criticizing ourselves and beating ourselves up. Compassionate self-support is a sympathetic attitude you have for yourself that is kind, encouraging, and soothing. During stressful events, this attitude helps prevent us from sliding into the vicious cycle we just described caused by self-criticism. Compassionate self-support also helps develop positive feelings that inhibit the negative ones.

Slide 70: The ability to compassionately support ourselves requires two foundational elements. The first is that *we place value on ourselves.* If we do not do this, it will be very difficult to compassionately support ourselves in times of distress. The second foundational element of compassionate self-support is that *we regularly take care of ourselves by engaging in activities that result in positive emotions.* By regularly engaging in positive activities, we strengthen the areas in the brain that are responsible for generating positive emotions. If these areas are strong, it will be far easier to activate positive emotions in times of distress.

Before we talk about the skill of compassionate self-support in challenging situations, let's first discuss how we can develop these two foundational elements of compassionate self-support. We will start with the first foundational element of compassionate self-support, which is learning to place value on ourselves. We will now go through an exercise to help us learn to value ourselves and to improve our self-esteem.

Note to the therapist:

Each participant is given a large sheet of white paper (e.g., $11'' \times 17''$ or $12'' \times 18''$). Then, participants are shown the Self-Esteem Building Worksheet (Appendix M) depicted on slide 71 and instructed to copy the worksheet onto their blank piece of paper. The therapist may also choose to print copies of the worksheet for the participants.

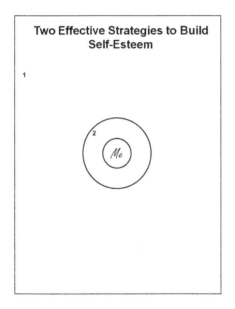

Slide 71

Next, the participants are asked to list their past successful achievements on the worksheet in the area indicated by the number "1." To inject some humor, the therapist may say something like, "You have 2 hours to complete this first part … (participants typically laugh) … and I know this is not nearly enough time, so feel free to pick this back up again later when you get home (this usually gets more laughter from the participants)."

After 5–10 min, the participants are asked to also write in the area marked by the number "1" the personal skills, strengths, and abilities (e.g., smart, hardworking, ambitious, resilient, good salesman, good listener, skilled writer, etc.) that helped them accomplish the achievements they just listed. After five to ten more minutes, the participants are then asked to list, also in the area marked by the number "1," everything else they like about themselves that is not related to their achievements and skills, such as a beautiful nose or a great sense of humor.

After the participants have finished, the ART therapist asks the participants to identify emotions they experienced as they reflected upon their achievements, abilities, and strengths. The participants commonly report emotions that range from joy and pride but also emotions such as sadness or shame.

When discussing these responses, the therapist first focuses on feelings such as joy and pride. The therapist asks the participants to describe what joy and pride feel like, how these emotions affect their energy level, and how these emotions affect their self-esteem. The participants will inevitably say that joy and pride feel positive and increase their energy level and self-esteem. This allows the therapist to reinforce the message that we can raise our mood, energy level, and self-esteem when we remind ourselves of our achievements, our abilities that contributed to our achievements, and our many positive qualities and attributes.

The therapist then turns attention to any negative emotions that participants may have experienced during the exercise. The therapist works collaboratively with the participants to help them understand that identifying achievements, abilities, and strengths can trigger a variety of responses that generate negative emotions. One common response that people have is a dismissive attitude toward their achievements and strengths. People who tend to dismiss their achievements and strengths typically do so because the standards they have set for themselves are impossibly high or are based on comparisons with others who have significant advantages. Since they will never be able to achieve their own self-imposed standards, they continue their pattern of devaluing themselves.

The following dialogue is presented as an example of an exchange that could take place between the therapist and a participant who is dismissive of his strengths and accomplishments:

Therapist:	"I haven't achieved anything in my entire life!"
Participant:	"Did you graduate from high school?"
Therapist:	"Sure, but everyone does that, and I did so poorly in college that I had to drop out."
	At this point, the therapist should help the patient see that he is devaluing himself, and that doing so has undesirable consequences.
Therapist:	"What are you doing right now to yourself?" "How does this feel?" "How does this affect your self-esteem?"
	The therapist is then able to begin to challenge the participant's dismissive thinking.
Therapist:	"As far as I know, not everyone does complete high school, correct?"
Participant:	"Yeah, that's right."
Therapist:	"…and if I remember correctly, you said earlier that in your childhood, your father had severe problems with alcohol and you also did not get a whole lot of support from your mother. Correct?"

Participant:	"Yeah, that's right."
Therapist:	"…and in spite of these circumstances you still graduated from high school?"
Participant:	"Yes."
Therapist:	"So what does this tell us?"
Participant:	"I don't know."
Therapist:	"Let's get the other participants to comment. So, what do you all think?"
Other participant:	"I think graduating from high school really is a big accomplishment, since he really had to do it all by himself!"
Therapist:	(to the dismissive participant) "What do you think about that comment?"
Participant:	"Yeah, maybe I do tend to downplay my achievements a bit…."
Therapist:	"What is the cost to you when you downplay your achievements?"
Participant:	"It makes me feel like I will never accomplish anything, so most times I don't even try."
Therapist:	"And is this how you want to feel about yourself?"
Participant:	"No, certainly not."
Therapist:	"So instead of downplaying your achievements, what could you do differently?"
Participant:	"I could validate and appreciate them."
Therapist:	"That is an interesting idea! How would you do that?"

In this scenario, the participant would then come up with specific ideas that are discussed in the group and a plan would be formulated to carry out these ideas. For example, at the end of each day the participant may choose to look back over the day and identify at least one success that occurred and identify what skills enabled the success to occur. While looking in a mirror, the participant may choose to congratulate himself and pat himself on his shoulder. This exercise will be introduced later as an exercise for all of the participants. This type of redundancy is purposefully used in ART to make sure that participants understand the crucial elements of the training.

Another common response that can occur when thinking about achievements and strengths is an internal voice that tells them that talking about their achievements and strengths is egotistical and arrogant. This response often leads to emotions such as shame and guilt. Another common response to noting achievements and strengths is the activation of a deep-seated negative self-image. For example, a participant may say, "If you want, I can write down all the successes I have had, but this feels like a lie. Deep down I know that I am a worthless person no matter what I achieve."

In this example, the person's negative self-image has been triggered, which activates a range of negative emotions and overrides the positive benefits that could result from acknowledging his/her achievements and strengths.

After pointing out that focusing on one's achievements and strengths is an effective but sometimes difficult strategy to build self-esteem, the ART therapist invites the participants to take turns presenting some of their achievements, skills, strengths, and abilities to the other participants. For those participants who are unable to identify any of these, the therapist's job is to help them discover at least one aspect of themselves that they can be proud of (e.g., "Earlier in the session, you had us all laughing with what you said. Would you agree that you are able to make others laugh with your good sense of humor?").

After the participants have taken turns sharing some of their achievements, abilities, and strengths, the therapist again asks the participants to describe emotions they experienced as they shared with the group. Again, participants commonly report emotions that range from joy and pride but also emotions such as sadness or shame. The ART therapist uses this opportunity to reinforce the point that noting achievements and strengths can result in positive emotions that elevate our mood and build our self-esteem. The therapist also reminds the participants that people can experience various responses that result in negative emotions as well.

The therapist continues speaking to the participants:

So we have discovered (*through the previous group discussion guided by the therapist*) there are many responses we could experience when we try to appreciate our strengths and achievements that may result in negative emotions. These responses become hindrances to our intentional efforts to use our achievements and strengths to enhance our self-esteem. Let's review the hindrances that we have discussed so far. (*The therapist lists the most important hindrances on a flip chart: e.g., a critical inner-voice, a belief that praising ourselves is arrogant, feeling the need to whip ourselves into shape, holding ourselves to impossibly high standards, etc.*) So we need to find ways to cope with these hindrances in order to receive the positive benefits that come with noting our strengths and achievements. Let's spend a few minutes brainstorming ways we can cope with the hindrances that we have here on our list.

The ART therapist then guides the participants in a brainstorming session to find potential ways of coping with the hindrances. At the end of this process the therapist skillfully leads the participants to the idea that ART Skill #3—Nonjudgmental Awareness can be used to cope with all of the hindrances.

When we focused on the sensation of our breathing during our practice of ART Skill #3—Nonjudgmental Awareness, we noticed any distractions (e.g., sounds, thoughts, emotions), labeled them (e.g., noise, thinking, anger), and redirected our focus back onto the sensation of our breathing. This technique can be used when we notice that hindrances are interfering with our attempts at focusing on our strengths, achievements, and abilities.

There is a helpful exercise we can practice daily at home that involves noting our strengths, abilities, and achievements. In this Daily Self-Esteem Building Exercise, we stand in front of a mirror at the end of each day and look back on what we achieved during that day, listing at least three examples. For example, our achievements may consist of meeting a deadline, acting kindly toward someone, or getting out of bed even though we didn't feel like doing so. For each achievement, we think of the strengths or abilities that enabled us to attain this achievement. As we do this, our minds may bring a hindrance to this exercise into your awareness. For example, when you are creating your list of achievements, an inner, critical voice in your mind may say, "You have done nothing important today!" or "This is a very stupid exercise!" or "These are all lies, the truth is that you are a complete failure!" When a hindrance like this occurs, we will try to simply label it (e.g., critical thought, judgmental voice from the past, etc.) and gently refocus our attention back onto the task of identifying our achievements and the strengths and abilities that enabled them to occur.

It is important to remember that the effect of these hindrances is completely dependent on the way in which we respond to them. If we give in to the hindrances and allow them to stop the exercise, we will not receive the boost to our self-esteem this exercise can provide.

If we rigidly fight the hindrances, we will be giving them even more attention, which could make them even stronger. However, if we are able to patiently observe the hindrances, label them, and then gently redirect our focus onto the exercise, we will find that over time these hindrances will become quieter. With practice managing the hindrances effectively, it will become easier to appreciate our strengths and achievements even though the hindrances may never disappear completely.

In summary, it is common to experience hindrances when we try to identify and appreciate our strengths and achievements, but these hindrances can be overcome with the help of nonjudgmental awareness as we redirect our focus back onto our strengths and achievements. Although appreciation of our achievements, strengths, abilities, and positive qualities is a helpful way to help build our self-esteem, there are some disadvantages of this self-esteem-building strategy. Does anyone have any ideas of what the disadvantages of this strategy could be? Right! Our self-esteem will become dependent on our achievements, strengths, abilities, and positive qualities. What would happen then to my self-esteem if my strengths decrease over time or I am no longer able to achieve what I once could? Yes, my self-esteem would decrease. Also, what would it feel like if I believe that my self-esteem is based on my achievements at my work? Right! I would feel intense pressure to continue to achieve in order to maintain my self-esteem. What could this feeling of pressure lead to? Yes, burnout and exhaustion, and I would probably lose the joy that I could have received from my job. Ultimately this pressure could lead me to be unsuccessful at work and take the joy out of my job.

So even though appreciating our achievements and strengths is a helpful way to build self-esteem, it also seems wise to complement this strategy with another strategy. If the problem with the first strategy is that it conditions our self-esteem on our achievements and strengths, what should be the core of a complementing strategy? Yes, building unconditional self-esteem that is not conditioned on our strengths and achievements. So how can we build unconditional self-esteem?

At this point there is usually a long silence, since most participants will acknowledge the importance of unconditional self-esteem but have no idea how to start to

*build it. To help them begin to develop unconditional self-esteem the therapist pro-
vides the following illustration*:

Let me ask you a question. If a child comes back from school with a good grade,
what do "good parents" do? Yes, they praise the child! What does this do for the
child? Yes, the child feels good, proud, and motivated to work hard in the future.
What does the praise do to the self-esteem of the child? Yes, it goes up, doesn't it?
So, this is how we recognize "good parents." They praise the child and give him/her
love and affection at times when the child is successful. But what happens if the
parents *only* give love and affection when the child is successful? Correct, the child
feels more and more pressure to always be successful, so he/she continues to receive
the parents' praise, which helps the child maintain a high self-esteem.

While good parents help build a child's conditional self-esteem, "excellent parents" help a child develop unconditional self-esteem. How do we recognize excellent
parents? Yes, by how the parents respond when the child comes home with a bad
grade. What do excellent parents do in such a situation to foster self-esteem that is
independent from factors such as success? Excellent parents may say that this bad
grade is certainly a setback, but at the same time they will take the child in their arms
and let the child know that they love him/her with all their heart regardless of the type
of grades he/she receives at school. This is how you recognize excellent parents.

Now, many of us may not have been so fortunate to have such excellent parents.
(*In clinical populations, there are often participants who experience grief and start
to cry when remembering how they were neglected during their childhood at this
point.*) However, as adults we have the opportunity to decide if we would like to be
excellent parents for ourselves and to treat ourselves as excellent parents would. So
what could you say to yourself that would express unconditional self-esteem for
yourself? Please take some time to develop a statement that an excellent parent
would say—something that expresses that you are a valuable person regardless of
your successes and abilities. For example, you may say to yourself "I love you, not
for what you do, but for who you are," or "I love everything about you: strengths,
flaws, and all," or "You are valuable—just the way you are." Now, please take some
time to create a statement that you can use to build unconditional self-esteem.

Note to the therapist:

The therapist gives participants approximately 5 min to develop a phrase that communicates unconditional self-esteem. The participants are then invited to share their
statements with the group. The therapist uses this opportunity to fine-tune the participants' affirmations and the delivery of their statements to encourage congruence
between the statement and their posture, tone of voice, facial expression, etc. The
therapist encourages each participant to repeat the sentence a couple of times and asks
the participants to what extent they *feel* the sentence building their unconditional self-
esteem. This reinforces the idea that building unconditional self-esteem is a two-step
process: first, developing a statement that expresses unconditional self-esteem and,
second, repeating that statement to intentionally build unconditional self-esteem.

One technique to encourage reflection on the concept that people have inherent or intrinsic worth outside of their achievements, strengths, and abilities is to show the participants a crisp $10 bill. The therapist or a participant then crumples it up and stomps on it. The therapist then asks how much the bill is worth. The participants will reply that the bill is still worth $10. The therapist then asks the participants to consider that just as the $10 bill has inherent value regardless of its appearance or whether it is used in an illegal transaction or in a manner that selflessly benefits someone, people also have a similar inherent value. While there is no single answer to the question of how we can unconditionally value ourselves, ART participants are invited to reflect on this question and to find an answer that is personally meaningful for them.

After each participant has identified and shared a statement that expresses unconditional self-esteem, the participants write these statements on the Self-Esteem Building Worksheet in the area marked by a number "2." This section on self-esteem is ended by returning to the Daily Self-Esteem Building Exercise and complementing conditional self-esteem with unconditional self-esteem.

Let's go back to the Daily Self-Esteem Building Exercise we discussed earlier that you could use to build self-esteem. Now we will add unconditional self-esteem to the exercise. So the exercise looks like this: At the end of the day, look at yourself in the bathroom mirror. Review the day in your mind and think of at least three achievements that you can be proud of (e.g., meeting a deadline, an act of kindness, or getting out of bed even though you didn't feel like it). Then, think about which of your strengths and abilities enabled you to attain these achievements. Next, look yourself in the eyes, pat yourself on the shoulder, and use some appropriate words to express that you are proud of yourself. If negative reactions cause resistance to doing this, label the negative reaction, and return your focus back to the exercise. Do this until you feel at least a little bit of pride toward yourself. Then give yourself a particularly warm smile, look deeply into your eyes, and repeat the unconditional affirmation statement you developed that in some way says that you love yourself regardless of your achievements and successes.

Participants are then invited to practice this Daily Self-Esteem Building Exercise each day at home. To reinforce the benefits of this exercise, the therapist hands out copies of the Self-Support Diary I: Appreciation of my Achievements and Strengths (Fig. 14.1, Appendix N). In this worksheet, participants are encouraged to record the achievements as well as the strengths and abilities that led to the various achievements that they identified during the Daily Self-Esteem Building Exercise. The worksheet also asks the participant to record if they were able to give themselves a signal of unconditional self-esteem. The participants can be encouraged to tape the Self-Support Diary I: Appreciation of my Achievements and Strengths worksheet to their bathroom mirror, as a reminder to practice the exercise, and so the worksheet will be readily available to record the thoughts they had during the exercise.

Day	Achievements	My Strengths & Abilities that Contributed to my Achievements	Unconditional Self-Esteem Signal (✓)
Monday			
Tuesday			
Wednesday			
Thursday			
Friday			
Saturday			
Sunday			

Fig. 14.1 Self-support diary I: appreciation of my achievements and strengths

The therapist continues with the presentation slides:

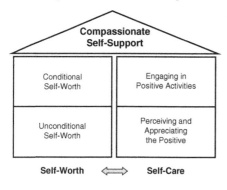

Slide 72: We have been talking about the first foundational element of compassionate self-support, <u>placing value on ourselves</u>. We will now talk about the second foundational element of compassionate self-support, which is <u>self-care by engaging in activities that result in positive emotions</u>. The rationale behind this second pillar of compassionate self-support is that it will be easier to improve our mood during times of distress if we have regularly practiced improving our mood during less challenging times.

Note to the therapist:

People often make lifestyle choices that lead to stress and result in physical and emotional problems. Some are insightful enough to realize they are experiencing stress related to their choices. Unfortunately many take an unhelpful approach in remedying the problem. Instead of making changes to their current lifestyle, they try to cope with it. People attending ART may fall into this category, so participants are challenged to look for practical changes they could make to reduce stressful activities while increasing healthy activities that result in positive emotional experiences.

To encourage ART participants to seek a more functional and balanced lifestyle, the Self-Support Diary II: Balanced Lifestyle and Appreciating the Positive (Fig. 14.2, Appendix O) is utilized.

Day:

Time: Duties/Work Leisure/Fun

08:00 – 09:00 _____ _____
09:00 – 10:00 _____ _____
10:00 – 11:00 _____ _____
11:00 – 12:00 _____ _____
12:00 – 01:00 _____ _____
01:00 – 02:00 _____ _____
02:00 – 03:00 _____ _____
03:00 – 04:00 _____ _____
04:00 – 05:00 _____ _____
05:00 – 06:00 _____ _____
06:00 – 07:00 _____ _____
07:00 – 08:00 _____ _____
08:00 – 09:00 _____ _____
09:00 – 10:00 _____ _____

When working on tasks or taking it easy: Try to appreciate the positive at least once every hour!

Fig. 14.2 Self-support diary II: balanced lifestyle and appreciating the positive

The participants are asked to think about what they typically do, hour-by-hour, during an average workday. These activities are then placed on the schedule in one of two categories: "Duties/Work" or "Leisure/Fun." Red and green colored pencils may be given to the participants to complete the worksheet. Activities in the "Duties/Work" category are written in red, while the activities in the "Leisure/Fun" category are written in green.

To illustrate how our lives can get "out of balance" the worksheet is viewed as a scale with each activity in the two columns having a perceived weight attributed to it. Participants are asked to decide which of the two categories (Duties/Work or Leisure/Fun) on the worksheet is "heavier." The therapist then asks the participants whether they are satisfied with how the worksheet does or does not balance. If the participants determine that their worksheets are not balanced, they are encouraged to add items, such as exercising, and delete items, such as an unnecessary stressful activity, in order to achieve balance between the categories.

The ART therapist suggests that the participants utilize this worksheet at the end of each day as an ongoing self-management tool. It can be helpful to tape this worksheet to the bathroom mirror next to the Self-Support Diary I: Appreciation of my Achievements and Strengths as a reminder to use both worksheets at the end of the day. The therapist explains to the participants that at the end of each day they could use the Self-Support Diary II: Balanced Lifestyle and Appreciating the Positive to record the "Duties/Work" and "Leisure/Fun" they took part in during that day.

The therapist explains that the purpose of doing so is twofold. First, writing down the stressful and positive experiences they had during the day allows the participants a chance to see if they are achieving proper balance between stressful and positive experiences. If it is realized that sufficient positive experiences did not occur during the day, the participants have a chance to use the time remaining in the day to do something (however small) that would be pleasurable. Also, plans can be made for the following day that would help them achieve the desired balance between stressful and positive experiences. Generally, people have more difficulty integrating positive experiences into their schedule, so the participants are encouraged to follow this rule of thumb: engage in at least one positive experience if you are feeling well and three positive experiences if you are feeling poorly.

The therapist may choose to give a set of Positive Activity Cards to each participant as a resource to help them identify activities that could foster positive emotions. These cards can be copied from Appendix P and cut into individual cards, using a paper cutter. Each card has a positive activity listed on it (e.g., go to the movies, call a friend, take a walk, etc.). Therapists may invite participants to create additional cards with activities they personally find pleasurable or enjoyable. Participants are encouraged to pick a card and engage in the activity described on the card when they are either experiencing a low mood or when they want to reward themselves.

The second purpose of using the worksheet to record the "Duties/Work" and "Leisure/Fun" that occurred during the day is so that the participants have an opportunity to remind themselves about the positive experiences that did occur during the day, so they can intentionally focus on the goodness of these positive experiences and experience positive emotions as a result. The therapist also discusses the importance of focusing on the goodness of positive experiences as they are occurring by pointing out that *just doing* a positive activity does not, in and of itself, result in positive emotions. As long as we keep thinking of all of our problems, even the most enjoyable activity or beautiful scenery will not improve our mood. Many people experience positive things (e.g., plenty of food to eat, a comfortable home, or family and friends that they care about), without an awareness of the inherent goodness of these things. Consequently, these positive experiences do not elevate their mood. Thus, it is important to consciously focus attention on the positive aspects of our present experiences and intentionally appreciate them in order for these enjoyable experiences to result in positive emotions.

Ideally this focus on positive things leads us to feel "thankful." Thankfulness is a powerful emotion that improves our sense of well-being. We can foster thankfulness by intentionally focusing on positive things and allowing the feeling of thankfulness to arise if it chooses to do so. It should be noted that thankfulness cannot be pressured, forced, or expected to occur. Many people have difficulties experiencing thankfulness as a result of past experiences when they have been shamed into "being thankful" by society, parents, or religious institutions. No one *has* to be thankful. However, since thankfulness has the capacity to improve our sense of well-being, we are wise to foster it.

After discussing these concepts with the participants, the therapist guides the participants in an "Exercise of Gratitude" they may utilize to focus on the positive aspects of their life in order to generate positive emotions, including possibly thankfulness.

The therapist may guide the "Exercise of Gratitude" using the "Exercise Four" audio that can be downloaded from the ART website, or the therapist may guide the exercise using the following instructions:

We will start the exercise after the sound of the bell.

Sound of the bell

Find a comfortable sitting position. Close your eyes. Exhale slowly. Relax your body, and bring your attention to your muscles. In a moment, we will begin tensing and then relaxing our muscles. (*3 s pause*) Now, tense the muscles in your body by doing the following: Clench your fists. Angle your fists inward. Angle your forearms toward your upper arms. Pull your fists to your shoulders. Clench your teeth. Pull the corners of your mouth outward. Press your tongue against the roof of your mouth. Carefully squeeze your eyes shut. Furrow your eyebrows. Pull your shoulders up and then back. Tilt your hips forward and arch your back. Press your buttocks together. Straighten and slightly lift your legs in front of you, and point your feet downward. Now hold the tension for a moment. (*slight pause*) Continue breathing as calmly and deeply as possible. (*slight pause*) Now, with the next out-breath … relax your muscles. Pay attention to the difference between the tension you felt before and the relaxation you feel right now. Keep breathing calmly and regularly, and let your muscles become more and more relaxed with each out-breath. (*5 s pause*)

Now, we will tense the muscles again, just like last time. Clench your fists. Angle your fists inward. Angle your forearms toward your upper arms. Pull your fists to your shoulders. Clench your teeth. Pull the corners of your mouth outward. Press your tongue against the roof of your mouth. Carefully squeeze your eyes shut. Furrow your eyebrows. Pull your shoulders up and then back. Tilt your hips forward and arch your back. Press your buttocks together. Straighten and slightly lift your legs in front of you, and this time point your feet back toward your face. Now hold the tension for a moment. (*slight pause*) Continue breathing as calmly and deeply as possible. (*slight pause*) Now, with the next out-breath … relax your muscles. Pay attention to the difference between the tension you felt before and the relaxation you feel right now. Keep breathing calmly and regularly, and let your muscles become more and more relaxed with each out-breath. (*5 s pause*)

Now, we will start to practice nonjudgmental awareness. Focus your attention on the sensations of your breath, the way it flows … in … and out again … without trying to control it. Say to yourself "in" when breathing in and "out" when breathing out, and do your best to focus on the sensation of your breathing in your abdomen. When you realize that you're getting distracted or that other thoughts cross your mind, use a word to label what is happening, such as "planning," "worrying," or "remembering," and gently bring your attention back to your breathing. Every time you become aware that you are distracted, praise yourself for noticing it, and then focus on your breathing again. We'll now spend a minute simply focusing on our breathing. Remember to say to yourself, "in" … and … "out" as you breathe. When you become distracted, use a word to label what is happening such as "planning," "worrying," or "remembering" and gently bring your attention back to your breathing. (*40 s pause*)

Now, gently shift your focus onto the good things in your life. Maybe begin by becoming aware that your basic needs are being met. For example, think about the food you have eaten today, and remind yourself that many people do not have enough to eat. (*15 s pause*) Now think of where you live. Remind yourself that many people in the world do not have proper housing, so this may not be something you wish to take for granted. (*15 s pause*) Think of the country you live in. Remind yourself that the safety, freedom, and daily comforts in this country do not exist in many others. (*15 s pause*) Then think of your own physical health. Remind yourself that many people suffer from extremely painful injuries or diseases and how fortunate you are not to suffer in this way. (*15 s pause*)

Now begin searching on your own for the good things in your life. Do your best to find these nuggets even if they are deeply buried under the tendency to take these good things for granted. What is going well in your life? (*15 s pause*) If you experience feelings of thankfulness, become aware of these feelings. Allow the feelings to expand and grow, since they can be an important source of positive energy and joy. (*15 s pause*)

And now at your own pace, shift your attention from your appreciation of the good things in your life to the present moment, here and now. (*5 s pause*) Focus your attention on any physical sensations occurring in your body right now. (*15 s pause*) Be aware of your breath as you breathe in … and … out. (*15 s pause*) As this exercise begins to close, take some time to stretch the muscles in your body, and when you are ready, you may open your eyes.

Sound of the bell

The participants are encouraged to share and discuss the experiences they had during the exercise.

Note to the therapist:

At this point, the therapist has discussed the foundational elements of compassionate self-support: (1) valuing ourselves and (2) continuously taking care of ourselves by engaging in activities and appreciating the positive. Exercises have also been introduced to foster both of these elements. Drawing heavily from Buddhist practices, the therapist now begins to teach the participants how to specifically provide compassionate self-support, which in ART consists of (1) fostering empathy for ourselves and (2) taking active steps to encourage and soothe ourselves. Since some participants may equate feelings of compassion with self-pity, the difference between the two should be discussed. Compassion is a warm, strong, and encouraging feeling which is associated with the desire to help. Therefore, compassionate self-support can provide motivation for constructive action. In contrast, self-pity is associated with feelings of helplessness, hopelessness, and passivity and, hence, impedes constructive action.

Two imaginative exercises are now introduced to the participants to generate compassionate self-support.

The therapist continues speaking to the participants:

I will now introduce two exercises to help increase your ability to compassionately support yourself. The first is a Compassion and Loving Kindness exercise and the second is a Sympathetic Joy exercise. I will first go through the steps of each exercise, and then after everyone understands them, we will go through the exercises together.

Compassion and Loving Kindness Exercise

1. Think of a difficult situation you were involved in recently, one in which you experienced negative emotions. Visualize yourself in this situation as it occurred.
2. Imagine that you are above this scene observing what is happening to you.
3. Try to see what triggered your negative emotions. Determine what emotions you are experiencing and how those emotions are being manifested (e.g., posture, facial expression, tone of voice, etc.).
4. Intentionally react to your negative emotional state with a warm and powerful feeling of empathy.
5. Visualize entering the situation directly and approaching yourself.
6. Communicate to yourself that this is a difficult situation. Normalize the negative emotions, and provide reassurance by saying that you are there to support and comfort yourself (not to give advice). If it seems appropriate, visualize giving yourself a physical gesture of compassion (e.g., laying a hand on your shoulder or giving yourself a hug).
7. Provide encouragement to yourself (e.g., You've gone through a lot in the past and you can get through this too. I'll be with you as you work through this. We will get through this together).
8. Give yourself a big, kind, reassuring smile.
9. Say goodbye to yourself for now with the understanding that you will gladly return again when needed.

Sympathetic Joy Exercise

1. Visualize yourself in a past situation in which you experienced happiness or any other form of positive emotion. Imagine that you are floating above this scene observing yourself.
2. As the observer, see how the positive emotions are expressed as joy in your facial expression and body posture.
3. As the observer, allow this joy to arise within yourself leading to "sympathetic joy," or in other words a feeling of happiness that you are seeing yourself happy in this scene. Allow the possibility that feelings of gratitude for this joy may arise within you.
4. Imagine that you are now entering this visualized scene.
5. Tell yourself you are happy for the positive emotions you experienced in this scene. Remind yourself that positive emotions are important sources of strength and energy. Tell yourself, "My wish for you is that you may be able to appreciate positive feelings and use the energy from these feelings to overcome difficulties and challenges in life" (Weissman & Weissman, 1996).

6. Give yourself another big, kind, reassuring smile. Say goodbye to yourself and then bring your attention back into this room.

Note to the therapist:

After explaining the exercise and answering questions from the participants, the two exercises to generate compassionate self-support ("Compassion and Loving Kindness" and "Sympathetic Joy") are integrated into the ART Sequence.

14.3   ART Sequence with ART Skills #1–5

The therapist continues speaking to the participants:

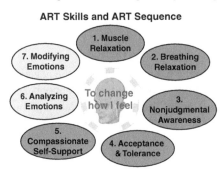

ART Skills and ART Sequence

Slide 73: At this point in the training we have now added ART Skill #5 (Compassionate Self-Support) to the other four ART Skills that we previously learned. We will now practice linking these skills together in the ART Sequence. We will again use the shortened version of muscle relaxation. We will also use a shorter version of "Acceptance and Tolerance" during this ART Sequence by focusing only on the Acceptance and Tolerance Statement instead of going through each of the five steps to develop the Acceptance and Tolerance Statement.

The therapist leads the participants in the ART Sequence with ART Skills #1–5:

The therapist may guide the exercise using the "Exercise Five" audio that can be downloaded from the ART website, or the therapist may guide the exercise using the following instructions:
We will start the exercise after the sound of the bell.

Sound of the bell

Find a comfortable sitting position. Close your eyes. Exhale slowly. Relax your body, and bring your attention to your muscles. In a moment, we will begin tensing and then relaxing our muscles. (*3 s pause*) Now, tense the muscles in your body by doing the following: Clench your fists. Angle your fists inward. Angle your forearms toward your upper arms. Pull your fists to your shoulders. Clench your teeth. Pull the corners of your mouth outward. Press your tongue against the roof of your mouth. Carefully squeeze your eyes shut. Furrow your eyebrows. Pull your shoulders up and then back. Tilt your hips forward and arch your back. Press your buttocks together. Straighten and slightly lift your legs in front of you, and point your feet downward.

Now hold the tension for a moment. (*slight pause*) Continue breathing as calmly and deeply as possible. (*slight pause*) Now, with the next out-breath … relax all of your muscles. Pay attention to the difference between the tension you felt before and the relaxation you feel right now. Keep breathing calmly and regularly, and let your muscles become more and more relaxed with each out-breath. (*5 s pause*)

Now, we will tense the muscles again, just like last time. Clench your fists. Angle your fists inward. Angle your forearms toward your upper arms. Pull your fists to your shoulders. Clench your teeth. Pull the corners of your mouth outward. Press your tongue against the roof of your mouth. Carefully squeeze your eyes shut. Furrow your eyebrows. Pull your shoulders up and then back. Tilt your hips forward and arch your back. Press your buttocks together. Straighten and slightly lift your legs in front of you, and this time point your feet back toward your face.

Now hold the tension for a moment. (*brief pause*) Continue breathing as calmly and deeply as possible. (*brief pause*) Now, with the next out-breath … relax your muscles. Pay attention to the difference between the tension you felt before and the relaxation you feel right now. Keep breathing calmly and regularly, and let your muscles become more and more relaxed with each out-breath. (*5 s pause*)

Now, we will start to practice nonjudgmental awareness. Focus your attention on the sensations of your breath, the way it flows … in … and out again … without trying to control it. Say to yourself "in" when breathing in and "out" when breathing out, and do your best to focus on the sensation of your breathing in your abdomen. When you realize that you're getting distracted or that other thoughts are crossing your mind, use a word to label what is happening, such as "planning," "worrying," or "remembering," and gently bring your attention back to your breathing. Every time you become aware that you are distracted, praise yourself for noticing it, and then focus on your breathing again. We'll now spend a minute simply focusing on our breathing. Remember to say to yourself, "in" … and … "out." When you become distracted, use a word to label what is happening such as "planning," "worrying," or "remembering," and gently bring your attention back to your breathing. (*40 s pause*)

Now we are going to practice shifting our focus and awareness onto other things. First, gently shift your attention from your breathing onto any sensations you are feeling in your body at the moment. (*20 s pause*) Now pay attention to what you are hearing at the moment. (*20 s pause*) Next, notice any smells you are aware of. (*20 s pause*) Now see what thoughts are crossing your mind. (*20 s pause*) Notice any desires you have right now. (*20 s pause*) Be aware of any emotions you are experiencing right now. Label each emotion. (*5 s pause*) Which of these emotions do you feel more strongly? (*20 s pause*) What other emotions are perhaps more subdued but are still present in the background? (*20 s pause*) Estimate the intensity of each emotion you have labeled on a scale from 0 to 10, and become aware of how you feel these emotions in your body. (*20 s pause*)

Now take a moment to develop an Acceptance and Tolerance Statement for a negative emotion that you have become aware of presently or one that has been challenging for you in the past. For example, you might say something to yourself like, "It's okay that I feel this way. These feelings are an important part of me, and they are trying to help me by providing me with valuable information. I can tolerate them for now because I know they won't last forever." (*1 min pause*)

We will now begin to shift our focus onto fostering compassionate self-support. Begin by imagining a situation that was difficult for you in the past or something more recently—some situation in which you experienced negative emotions. Now do your best to visualize that you are observing yourself from above this scene. (*5 s pause*) What do you see as you are looking down at this scene? (*brief pause*) Where are you? (*brief pause*) What is happening that is triggering your negative emotions? (*brief pause*) Which negative emotions are you experiencing? (*brief pause*) How are your negative emotions reflected in your body posture, facial expression, tone of voice, etc.? (*5 s pause*)

Now do your best to let the feeling of compassion toward yourself arise within you … a strong and warm feeling of empathy for yourself that is accompanied by the desire to help yourself and a desire to end your suffering. (*5 s pause*) Visualize yourself entering this scene as well, and approach yourself, who is in some way hurting in this scene. (*5 s pause*) Communicate to yourself that this is a difficult situation. Normalize the negative emotions, and provide reassurance by saying that you are there to support and comfort yourself (not to give advice). (*10 s pause*) If it seems appropriate, visualize giving yourself a physical gesture of compassion (e.g., laying a hand on your shoulder or giving yourself a hug). (*10 s pause*) Provide encouragement to yourself. Maybe you could say something like, "You've gone through a lot in the past, and you can get through this too! I'll be with you as you work through this. We will get through this together!" (*10 s pause*) Give yourself a big, kind, reassuring smile. (*5 s pause*) Take your time as you give yourself all the support you need in this situation. (*15 s pause*)

Then, when the moment feels right, you can … at your own pace … begin mentally saying goodbye to yourself. Be aware that this is not goodbye forever. You will always be able to mentally come back to this place and provide support for yourself when needed. If there is something you want to say to yourself before parting … feel free to do so now. (*10 s pause*) Now, at your own pace, bring your attention back to this room. Allow your muscles to relax. Take a deep breath, and on the exhale, allow your muscles to relax even further. (*5 s pause*)

You may keep your eyes closed, as we continue on, shifting our focus onto a positive experience in order to foster feelings of joy. Start by imagining a situation from the past week that was pleasant for you. Pick any pleasant situation. It does not have to be some extremely euphoric experience. Any slightly positive feeling is fine. (*10 s pause*)

Once you have remembered a situation involving a pleasant experience, imagine you are floating above this scene observing yourself. As the observer, notice how the positive emotions are expressed as joy in your facial expression and body posture. (*10 s pause*) As the observer, allow this joy to arise within yourself leading to "sympathetic joy" or a feeling of happiness that you are seeing yourself happy in this scene. (*10 s pause*) Allow the possibility that feelings of gratitude for this joy may arise within you. (*10 s pause*)

Now imagine that you enter this visualized scene. Tell yourself you are happy for the positive emotions you experienced in this scene. (*10 s pause*) Remind yourself that positive emotions are important sources of strength and energy. Tell yourself,

"My wish for you is that you may be able to appreciate positive feelings and use the energy from these feelings to overcome difficulties and challenges in life." (*10 s pause*) Give yourself another big, kind, reassuring smile. Maybe there is something you want to say to yourself before you go. If so, feel free to do so now. (*10 s pause*) When you are ready, say goodbye to yourself. (*10 s pause*) Now, at your own pace, slowly begin bringing your attention to your body again. Bring your attention to your breathing. Notice how the breath flows in and out. (*brief pause*) Now bring your attention from this exercise into the present moment. Stretch your body. Open your eyes, and return to the present experience of being in this room.

Sound of the bell

As usual, a debriefing occurs at the end of the exercise.

Reference

Weissman, S., & Weissman, R. (1996). *Meditation, compassion & lovingkindness. An approach to vipassana practice*. York Beach, ME: Samuel Weiser.

Chapter 15
Module Seven: Analyzing Emotions

15.1 Vicious Cycle #6: Amygdala Activation and Difficulty Analyzing Emotions

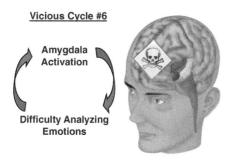

Vicious Cycle #6

Amygdala Activation

Difficulty Analyzing Emotions

Slide 74: We will now discuss yet another vicious cycle that maintains negative emotions. When we are under stress, the amygdala initiates the release of stress hormones into our brain and body. These stress hormones strengthen amygdala functioning but weaken other areas in the brain including the prefrontal cortex and the hippocampus, which play important roles in the analysis of what cued our emotions. The ability to analyze and understand why we feel the way we do provides a sense of mastery and control that reduces activation in the amygdala.

If, through weakened prefrontal and hippocampal functioning, we lose our ability to analyze our emotions, we will probably feel confused and out of control. A vicious cycle now develops, since feeling confused and out of control unfortunately triggers the amygdala to sound the danger alarm even louder. Now even more stress hormones are released and the vicious cycle is repeated as the stress hormones further weaken prefrontal and hippocampal functioning and increase amygdala activation.

M. Berking and B. Whitley, *Affect Regulation Training: A Practitioners' Manual*,
DOI 10.1007/978-1-4939-1022-9_15, © Springer Science+Business Media New York 2014

15.2   ART Skill #6: Analyzing Emotions

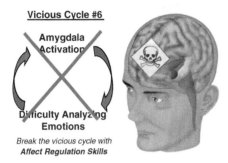

Slide 75: We can prevent or break this vicious cycle by analyzing our emotions during times of distress. By analyzing our negative emotions we gain a better understanding of why we feel the way we do. This knowledge reassures us that we are in control of our emotions, which calms the amygdala activation and facilitates effective emotion regulation.

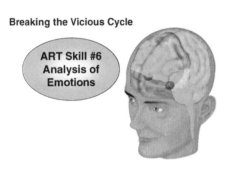

Slide 76: The good news is that we can practice the ability to analyze and understand our emotions. ART Skill #6—Analyzing Emotions—consists of a series of steps we can take to better understand how and why we feel the way we do. These steps can be practiced until we are able to conduct an analysis of our emotions, almost automatically, even during times of stress.

Before we get into the specific steps of analyzing our emotions, we are going to do an exercise to help us look at our emotions from a different angle. Let's start the exercise by thinking of a negative emotion that we had in the past week. I am going to ask you to draw this emotion in any way that feels best for you. Any way you would like to express the emotion through drawing is fine. After everyone is finished, we are going to discuss the drawings. If some of you feel anxious about this exercise because you believe you are not good at drawing, please bear in mind that the intention of this exercise is definitely *not* to produce an art masterpiece! Instead, it is an opportunity for your mind to express an emotion in a unique way. We will have about 15 min to work on these drawings.

Note to the therapist:

At this point, the therapist passes out a piece of flip chart paper to each participant. Colored pencils, crayons, markers, colored chalk, and watercolor paints should be made available to use. It may be helpful to play music that is relaxing or that fosters other positive emotions in order to inspire creativity and reduce anxiety regarding the exercise.

After 15–30 min, the participants take turns presenting their work. As the participants present their drawings, the therapist helps them understand the emotions represented in the drawings by asking questions and making observations, similar to what a therapist would do during a psychotherapy session utilizing art therapy.

While the participants are presenting their pictures, the therapist also uses the drawings to illustrate concepts that are important for analyzing emotions. These concepts, listed below, will later be incorporated into a step-by-step process for analyzing emotions that will be explained to the participants:

- Challenging situations normally trigger more than one "negative" emotion. However, since it is difficult to analyze more than one emotion at a time, it is important to be aware of the various emotions we are experiencing but pick only one at a time to analyze. *As the participants present their drawings to the group, the ART therapist may say, "So, this drawing represents the anger you feel when your boss makes unreasonable demands on you, as well as fear about what could happen if you talk back to your boss. This is a good example of how we often experience several emotions simultaneously. Since it is impossible to analyze different emotions at the same time, the first step when analyzing emotions is to decide which emotion we want to analyze first. After we choose an emotion and analyze it, we can then pick another one and analyze it as well. Which emotion would you like to focus on now as we talk about your picture?"*

- Our emotions are often triggered by specific events, circumstances or situations. *"So this section of your drawing here shows your boss telling you that you must work double-shifts for 2 weeks? Is your boss' statement the specific part of this situation that led you to become really angry?"*

- Our emotions are influenced by our current physical and emotional state. *"It sounds like you were feeling tired and on-edge just before this interaction with your boss. I wonder if that made this situation even more difficult."*

- Our emotions are determined by how we appraise situations. *"So at the time you believed you were being forced to do something you did not want to do. You felt this was not fair and that he was not being considerate of your needs. Did I get this right?"*

- Our appraisals are determined by how our needs, wishes, and goals are impacted by a situation. *"It sounds like you were concerned at the time that your boss' demand to work double-shifts would prevent you from important things you had planned to do, such as spending time with friends and family. Is that what was at stake in this situation?"*

- Our emotional response can be influenced by how we have reacted to past situations in a similar manner. *"It sounds like you have felt angry in the past during similar situations. So, do you think this emotional response that you are describing is repeating an old pattern? If so, what could you call this pattern?"*

- The primary emotional response can also be appraised and trigger secondary emotions. *"It seems as though in this situation you thought you should not be angry and consequently you were angry at yourself for being angry. Correct? How did this affect your primary or initial feelings of anger? Okay, I see that it made them even worse."*

- Specific body sensations accompany emotions. *"Did you notice any changes in your body (e.g., heart racing, faster breathing, etc.) when you became angry?"*

- Emotions can compel us to engage in various behaviors. *"What did the anger tell you to do? Oh ... I see. You felt like punching your boss in the face."*

- While our emotions can compel us to engage in various behaviors, we always retain the option of choosing actions that are different than the actions that our emotions compel us to do. *"So you felt like punching your boss ... and what did you actually do? I see ... you agreed to work the double-shifts? And what did you do with all the energy from the anger?"*

Since the participants' exploration of emotions in front of the group is likely to elicit feelings of vulnerability, the therapist should work to provide support and validation to foster a sense of safety and control during the next exercise. The therapist then passes out copies of the Analyzing Emotions Worksheet (Appendix Q) to the participants. This worksheet outlines a step-by-step process to analyze emotions and incorporates the concepts that were just explained.

The therapist continues speaking to the participants:

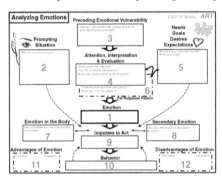

Slide 77: This worksheet will be our guide for thoroughly understanding how and why we feel the way we do. If you are thinking, "This sure is complex!" you are correct. It is! Emotions are complicated things, but don't worry, we will get through this together. No one expects you to have this whole thing mastered today. We will look at this worksheet together and go through it step-by-step, and eventually you will understand the concept. In order to practice going through the steps on the worksheet, we will work right now with the emotion "anxiety" that has resulted from a hypothetical situation that happened to us at work. In this situation our boss told us to increase our sales numbers by 10 %.

Okay, here we go. To start with, we need to remember that we can only analyze one emotion at a time. This means that the first step in analyzing an emotion is to be aware of the different emotions we are experiencing and then to decide which specific one we would like to analyze. Using our hypothetical situation at work, we may have felt a mixture of fear, anger, and anxiety. Since we cannot analyze all of these different emotions at once, I will choose "anxiety" to analyze. So I would write "anxiety" in Box #1 on the Analyzing Emotions Worksheet.

Then, I determine what situation triggered the emotion. This should only include the facts of what occurred. "My boss told me to increase my sales numbers by

10 %." Be careful *not to include* opinions or interpretations of what occurred. So for Box #2, I would write the objective facts of what occurred such as "told to increase sales by 10 %."

I next look at how I felt, both emotionally and physically, just before I experienced the anxiety, since our <u>emotional vulnerability</u> often plays a role in our reactions. For example, at the time that my boss told me to increase my sales numbers, I may have been fighting a cold or had been in a heated argument with my spouse earlier that morning. These types of emotional and physical states can cause us to view difficult situations more negatively than we would if we were healthy and happy at the time. For Box #3, I would describe my physical and emotional state at the time. For example, I could write in Box #3 that "I was already irritated from an earlier argument with my spouse," or "I was fighting a cold at the time."

The next step is to examine how I <u>appraised</u> the situation. This can be broken down by asking three questions:

1. What did I focus my attention on during the situation?
2. How did I interpret the thing that caught my attention?
3. How did I evaluate the overall situation based on how I interpreted the thing that caught my attention?

Note to the therapist:

The second question asks "How did I interpret the thing that caught my attention?" *Interpretation* involves at least three components that should be mentioned because each component can be a target for cognitive interventions. First, interpretation involves labeling or categorizing the situation (e.g., serious health problem). Second, interpretation involves attributing the situation to an assumed cause (e.g., because of the stress I am under). Third, interpretation involves a prediction of what will happen next in the situation (e.g., I will never get well again). Unhelpful cognitions in any of these three components of interpretation can lead to dysfunctional affective responses.

The therapist continues speaking to the participants:

For example, as my boss told me to increase my sales numbers, I could have focused on the irritated tone in his voice. Maybe I interpreted his irritated tone of voice as a signal of his displeasure with my overall performance. Since I believed at the time that he viewed my overall job performance poorly, I evaluated this interaction with my boss negatively. In Box #4, I would write down my appraisal of the situation. More specifically, I would write (1) what caught my attention (e.g., boss' irritated tone of voice), (2) how I interpreted the situation ("My boss thinks I am a bad employee!")", and (3) my evaluation of the overall situation—"This is awful!"

The evaluation of a situation has a crucial impact on our emotions. As soon as we evaluate something, we generate an emotion. If we evaluate something as negative, we generate a negative emotion. If we evaluate something as positive, we generate a positive emotion. Situations are not inherently "good" or "bad." Instead, we evaluate situations as good or bad according to how a situation either facilitates or hinders the attainment of goals that are important to us.

Using our example, if my boss demands increased sales numbers, I might believe that I may be fired soon. If I am the sole provider of income for my family of five and my primary goal is to create financial security for my family, the possibility I could be fired would probably cause me to feel anxious. In this case, I would write down my goal that is being threatened, "ensure financial security for my family" in Box #5. On the other hand, if I am unhappy because I hate my job, I have plenty of money saved up, and my goal is "to have more time for myself," then the possibility that I may be fired could actually bring relief instead of anxiety. This example illustrates the point that the type of goals we have impact how we feel about various situations. Therefore, it is important to identify the goals that are related to the emotion we are analyzing.

In the next step, we explore the possibility that our response to this situation is similar to how we have typically responded in the past in similar situations. This old response pattern could consist of thoughts, emotions, and behaviors that we have consistently used in the past. If we believe that our present response to this current situation is part of an old response pattern, we try to label it and then write the label in Box #6. For example, using our hypothetical scenario at work, I may realize that my anxiety in this situation is related to an old response pattern to difficult situations in which I typically believe, "Bad things are going to happen to me!" I could use this thought to label my old response pattern and write, "Bad things are going to happen to me!" in Box #6.

It is important to remember that not every response to a situation is based on an old response pattern, so in these cases, Box #6 would simply be left blank. While old response patterns will not be relevant for every situation, this is still an important step to explore. The identification of an old response pattern can provide a sense of understanding and order when our own responses feel confusing and disorganized. The awareness of these patterns also provides us with ways that we can positively intervene in these types of situations. (For further information on contributing elements of response patterns, refer to Beck, 1964, 1995; Ellis, 1977; and Young, Klosko, & Weishaar, 2003).

After we look for old response patterns that may be contributing to our current reactions, we look at how the emotion manifests itself in our body, such as increased heart rate and respiration. This is an important step in the analysis process since many physical complaints are related to emotional responses. In these cases, the physical symptoms will persist unless the emotion is effectively regulated. In Box #7 we describe how and where the emotion is experienced in the body, such as "tightness in my chest and a pit in my stomach." (The therapist is encouraged to review Appendix J and Appendix K for examples of physical manifestations of emotions.)

In the next step, we identify the emotions that were triggered as we evaluated our emotional state. The human brain tends to evaluate significant experiences. Since intense emotions feel significant, they are very likely to be evaluated. As we have said before, "Every evaluation triggers an emotion." Thus, assigning a negative evaluation to a challenging emotion will inevitably trigger a "secondary" challenging emotion.

We can identify secondary emotions by asking "How do I feel about my emotional reaction?" Examples of common secondary emotions include feeling helpless about being anxious or feeling shame for becoming angry. So in Box #8, I would write something like "felt hopeless about being anxious." Since negative secondary emotions hinder efforts to regulate the initial emotional response (see Greenberg, 2002), it is important to identify and eventually learn to reduce negative secondary emotions.

The next step in this process is to identify the urges or <u>impulses to act</u> that are triggered by our emotional response. These urges can be viewed as knee-jerk reactions. For example, my impulse in the hypothetical scenario may have been to "work through the night, so I could increase my sales numbers," which I would write in Box #9. Just because we have an impulsive urge to do something does not mean that we must carry it out. This is the point at which we are able to choose either to follow our impulse or to act differently. For example, although my impulse in the hypothetical scenario may have been to "work through the night, so I could increase my sales numbers," I actually chose to go home at 11 pm. I would write my <u>actual behavior</u> "going home at 11 pm" in Box #10.

Finally, it is important to consider the <u>short- and long-term advantages and disadvantages</u> of my emotional response. This is important information we can use to decide whether and how we want to modify our emotion. Using our current example, a short-term advantage of my anxiety could be that it motivates me to stay more focused at work, which in the long-term could help me keep my job. I would list these short- and long-term advantages in Box #11. On the other hand, a short-term disadvantage could be that anxiety causes me to miss having dinner with my family. A long-term disadvantage could be that anxiety causes me to end up hating my job. I would write these short- and long-term disadvantages of my emotional response in Box #12.

Note to the therapist:

After describing the steps of the Analyzing Emotions Worksheet (Appendix Q), the participants are given an opportunity to ask questions about the analysis process. The therapist should explain that with practice, they will be able to learn the steps in this analysis process and apply them to their emotions in real time.

The therapist then invites one of the participants to share a personally challenging emotion, which the participants can use as a group to practice the steps of the Analyzing Emotions Worksheet. Using the participant's example, the therapist works collaboratively with all of the participants to work through each step of the worksheet. The therapist records the participants' responses in the boxes that correspond to each step of the worksheet on a large poster-board-size version of the Analyzing Emotions Worksheet. If this enlarged copy of the worksheet is laminated, the therapist can use dry-erase markers to record the participants' responses. The laminated worksheet can be erased and reused during future training sessions.

Next, the participants are asked to use the Analyzing Emotions Worksheet to analyze one of the important negative emotions they depicted in the drawing they made earlier. They should write the information related to each step of the analysis process in the various boxes on the worksheet. After they complete the worksheet, they may discuss it in pairs. The therapist should spend a few minutes working with each pair to provide support and to clarify any questions they may have. When the pairs have finished reviewing their worksheets, the therapist may either elect to ask individual participants to present their Analyzing Emotions Worksheet to the group or choose instead to offer some time for the participants to ask questions or make comments about the worksheet.

It should be noted that the steps listed in the Analyzing Emotions Worksheet can be modified or simplified in order to make it easier to use. For example, if a participant has difficulty with Box #4 (Attention, Interpretation, and Evaluation), the therapist may instead ask the participant to simply say what "thoughts" crossed his/her mind during the situation that triggered the emotion. The therapist can then use these thoughts to help the participant discover what goals were threatened by this situation (Box #5).

As the participants learn the process of analyzing emotions, the therapist should be sure to provide sufficient empathy and support to each participant. For example, if a participant has difficulty determining how and where he experienced the emotion in his body (Box #7), the therapist might say, "It seems as though it is hard to locate where this feeling is located in your body. It sure is tough to figure out how emotions manifest in our bodies. Sometimes it can help if you visualize the situation for a moment. Do you have it? Good! Now focus your attention to your body. What changes do you notice in your body?"

While helping participants to understand and analyze their emotions, it is also important to normalize the difficult nature of this process. The participants should be reminded that, as they are learning to analyze their emotions, it is fine if they do not have answers for each and every box on the worksheet. With time and practice they should feel more and more confident with the steps involved in analyzing their emotions.

15.3   ART Sequence with ART Skills #1–6

At this time, ART Skill #6 is integrated into the ART Sequence.

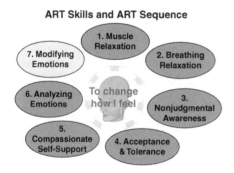

ART Skills and ART Sequence

The therapist continues speaking to the participants:

Slide 78: We will now include ART Skill #6 into the ART Sequence. During the last several ART Sequence Exercises, we tensed several specific muscles together at one time and then relaxed them. Starting with this next ART Sequence Exercise we will shorten the muscle relaxation technique even further by consciously relaxing specific muscles without tensing them first. Does anyone have questions about this change?

The therapist may guide the ART Sequence Exercise using the "Exercise Six" audio that can be downloaded from the ART website, or the therapist may guide the exercise using the following instructions:

We will start the exercise after the sound of the bell.

Sound of the bell

Find a comfortable position. Close your eyes. Allow your body to relax as much as possible. Focus your attention on your muscles. Breathe in … and out. As you exhale, relax the muscles in your hands … forearms … upper arms … face … neck … shoulders … back … belly … buttocks … and legs. (*slight pause*) Now focus your attention on your breathing. Breathe in … and out. With each exhale, allow your muscles to relax even more. (*5 s pause*)

Now, shift into the state of nonjudgmental awareness by observing your breath without trying to control it. (*5 s pause*) Simply notice how it feels when you breathe in and out. (*5 s pause*) Now prepare to broaden the focus of your attention. Remember that when you realize you're getting distracted or that thoughts are crossing your mind, use a word to label what is happening, such as "planning," "worrying," or "remembering," and then gently refocus your attention. Be aware of any sensations in your body (*5 s pause*), any sounds you can hear (*5 s pause*), or any odors you can smell. (*5 s pause*) Notice what you can see even though your eyelids are closed. Maybe you see patterns or maybe you notice lighter and darker areas. (*5 s pause*) Notice what thoughts are coming into your mind … (*5 s pause*) what needs, desires, goals, or impulses to act are currently activated in your mind. (*5 s pause*) Notice what emotions or moods you are currently experiencing. (*5 s pause*) Briefly label these feelings. (*5 s pause*) Rate the intensity of your feelings on a scale from 0 to 10. Be aware of the places where you feel these emotions in your body. (*10 s pause*)

Now take a moment to develop an Acceptance and Tolerance Statement for a negative emotion that you have become aware of presently or one that has been challenging for you in the past. For example, you might say something to yourself like "It's okay that I feel this way. These feelings are an important part of me, and they are trying to help me by providing me with valuable information. I can tolerate them for now because I know they won't last forever." (*1 min pause*)

We will now begin to shift our focus onto fostering compassionate self-support. Begin by imagining a situation that was difficult for you in the past or something more recently, some situation in which you experienced negative emotions. Now do your best to visualize that you are observing yourself from above this scene. (*5 s pause*) What do you see as you are looking down at this scene? (*brief pause*) Where are you? (*brief pause*) What is happening that is triggering your negative emotions? (*brief pause*) Which negative emotions are you experiencing? (*brief pause*) How are your negative emotions reflected in your body posture, facial expression, tone of voice, etc.? (*5 s pause*)

Now do your best to let the feeling of compassion toward yourself arise within you … a strong and warm feeling of empathy for yourself that is accompanied by the desire to help yourself and a desire to end your suffering. (*5 s pause*) Visualize yourself entering this scene as well, and approach yourself, who is in some way hurting in this scene. (*5 s pause*) Communicate to yourself that this is a difficult situation. Normalize the negative emotions, and provide reassurance by saying that you are there to support and comfort yourself (not to give advice). (*10 s pause*) If it seems appropriate, visualize giving yourself a physical gesture of compassion (e.g., laying a hand on your shoulder or giving yourself a hug). (*10 s pause*) Provide encouragement to yourself. Maybe you could say something like, "You've gone through a lot in the past, and you can get through this too! I'll be with you as you work through this. We will get through this together!" (*10 s pause*) Give yourself a big, kind, reassuring smile. (*5 s pause*)

Now, let's practice the skill of analyzing a negative emotion. Maybe you would like to analyze a negative emotion that was triggered in the scene you just visualized. Maybe you would like to analyze a negative emotion from a situation in the past or even one you are currently experiencing. Select a feeling that you want to analyze. (*10 s pause*) I will guide you through the analysis process by suggesting a series of questions that you can ask yourself based on the worksheet we just completed. Imagine that you are asking these questions of the part of you that is experiencing challenging emotions. Try to give your attention to each question.

First, what situation prompted this feeling? (*10 s pause*) Did a particular emotional or physical state leave you vulnerable to this emotional reaction? (*10 s pause*) What in particular caught your attention about the situation that triggered the emotion? (*10 s pause*) Also, how did you interpret and evaluate the situation? (*10 s pause*) Which needs, goals, desires, or expectations were associated with this interpretation and evaluation? In other words, what was at stake in this situation? (*10 s pause*) Was your interpretation and evaluation related to ways you have commonly responded in the past during similar situations? What label could you give to these old response patterns? (*10 s pause*) How do you feel about having this emotion? (*10 s pause*) How and where do you feel this emotion in your body? (*10 s pause*) Do these body sensations cause the emotion to last longer or feel more intense? (*10 s pause*) What impulses to act are triggered by the emotion? (*10 s pause*) If you have already acted on these impulses, what did you end up doing? (*10 s pause*) What are the short-term and long-term advantages of this emotion? (*10 s pause*) What are the short-term and long-term disadvantages of this emotion? (*10 s pause*) Take some time now to review and reflect on what you have discovered in the analysis process. (*30 s pause*)

Now, at your own pace, bring your attention back to this room. Allow your muscles to relax. Take a deep breath, and on the exhale, allow your muscles to relax even further. (*5 s pause*) You may keep your eyes closed, as we continue on, shifting our focus onto a positive experience in order to foster feelings of joy. Start by imagining a situation from the past week that was pleasant for you. Pick any pleasant situation. It does not have to be some extremely euphoric experience. Any slightly positive feeling is fine. (*10 s pause*)

Once you have remembered a situation involving a pleasant experience, imagine you are floating above this scene observing yourself. As the observer, notice how the positive emotions are expressed as joy in your facial expression and body posture. (*10 s pause*) As the observer, allow this joy to arise within yourself leading to "sympathetic joy" or a feeling of happiness that you are seeing yourself happy in this scene. (*10 s pause*) Allow the possibility that feelings of gratitude for this joy may arise within you. (*10 s pause*)

Now imagine that you enter this visualized scene. Consider telling yourself that you are happy for the positive emotions you have experienced in this scene. (*10 s pause*) Ask yourself to consider which of your strengths and abilities contributed to these positive feelings. Maybe it was your courage to try something new that led to these positive feelings. You may want to say to yourself, "My wish for you is that you may be able to appreciate positive feelings and use the energy from these feelings to overcome difficulties and challenges in life." (*10 s pause*) Now try to give yourself another big, kind, reassuring smile. Maybe there is something you want to say to yourself before you go. If so, feel free to do so now. (*10 s pause*)

When you are ready, say goodbye to yourself. (*10 s pause*) Now, at your own pace, slowly begin bringing your attention to your body again. Bring your attention to your breathing. Notice how the breath flows in and out. (*brief pause*) Now bring your attention from this exercise into the present moment. Stretch your body. Open your eyes, and return to the present experience of being in this room.

Sound of the bell

As usual, a debriefing occurs at the end of the exercise.

References

Beck, A. T. (1964). Thinking and depression: II. Theory and therapy. *Archives of General Psychiatry, 10*(6), 561–571.

Beck, J. S. (1995). *Cognitive therapy: Basics and beyond*. New York, NY: Guilford Press.

Ellis, A. (1977). *Reason and emotion in psychotherapy*. Secaucus, NJ: Citadel.

Greenberg, L. S. (2002). *Emotion-focused therapy: Coaching clients to work through their feelings*. Washington, DC: American Psychological Association.

Young, J. E., Klosko, J. S., & Weishaar, M. E. (2003). *Schema therapy: A practitioner's guide*. New York, NY: Guilford Press.

Chapter 16
Module Eight: Modifying Emotions

16.1 Vicious Cycle #7: Amygdala Activation and Difficulty Modifying Emotions

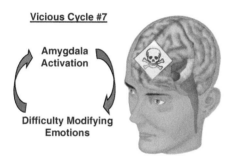

Vicious Cycle #7

Amygdala Activation

Difficulty Modifying Emotions

Slide 79: We will now discuss one last vicious cycle and the seventh and final ART Skill we can use to interrupt it. This vicious cycle is in some ways related to the last one that we discussed. To review, when we are under stress, the amygdala begins processes that release stress hormones into our brain. These stress hormones strengthen amygdala functioning, but weaken other areas in the brain including the prefrontal cortex and the hippocampus. As we discussed before, both the prefrontal cortex and hippocampus play important roles in the analysis of emotions. These regions also play important roles in our ability to systematically find solutions to problems. When we are able to use problem-solving techniques to modify our emotions, we achieve a sense of mastery and control over our emotions.

If, however, through weakened prefrontal and hippocampal functioning, we lose our ability to modify our emotions, we are likely to feel out of control. A vicious cycle now develops, since feeling out of control triggers the amygdala to sound the danger alarm even louder. Now even more stress hormones are released, which further weakens prefrontal and hippocampal functioning and increases amygdala activation even more.

M. Berking and B. Whitley, *Affect Regulation Training: A Practitioners' Manual*,
DOI 10.1007/978-1-4939-1022-9_16, © Springer Science+Business Media New York 2014

16.2   ART Skill #7: Modifying Emotions

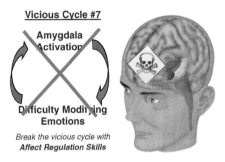

Slide 80: We can prevent or break this vicious cycle through the ability to modify our emotions during times of distress. The availability of effective modification skills helps us maintain or regain a sense of mastery and control and thus reduces the stress response in the amygdala.

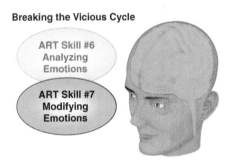

Slide 81: ART Skill #7—Modifying Emotions consists of a series of steps we can take to change our negative emotions. With practice, we can learn to modify our emotions, almost automatically during times of stress.

General Problem Solving Steps

1) Approach the problem with a positive attitude
2) Describe and analyze the problem
3) Set a goal
4) Brainstorm ways to achieve the goal & create a plan
5) Put the plan into action
6) Evaluate the outcome
7) Praise yourself for successes

Slide 82: Any type of problem, including persistent negative emotions, can be addressed using a set of general problem-solving steps. Let's go through these general problem-solving steps together. Afterward, we will see how the ART Skills we have learned so far, and the new one (ART Skill #7) we are learning today, help us implement these general problem-solving steps in order to effectively manage our negative emotions.

General Problem-Solving Step #1: Approach the problem with a positive attitude

Developing a positive attitude toward our problems is critical to reduce feelings of shame and inadequacy that can prevent us from dealing openly and effectively with our problems. It is important to understand that it is okay to have problems; we do not need to be ashamed of them. However, we do have a responsibility to ourselves to work through our problems in healthy ways. ART Skills 1–5 (Muscle and Breathing Relaxation, Nonjudgmental Awareness, Acceptance and Tolerance, and

Compassionate Self-Support) all help us develop and maintain a positive attitude toward the "problem" of persistent, challenging emotions.

General Problem-Solving Step #2: Describe and analyze the problem

Regardless of the type of problem you want to solve, you first need to understand what the problem is and how it is maintained. With the help of ART Skill #6 (Analysis of Emotions), you can develop a better understanding of a problem involving unwanted emotions. The information gained from the analysis forms the basis for effectively modifying an emotion.

General Problem-Solving Step #3: Set a goal

The next step in the general problem-solving model is to set a goal for resolving the problem. Sometimes we spend so much time trying to get rid of a problem we become completely focused on it. If this focus leads to ruminating on its causes and consequences, we are likely to get stuck in the problem. Instead, at some point it is important to proceed from thinking about the problem to setting a goal for resolving it. This is where our new skill, ART Skill #7—Modifying Emotions, comes into play. ART Skill #7 begins with setting a goal to experience a positive emotion that we would like to feel instead of the one that is causing us problems. We will discuss ART Skill #7 in more detail after we finish reviewing the general problem-solving model.

General Problem-Solving Step #4: Brainstorm ways to achieve the goal and create a plan

After setting a goal for resolving a problem, the next step is to brainstorm various ways to achieve the goal and then to use the most appropriate options to create a plan. When we are in the middle of a problem, it often feels as though we have very few options for getting out of the mess we are in. However, there are usually many options available to us that we have not discovered because we have not intentionally sought them out. Sifting through the options and creating a plan to achieve our goal gives us the best chance of efficiently and effectively resolving our problem. ART Skill #7— Modifying Emotions provides a step-by-step process that can be used to build a thoughtful plan to achieve the goal of modifying a challenging emotion.

General Problem-Solving Step #5: Put the plan into action

Plans in and of themselves do not solve problems. A plan that we have developed must be implemented in order to achieve our goal of resolving a problem. This requires courage and motivation to take the necessary steps to achieve a goal.

General Problem-Solving Step #6: Evaluate the outcome

After the plan has been put into action, it should be evaluated to see if it has been successful in achieving the goal. If the goal has in fact been achieved, the plan was successful! If the goal has *not* been achieved, it might be helpful to put more effort into implementing the plan, or maybe the plan needs to be modified to achieve the desired goal. If neither of these strategies is successful, thoughtful consideration should be directed at deciding whether or not the goal is attainable. If the goal is determined to be unattainable, the goal can be modified. When trying to modify an emotion, sometimes it can be helpful to change the original goal to "acceptance of the current negative emotion" and flexibly switch from using ART Skill #7 (Modifying Emotions) to using ART Skill #4 (Acceptance and Tolerance).

General Problem-Solving Step #7: Praise yourself for successes

The final step in the general problem-solving model is to praise yourself for any and all types of successes that have occurred. While it is important to remember to praise yourself in the final stage of the problem-solving model, you should be looking for successes and praising yourself during all of the steps of the general problem-solving model. The more difficult it is to modify an emotion, the more important it becomes to praise yourself solely for trying.

To summarize, the general problem-solving model can be used to solve any type of problem, and the ART Skills can help us implement the steps of the problem-solving model to resolve persistent, challenging emotions. ART Skill #7—Modifying Emotions can specifically help us work through the final steps of the problem-solving model.

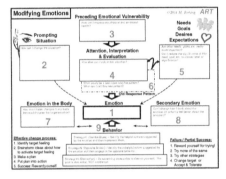

Slide 83: ART Skill #7 utilizes the Modifying Emotions Worksheet (Appendix R) as a guide. *The therapist gives each participant a copy of the Modifying Emotions Worksheet.* The Modifying Emotions Worksheet uses the information learned from the steps in the Analyzing Emotions Worksheet to explore various ways a negative emotion could be modified.

Let's go through the steps of the worksheet together. To explain the steps, I will use the same hypothetical situation that I used to explain the steps for Analyzing Emotions in the previous module. If you remember, in this situation, my boss told me to increase my sales by 10 %.

The Modifying Emotions Worksheet begins with setting a goal. Setting a goal using the Modifying Emotions Worksheet involves selecting a *target* emotion, which is how the person would rather feel. The target emotion must be realistically possible to achieve. Examples of *unrealistic* target emotions include wanting to feel "completely calm" before an important job interview or "happy" immediately after something unfortunate happens. A realistic target emotion can provide motivation for changing a negative emotion. It also clarifies the question, "What exactly am I working toward?" that guides decisions on how best to achieve the target emotion.

The target emotion may simply be a reduction in the intensity of the present negative emotion. For example, someone who is feeling "extremely anxious" could realistically set a target emotion of "slightly anxious." Since it is most helpful to form *positive* goals, it is best to combine goals that simply reduce the intensity of a negative emotion with a positive goal of experiencing a positive emotion. For example, the person who is feeling "extremely anxious" could make a target emotion of "less anxiety and more peace." Other examples include "less tension, more relaxation" and "less fear, more courage."

Note to the therapist:

The intent here is to engage the approach orientation by adding a positive or approach goal to target emotions that only involve a reduction in negative affect.

The therapist continues speaking to the participants:

If you remember, during the analysis of my emotion in the hypothetical situation, I identified that I felt "anxious." I may decide that for my target emotion, I would like to decrease the amount of anxiety I feel (i.e., "less anxious"). I may also want to add a goal of experiencing a positive emotion to my original target emotion of "less anxious," so I could add something like "more calm." My target emotion, therefore, would be "less anxious, more calm," which I would write in Box #1 of the worksheet.

In the next step of the Modifying Emotions Worksheet, we think of ways we could change the situation (identified in our analysis as the situation that originally triggered our negative emotion), which would facilitate our current target emotion. For example, using my hypothetical situation, I could write "quit my job" in Box #2. How else could I change the situation in order to become "less anxious, more calm?" What other ideas do you all have?

Next, we think of ways we can improve our physical and emotional health, so we are less likely to experience the negative emotion we identified in our analysis and more likely to experience our target emotion. For example, in Box #3 I could write something like "improve my diet," "exercise," or "spend time with friends."

In the next step, we review from our previous analysis how we appraised the situation at the time, and we consider all of the ways we could appraise the situation differently that would help us achieve our target emotion. For example, in Box #4, I could write, "My boss thinks I am up for the challenge. It would not be hard to increase my sales by 10 %." I could also write, "My boss is just having a bad day. My job is not really in jeopardy." These modified appraisals would likely lead me to feel my target emotion of "less anxious, more calm."

In the following step of the worksheet, we explore ways we can reduce the importance of our needs, goals, desires, and expectations (identified in our analysis) that originally facilitated the negative emotion. One way to do this is to critically examine why we consider the needs, goals, etc. that are related to the negative emotion to be so important. Maybe we have overestimated the importance of these goals. It could be that while it would be disappointing for me to lose my job, it would not actually be as catastrophic as it feels it would be. In Box #5, I could write "maybe losing my job would not be a catastrophe."

Another way to reduce the importance of our needs, goals, etc., which originally triggered the negative emotion, is to set *new* goals that *can* be attained in the problematic situation. For example, I may choose to <u>set new goals</u> for myself in Box #5, such as "being a good father" or "living an exciting life." I could attain both of these goals even if I lose my job. In fact, losing my job would actually help me attain these goals. If I am able to refocus on these new goals, the situation becomes less threatening and may be actually viewed as a good opportunity. This reorientation of my goals would foster my target emotion of "less anxious, more calm."

In the next step, we check to see if our negative emotion is part of an old response pattern that we labeled during the analysis process. If the negative emotion is in fact part of a response pattern, we can <u>brainstorm new, more positive patterns</u> we could begin instead. For example, if my anxiety was part of an old response pattern to difficult situations in which I typically believe "Bad things are going to happen to me!", I would try to come up with a new pattern I would rather experience instead that would foster my target emotion. Then I would attempt to label this new pattern. This new pattern may be that when faced with difficult situations I choose to believe "I am a survivor!" I would write the label for this new pattern "I am a survivor!" in Box #6.

In the next step, we review from our previous analysis how our emotion was expressed in our body. We then look at how we can <u>make changes in our body</u> that would likely trigger the target emotion. For example, I could write "muscle and breathing relaxation to induce feeling less anxious, more calm" in Box #7.

In the following step, we review our analysis for the ways we evaluated our negative emotion in unhelpful ways. We then think of ways we could <u>evaluate the negative emotion differently</u> that would foster positive secondary emotions and would facilitate our target emotion. For example, I could remind myself that the anxiety I felt in my situation is a good thing in that it keeps me from overlooking the threat of being fired. Thus, in Box #8 I may choose to write, "My anxiety is helpful, since it alerts me to the risk of losing my job. It encourages me to take steps to ensure this does not happen." This new evaluation could lead to feeling grateful for my anxiety and help me achieve my target emotion of "less anxious, more calm."

In the final step of the worksheet, we review, in our previous analysis, the impulses to act that were triggered by our negative emotion. We then <u>brainstorm other behaviors</u> we could implement instead that would likely trigger our target emotion. Strategies to brainstorm helpful behaviors include:

1. **Strategy #1 (Use the Blues):** Identify the *helpful* behavior the emotion suggests and then engage in this behavior (e.g., listening to the urgency in my anxiety, I decide to call a few old business contacts to make some sales deals, which would help me feel "less anxious, more calm").
2. **Strategy #2 (Opposite Action):** Identify the *unhelpful* behavior the emotion suggests and then do the opposite. (e.g., even though my anxiety prompts me to rush around my office I will intentionally slow down and take my time in order to "reduce my anxiety and experience more calm"). This strategy is a key component of dialectical behavior therapy (Linehan, 1993).
3. **Strategy #3 (Distraction):** Do something pleasurable to distract yourself (e.g., I decided to take a walk outside). Remember that the intent of doing something

pleasurable is distraction, NOT avoidance! Distraction is an effective emotion regulation technique that intentionally directs attention away from a negative emotion while still *being willing* to experience the negative emotion if necessary. On the other hand, avoidance is used when a negative emotion is feared and there is an *unwillingness* to experience it. While distraction can reduce a negative emotion, avoidance paradoxically intensifies and maintains it.

Having explored these three behavioral strategies to achieve my target emotion, I would write down a few options in Box #9.

Ideally, we have brainstormed multiple options for each of the steps on the Modifying Emotions Worksheet. We then select the idea or ideas from each step that have the highest chance of success at achieving our target emotion by circling these options on the worksheet. Finally, we number the options on the worksheet in the order in which we intend to carry them out.

By selecting the brainstorming options that have the highest chance of success and determining the order for implementing the options, we have created our very own personalized emotion modification plan. However, the process is not quite finished. The plan must be implemented, and after the plan has been put into place, it should be evaluated.

The plan is evaluated by determining the degree to which the target emotion has been achieved. If the target emotion has in fact been achieved, the plan was successful. In this case, we should appreciate all of our hard work! If the goal was NOT achieved or only partially achieved, it is important to remember not to give up. The following steps can help deal constructively with setbacks:

General Problem Solving Steps – Insufficient Progress

1) Reward yourself for trying

2) Keep working your same plan

3) Make adjustments to the plan

4) Modify the target emotion – maybe make "acceptance & tolerance" the goal

Slide 84:

1. Reward yourself for trying!
2. Keep working the same plan with increased intensity.
3. Modify the plan; try other strategies.
4. Modify the target emotion. Maybe make "Acceptance and Tolerance" (ART Skill #4) the goal.

General Problem Solving Steps

1) Approach the problem with a positive attitude

2) Describe and analyze the problem

3) Set a goal

4) Brainstorm ways to achieve the goal & create a plan

5) Put the plan into action

6) Evaluate the outcome

7) Praise yourself for successes

Slide 85: The final step in the Modifying Emotions Worksheet is to praise yourself for any and all types of successes that have occurred during the modification process. Praising ourselves for successes gives us the encouragement we need to continue to work hard to modify our emotions.

Note to the therapist:

After presenting the steps listed in the Modifying Emotions Worksheet (Appendix R), the participants are given an opportunity to ask questions about the process of modifying emotions in ART Skill #7. The therapist should explain that with practice, they will be able to learn the steps in this process and modify their emotions in real time.

The therapist then invites one of the participants to share a personally challenging emotion that the therapist and participants can use to practice the steps of the Modifying Emotions Worksheet. Using the participant's example, the therapist works collaboratively with all of the participants to work through each step of the worksheet. The therapist records the participants' responses in the boxes that correspond to each step of the worksheet on a large poster-board-size version of the Modifying Emotions Worksheet. If this enlarged copy of the worksheet is laminated, the therapist can use dry-erase markers to record the participants' responses. The laminated worksheet can be erased and reused during future training sessions.

The participants are then asked to use the Modifying Emotions Worksheet to practice modifying one of the important negative emotions they depicted in the drawing they made earlier. They should write the information related to each step in the modification process in the various boxes on the worksheet. After they complete the worksheet, they may discuss it in pairs. The therapist should spend a few minutes working with each pair to provide support and clarify any questions they may have. When the pairs have finished reviewing their worksheets, the therapist may elect either to ask each participant to present their Modifying Emotions Worksheet to the group, or the therapist may choose instead to offer some time for the participants to ask questions and make comments about the worksheet.

It is common for participants to have difficulty with the modification process, so the therapist should be sure to provide empathy and support as the participants describe problems they are experiencing with this process. The therapist can best assist the participants in these situations by normalizing the difficult nature of this process and by asking empathic questions related to challenges or difficulties they are having. For example, "It sure is hard to look at this situation from another angle. How do you suppose someone else could interpret this situation?" or "How would you advise someone in this same situation who is trying to change how they feel?"

It is common for participants to discount their own brainstorming ideas by saying that the options they came up with for modifying their emotion "would never actually work." The therapist should respond to these participants by gently pointing out their hopeless feelings, providing empathic support, and helping them realize that just because they feel that something is hopeless does not actually mean that it is in fact hopeless. In these instances, participants need to understand that instantly discounting their potentially helpful ideas leaves them with no ideas at all, which is the perfect setup for hopelessness and depression. Sometimes, participants may be more open to consider input from the other participants than from the therapist. In these cases, the therapist can elicit brainstorming ideas from the group.

16.3   ART Sequence with ART Skills #1–7

At this time, ART Skill #7 is integrated into the ART Sequence.

The therapist continues speaking to the participants:

ART Skills and ART Sequence

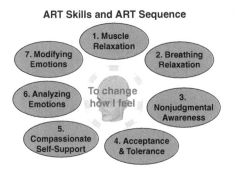

Slide 86: We will now include ART Skill #7 into the ART Sequence.

The therapist may guide the ART Sequence Exercise using the "Exercise Seven" audio that can be downloaded from the ART website, or the therapist may guide the exercise using the following instructions:

We will start the exercise after the sound of the bell.

Sound of the bell

Find a comfortable position. Close your eyes. Breathe in … and out. Exhale slowly. Relax your body, and focus your attention on your muscles. Relax the muscles in your hands … forearms … upper arms … face … neck … shoulders … back … belly … buttocks … and legs. (*slight pause*) Focus your attention on your breathing. Breathe in … and … out. With each exhale, allow your muscles to relax even more. (*5 s pause*)

Now, shift into the state of nonjudgmental awareness by observing your breath without trying to control it. (*5 s pause*) Simply notice how it feels when you breathe in … and … out. (*5 s pause*) Now broaden the focus of your attention. Remember that when you realize you're getting distracted or that thoughts are crossing your mind, use a word to label your thoughts, such as "planning," "worrying," or "remembering," and gently refocus your attention. Be aware of any sensations in your body, (*5 s pause*) of any sounds you can hear, (*5 s pause*) or any odors you can smell. (*5 s pause*) Notice what you can see even though your eyelids are closed. Maybe you see patterns or maybe you notice lighter and darker areas. (*5 s pause*) Notice what thoughts are coming into your mind, (*5 s pause*) and what needs, goals, desires, or impulses to act are currently in your mind. (*5 s pause*) Notice what emotions or moods you are currently experiencing. (*5 s pause*) Briefly label these feelings. (*5 s pause*) Rate the intensity of your feelings on a scale from 0 to 10, and be aware of the places you feel these emotions in your body. (*10 s pause*)

Now take a moment to develop an Acceptance and Tolerance Statement for a negative emotion that you have become aware of presently or one that has been challenging for you in the past. For example, you might say something to yourself like, "It's okay that I feel this way. These feelings are an important part of me, and they are trying to help me by providing me with valuable information. I can tolerate them for now because I know they won't last forever." (*1 min pause*)

We will now begin to shift our focus onto fostering compassionate self-support. Begin by imagining a situation that was difficult for you in the past or something more recently, some situation in which you experienced negative emotions. Now do your best to visualize that you are observing yourself from above this scene. (*5 s pause*) What do you see as you are looking down at this scene? (*brief pause*) Where are you? (*brief pause*) What is happening that is triggering your negative emotions? (*brief pause*) Which negative emotions are you experiencing? (*brief pause*) How are your negative emotions reflected in your body posture, facial expression, tone of voice, etc.? (*5 s pause*)

Now do your best to let the feeling of compassion toward yourself arise within you … a strong and warm feeling of empathy for yourself that is accompanied by the desire to help yourself and a desire to end your suffering. (*5 s pause*) Visualize yourself entering this scene as well, and approach yourself, who is in some way hurting in this scene. (*5 s pause*) Communicate to yourself that this is a difficult situation. Normalize the negative emotions, and provide reassurance by saying that you are there to support and comfort yourself (not to give advice). (*10 s pause*) If it seems appropriate, visualize giving yourself a physical gesture of compassion (e.g., laying a hand on your shoulder or giving yourself a hug). (*10 s pause*) Provide encouragement to yourself. Maybe you could say something like, "You've gone through a lot in the past, and you can get through this too! I'll be with you as you work through this. We will get through this together!" (*10 s pause*) Give yourself a big, kind, reassuring smile. (*5 s pause*)

Now, let's practice the skill of analyzing a negative emotion. Maybe you would like to analyze a negative emotion that was triggered in the scene you just visualized. Maybe you would like to analyze a negative emotion from a situation in the past or even one that you are currently experiencing. Select a feeling you want to analyze. (*10 s pause*) I will guide you through the analysis process by suggesting a series of questions that you can ask yourself. Imagine that you are asking these questions of the part of you that is experiencing challenging emotions. Try to give your attention to each question.

First, what situation prompted this feeling? (*10 s pause*) Did a particular emotional or physical state leave you vulnerable to this emotional reaction? (*10 s pause*) What in particular caught your attention about the situation that triggered the emotion? (*10 s pause*) Also, how did you interpret and evaluate the situation? (*10 s pause*) Which needs, goals, desires, or expectations were associated with this interpretation and evaluation? In other words, what was at stake in this situation? (*10 s pause*) Was your interpretation and evaluation related to ways you have commonly responded in the past during similar situations? What label could you give to these old response patterns? (*10 s pause*) How did you feel about having this emotion? (*10 s pause*) How and where did you feel this emotion in your body? (*10 s pause*) Did these body sensations cause the emotion to last longer or feel even more intense? (*10 s pause*) What impulses to act were triggered by the emotion? (*10 s pause*) If you have already acted on these impulses, what did you end up doing? (*10 s pause*)

What are the short-term and long-term advantages of this emotion? (*10 s pause*) What are the short-term and long-term disadvantages of this emotion? (*10 s pause*) Take some time now to review and reflect on what you have discovered in the analysis process. (*30 s pause*)

As soon as you have gained a more thorough understanding of this particular feeling, you can go one step further and encourage the part of you that is experiencing difficult emotions to practice actively modifying the problematic emotion. To modify the emotion, encourage the part of you that is experiencing the challenging emotion to follow the steps listed on the modifying emotions worksheet we reviewed together. Visualize the worksheet (*5 s pause*) and begin this process by first asking yourself how you actually want to feel in this situation. What is your "target emotion?" (*10 s pause*)

I will now guide you through a series of questions you can ask yourself in order to brainstorm ways you could achieve your target emotion. First, how could I change the situation in order to achieve my target emotion? (*10 s pause*) How could I improve my physical and emotional health in order to foster my target emotion? (*10 s pause*) Are there other ways I could look at this situation that would facilitate my target emotion? (*10 s pause*) In order to encourage my target emotion, could I consider the possibility that other needs, goals, etc. are really more important than the ones I currently have that are related to my situation? (*10 s pause*) Could I reduce the significance of my threatened need, goal, etc. to a lower level of significance in order to foster my target emotion? (*10 s pause*) Which old response patterns could be modified that would encourage my target emotion? (*10 s pause*) What label could I use for these new response patterns? (*10 s pause*) Could I change how I feel about my emotion in order to foster my target emotion? (*10 s pause*) How could I facilitate changes in my body that would trigger the target emotion? (*10 s pause*) What behavior could I engage in that would cue the target emotion? (*10 s pause*)

Considering all of the ideas you thought of to achieve your target emotion, which ideas have the highest chance of successfully cueing your target emotion? (*10 s pause*) In your mind, make a specific plan of how, when, and where you will put these ideas into action. (*15 s pause*) Now, imagine yourself implementing the plan. Do your best to visualize yourself putting your plan into action. Imagine every single step of your plan. (*20 s pause*) Now check if maybe you can already feel your target emotion appearing even a little bit. (*5 s pause*) If so, be aware of your success, and praise yourself. Give yourself a pat on the back. It is okay to feel proud of yourself. Remind yourself that it is important to praise yourself for any progress you have made … or, if you did not make any progress, to praise yourself for the effort you spent trying. (*5 s pause*)

If you do not get closer to your target emotion, remember that you have three options. First, try the same plan with even more dedication than before. If this does not work, choose other strategies and try a different plan. If this still does not work, you can always modify your target emotion and increase your level of acceptance and tolerance.

As we prepare to end this exercise, briefly focus on any positive emotion you may have experienced while working through the emotion modification process. Do your best to become aware of even the smallest positive emotion that you may have experienced. When you have found such an emotion, gently encourage the feeling of joy to arise. Appreciate your positive feeling. Remind yourself to appreciate positive feelings such as these and to use the energy from these feelings to overcome difficulties and challenges in life. (*10 s pause*) Ask yourself to consider which of your strengths and abilities contributed to these positive feelings. Maybe it was your courage to try something new that led to these positive feelings. (*10 s pause*)

Now bring this exercise to an end by saying goodbye to yourself. Maybe there is something you want to say to yourself before you go. If so, feel free to do so now. (*5 s pause*) Now, at your own pace, slowly begin bringing your attention to your body again. Bring your attention to your breathing. Notice how the breath flows in and out. (*brief pause*) Now bring your attention back from this exercise and into the present moment. Stretch your body ... open your eyes ... and return back to the present and into this room.

Sound of the bell

As usual, a debriefing occurs at the end of the exercise.

Reference

Linehan, M. M. (1993). *Cognitive-behavioral treatment of borderline personality disorder*. New York: Guilford.

Chapter 17
Module Nine: Additional Practice Coping with Particularly Important Affective States

17.1 Recognizing and Understanding Particularly Important Affective States

In this final training module, participants practice how to best cope with affective states that we consider particularly important for mental health. According to our review of the literature and our clinical experience, these states include stress/tension, fear/anxiety, anger, shame, guilt, sadness, and disappointment, as well as depressed mood (see slide 87). We refer to these here as "affective states," since stress/tension and depressed mood are generally not considered to be distinct emotions in the scientific literature. However, from a practical standpoint the ART therapist might choose to refer to these affective states as "feelings" or even "emotions," because these terms are consistent with the everyday language of the participants. Also, distinguishing between the terms "stress," "emotions," and "moods" is often less important in a therapeutic setting than in a research setting, since these states can all be successfully managed with the same or similar strategies (e.g., ART Skills #1–7).

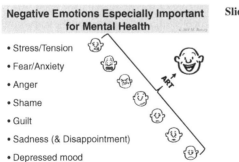

Slide 87

After introducing the affective states that have a significant impact on mental health and well-being, the therapist asks each participant to identify which of these states they have had the most experience with in the past, since an "expert" for each state is needed for the next segment of the training. Naturally, participants often express reluctance to take on the "expert" role saying that if they were an expert, they would not have struggled so much with this affective state. If this happens, the therapist can ask a participant questions such as: "How long and how often have you struggled with this particular emotion? How many self-help books have you read to conquer this emotion? How much psychotherapy have you received to help you with this particular emotion?" With the information gained from questions such as these, the therapist can then ask the participant, "Who else but you truly has an 'expert' level of knowledge about this emotion? Who else but you knows how difficult it is to cope with this emotion? Who else but you knows which strategies are helpful to use to cope with this emotion and which strategies are not? So, I wonder who else but you should be our 'expert' on … (anxiety, depression, anger, etc.)?" Since this reframe is somewhat flattering, the participant will often accept the new expert role and may also help the participant see him/herself as a master of the undesired affective state instead of a victim of it.

After participants have been guided to choose one of the seven affective states they have trouble with (or are an "expert" of), they individually utilize the Analyzing Emotions Worksheet (Appendix Q) to determine how to recognize these affective states and understand what cues them. If possible, the participants should conduct the analysis of the emotion in general and not as it pertains to a specific situation. For example, if the participant is analyzing "anxiety" in step two of the analysis process, the participant should brainstorm various situations that likely trigger anxiety and identify the common or *generic* core of these situations (e.g., not being prepared, facing the possibility of danger, etc.) (Fig. 17.1).

After the analysis of the emotion is conducted, each participant is directed to present the results of their analysis to the group while the other participants follow along, contribute examples from their own experiences, and record relevant information on a blank Analyzing Emotions Worksheet (one worksheet for each affective state that is discussed). Through this process, all of the participants learn how to recognize each of the particularly important affective states and what typically cues them. If there are fewer than seven participants, some participants could analyze more than one of the seven affective states that have a substantial impact on mental health and well-being.

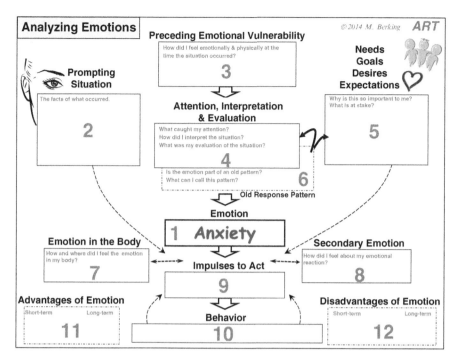

Fig. 17.1 Using the Analyzing Emotions Worksheet with emotions that have a significant impact on mental health and well-being

17.2   Modifying Affective States that Are Particularly Important for Mental Health

To begin the process of modifying particularly important affective states, the therapist first asks the participants how they would decide when it would be helpful to try to modify these states. In order to guide this discussion, the therapist gives copies of the Evaluating Emotions Worksheet (Appendix S) to the participants. The participants provide feedback regarding when each of the seven states listed on the worksheet are helpful and when they are not. The therapist points out that generally, emotions become unhelpful when they last too long or become too intense and reminds the participants that when an emotion becomes unhelpful we have an opportunity to take steps to modify it.

When we have determined that an emotion is unhelpful and we would like to modify it, we can then ask ourselves how we would like to feel instead of the way we do at the time. Setting a positive goal for a target emotion can sometimes be a difficult task. To help the participants set target emotions for the seven affective states that are important for well-being, the therapist passes out the Identifying Target Emotions Worksheet (Appendix T). The therapist asks the participants to

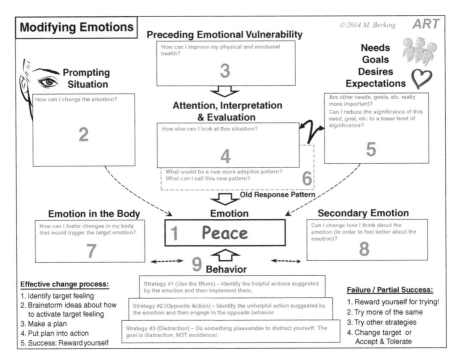

Fig. 17.2 Using the Modifying Emotions Worksheet with emotions that have a significant impact on mental health and well-being

brainstorm potential target emotions for each of the seven emotions. If the participants identify target emotions that only involve a reduction in the undesired emotion, such as less depressed, the therapist should encourage the participants to add a positive goal to it (e.g., less depressed and more happy).

Now that the participants have had some additional practice setting target emotions, the participants are then instructed to individually utilize the Modifying Emotions Worksheet (Appendix R) to modify, toward a target emotion, the same affective state(s) they previously analyzed. Just as before, participants should conduct the modification process for the emotion in general and not only as it pertains to a specific situation. If a participant discusses the modification process using a specific situation, the therapist should help the participant identify the general concept involved that could be applied to other situations.

To assist the participants with the Modifying Emotions Worksheet, the therapist may choose to pass out copies of the Regulation Cheat Sheet (Appendix U), which lists a variety of effective short- and long-term regulation strategies.

After the modification of the emotion is conducted, each participant is directed to present the results of their modification process to the group as the other participants, add their own examples, ask questions, and record information they consider important on a blank Modifying Emotions Worksheet (one worksheet for each affective state that is discussed). At the end of this entire process, each participant should have a completed Analyzing Emotions Worksheet and a completed Modifying Emotions Worksheet for each of the seven affective states that are especially important for mental health.

17.3 Closing Words for Participants

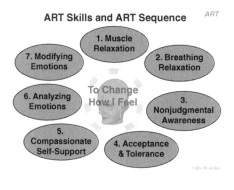

Slide 88: During this training you have learned a lot about how our brains and bodies work and the roles they play in our emotions. You have learned the seven ART Skills that can help you manage your emotions. You have also learned how to chain these skills together into the ART Sequence. The ART Sequence provides an organizing step-by-step process to help you implement the ART Skills. The ART Skills and the ART Sequence can be practiced at home using the audio exercises. Remember, these skills must be practiced to become effective emotion regulation tools.

When working through the ART Sequence in a real-life situation, you may find it helpful to cue yourself with a phrase such as "To change how I feel, I will …"

• Take a few moments to relax my muscles (ART Skill #1).
• Calmly and consciously breathe in and out a few times (ART Skill # 2).
• Observe what is happening within me, without judgment. I will try to label my emotions as specifically as possible (ART Skill #3).
• Accept my emotions as they are occurring in the moment. I am aware that emotions are not permanent and that I can tolerate unpleasant emotions for a time (ART Skill #4).
• Actively support myself in a compassionate and caring way (ART Skill #5).
• Constructively analyze why I feel the way I do (ART Skill #6).
• Identify how I want to feel and switch to a problem-solving mode to modify my emotions (ART Skill #7).

It works best at first to go through the entire ART Sequence when applying the ART Skills to a challenging emotion. Later, when you are more comfortable with all of the ART Skills and the ART Sequence, you may begin to pick and choose which skills are most helpful for you. You may also decide the skills in the ART Sequence are more helpful for you in a different order. Again, please become very familiar with the ART Skills and applying the ART Sequence in its entirety and in its original order before you begin making adjustments to it. It is very common to become distracted as you are working through the ART Sequence. When this occurs, utilize ART Skill #3 (Nonjudgmental Awareness), by noticing what has occurred (e.g., "I am planning, worrying, thinking, etc."), and then gently shift your attention back to the ART Sequence. Please remember that while emotions are the "spice of life," we are wise to manage them skillfully in times of distress in order to maintain good health and well-being. Our hope is that the skills you have learned during this training will help you to do so in a lifelong pursuit of growth and wellness.

Part III
Evaluation and Future Prospects

Chapter 18
Program Evaluation, Efficacy Findings, and Future Directions

In part one of this manual, we reviewed the extensive empirical research on emotion regulation and mental health and presented a conceptualization model of adaptive emotion regulation (Adaptive Coping with Emotions Model). We also explored the ways in which emotion regulation skills deficits may occur (ART Developmental Model of Emotion Regulation Deficits) and potential pathways by which emotion regulation skills deficits may negatively impact mental health. In part two, we described the ART program in detail to enable mental health professionals to effectively use the program to help their patients. Here in part three of the manual, we will present some of our clinical experiences delivering ART. We will also review findings from the scientific studies we have conducted to evaluate the efficacy of the program. Finally, we will discuss limitations of ART and the ongoing efforts to further improve the program.

18.1 Feedback from Participants and ART Therapists

In the development phase of ART, the training was tested repeatedly with students at the University of Bern, Switzerland, and with patients treated in the university's outpatient clinic. Revisions to the training program were made based on experiences during the development phase. The revised version of the program has now been utilized in many different settings across Europe, including psychotherapy outpatient clinics, psychiatric hospitals, psychosomatic rehabilitation centers, neurological rehabilitation facilities, addiction treatment centers, private businesses, government service agencies, and educational institutions. It is estimated that approximately 10,000 people have participated in the training over the past 8 years.

During this time, we have received feedback about the program from therapists and participants through various letters, emails, and phone calls. In general, feedback from participants has been extremely positive. Participants particularly praise (1) the way in which the various skills are integrated ("I knew some individual skills, but before the class I was not able to combine them like I can now."), (2) the

M. Berking and B. Whitley, *Affect Regulation Training: A Practitioners' Manual*,
DOI 10.1007/978-1-4939-1022-9_18, © Springer Science+Business Media New York 2014

explanation of the positive aspects of negative emotions ("It had never occurred to me before that negative emotions have important information to give me and that they can help me reach my goals!"), and (3) the e-coaching tools ("Getting short, quick exercises in text messages allowed me to practice the skills as I went about my day"). Participants also often have praise for the Analyzing Emotions and the Modifying Emotions Worksheets, even though they sometimes describe being overwhelmed when they are first introduced to the worksheets. These participants tend to report that seeing all of the various aspects of analyzing or modifying emotions on one piece of paper helps them understand the steps they could take to analyze and modify their emotions.

When asked how ART might be improved, the most common suggestion from participants has been to provide less theory and more time spent working out individual solutions for undesired emotions in specific situations. In settings where ART has been delivered in daylong sessions, some participants have reported feeling exhausted after learning several skills in one day. Others have reported that the material in ART is sometimes presented too quickly for them to fully absorb it.

Therapists who deliver the ART program often praise the approach in ART of focusing on general emotion regulation deficits to restore mental health. These therapists have told us they consider emotion regulation to be crucial for mental health and are often disappointed with disorder-specific treatments that do not adequately address *general* affect regulation skills. Therapists often praise the systematic integration of various effective therapeutic strategies into a coherent training program.

Positive feedback is also frequently received for the components of the ART program, including the presentation slides, the participant manual, and the e-coaching tools. The therapists have stated that the high quality of these components increases the validity of the program and encourages engagement from the participants. Moreover, therapists often praise the warm, positive, and encouraging style of ART that utilizes and builds upon the participants' strengths during the program. Finally, therapists report that if they succeed in engaging participants in the training, they observe a positive cycle in which fulfilling experiences in ART encourage the participants' motivation to engage more deeply in the training, providing more positive experiences, and so on. While the participants undoubtedly benefit from this positive cycle, therapists describe this as personally meaningful and rewarding to observe.

Some therapists who have delivered ART, especially those exclusively rooted in behavioral therapy, have reported difficulties understanding and teaching the skills of "nonjudgmental awareness" and "acceptance and tolerance." Participation in mindfulness training can be beneficial in providing greater mastery of these concepts. Additionally, therapists have voiced concerns similar to the ones raised by participants regarding the complexity of the entire ART program. These therapists have proposed that more time than 18 hours is needed to deliver the entire program effectively. We share these concerns and agree that when delivering the training to more challenging populations or when time is not restricted, it would be preferable to extend the training time to 25 hours. Unfortunately, therapists are often forced to simply use the time that is available due to financial or health insurance constraints. Finally, some therapists with a limited background in neuroscience have reported feeling insecure when explaining the neurological vicious cycles that contribute to emotion dysregulation.

18.2 Efficacy Findings

Systematic research on the effectiveness of ART is still in the early stages. However, early results are quite promising, and several studies have been conducted in a variety of settings. With regard to nonclinical populations, ART has been found to enhance affect regulation skills in college students (Schwarz, Kowalsky, & Berking, 2013). Also, a study was conducted in which the ART program was given to a group of police officers, whose profession is associated with many emotional challenges. According to Evans and colleagues, "Officers typically use problem-focused, direct action, coping strategies to deal with occupational stress but may not deal effectively with their emotional reactions to occupational stress" (Evans, Coman, Stanley, & Burrows, 1993, p. 243). Consistent with this statement, it was found that prior to the training, the officers' emotion regulation skills were significantly lower than a control population. After the training, however, the police officers' emotion regulation skills had increased to the point where they no longer differed from the control population (Berking, Meier, & Wupperman, 2010).

ART has also been evaluated within clinical settings. One study integrated ART into a CBT-based inpatient treatment to determine if the inclusion of ART would enhance treatment outcome (Berking et al., 2008). The 289 patients who met criteria for various mental disorders received 6 weeks of CBT-based therapy. A subgroup of these patients was offered the option to replace parts of the CBT-based treatment with an abbreviated version of ART. Comparing outcomes across these two groups showed that the patients who had participated in ART improved their emotion regulation skills significantly more than those who had received only the traditional CBT-based treatment. Moreover, the patients who participated in ART showed significant decreases in depression and negative affect and greater increases in positive affect.

Although the results from this study appear promising, they are preliminary because participants were not completely randomized to treatment conditions. Thus, we recently conducted a completely randomized, controlled, prospective, clinical trial with a sample of 432 participants who were receiving inpatient treatment at a psychiatric hospital and who met diagnostic criteria for major depressive disorder (Berking, Ebert, Cuijpers, & Hofmann, 2013). The participants received either traditional CBT-based therapy or a modified version of this therapy in which some of the components were replaced with a shortened version of ART. Comparisons across the two groups indicated that integrating ART into the CBT-based treatment was associated with greater gains in the acquisition of emotion regulation skills including modification, acceptance and tolerance of emotions, and compassionate self-support, as well as greater reduction in the severity of depressive symptoms. More specifically, 65% of participants who received the CBT+ART treatment attained remission status compared to only 51% of participants who received the traditional CBT treatment.

Similar results have been found in a preliminary data analysis of a study that investigated the effectiveness of ART in reducing depressive symptoms in individuals meeting criteria for major depressive disorder and examined if participation in

ART enhanced the treatment effects of subsequent individual CBT (Ehret, Kowalsky, Rief, Hiller, & Berking, 2014). Moreover, in a recent, quasi-experimental study, a combination of ART and CBT was shown to be effective for patients suffering from medically unexplained somatic symptoms (Gottschalk, Bleichhardt, Kleinstäuber, Berking, & Rief, in press).

Further evidence for the efficacy of ART comes from experimental studies in which we evaluated the short-term efficacy of the skills practiced in ART. For these studies, we developed an experimental paradigm in which depressive mood states are repeatedly induced with a combination of mood-inducing music and typed statements ("Velten items"; Velten, 1968) read by the participants. After each induction phase, participants are given audio instructions to utilize certain ART Skills to regulate their emotions. Before and after each mood induction and regulation, participants are asked to rate the intensity of their affective state. Using this experimental paradigm with a healthy sample of graduate students and another sample that met criteria for major depressive disorder, the study results indicated that in both samples, the ART-based audio instructions were more effective in reducing the intensity of the induced depressed mood than the spontaneous regulation control condition (Diedrich, Kandl, Hofmann, Hiller, & Berking, 2014).

18.3   Limitations of the Research Assessing the Efficacy of ART

There are several limitations of the research that has been conducted to evaluate the ART program. First, the efficacy research has exclusively relied on retrospective self-report measures such as the ERSQ (see Sect. 3.3). These types of measures rely on a person's ability to understand and report his/her emotional state, which is the very skill that many people lack. Another specific drawback for the ERSQ is that this self-report measure asks if a person has been able to apply various regulatory skills to his/her emotions in general. Since each person experiences emotions differently based on his/her unique affect regulation capacities, the measure does not uniformly assess regulatory strategies for each person taking the ERSQ. It is unclear if assessing emotion regulation skills in this manner provides an accurate picture of a person's capacity to regulate a wide range of emotions. To address this specific limitation of the ERSQ, we have recently developed and validated a modified version of the ERSQ, which assesses affect regulation skills separately in the context of various affective states (Affect Regulation Skills Questionnaire,[1] ARSQ; Ebert, Christ, & Berking, 2013). This measure will help clarify how individuals differ in their use of affect regulation skills across affective states and will identify which skills are most important for regulating each affective state.

---

[1] An English version of the ARSQ can be obtained from the first author.

Another limitation of the efficacy research is that, in clinical populations, ART has been evaluated primarily as an adjunctive instead of as a stand-alone intervention. This has been done purposefully because of our belief that the unique characteristics of various disorders should be considered when utilizing transdiagnostic interventions such as ART. Because of the lack of studies evaluating ART as a stand-alone intervention, it is unclear which disorders can be treated effectively with ART's exclusive focus of enhancing affect regulation skills. Moreover, when ART has been studied as an adjunctive treatment, we have not systematically varied the time period at which ART is added to other treatments. As a result, we do not yet know whether adding ART at specific phases of various treatments is more or less effective. For example, it is unknown whether ART would be more or less effective as a treatment for severe depression before or after evidence-based interventions, such as behavior therapy, have been applied. Finally, the efficacy research is also limited by its focus on heterogeneous clinical samples and samples of depressed patients. Thus, it is unclear to what extent the efficacy of ART varies across disorders.

References

Berking, M., Ebert, D., Cuijpers, P., & Hofmann, S. G. (2013). Emotion regulation skills training enhances the efficacy of inpatient cognitive behavioral therapy for major depressive disorder: A randomized controlled trial. *Psychotherapy and Psychosomatics, 82*(4), 234–245.

Berking, M., Meier, C., & Wupperman, P. (2010). Enhancing emotion-regulation skills in police officers: Results of a pilot controlled study. *Behavior Therapy, 41*(3), 329–339.

Berking, M., Wupperman, P., Reichardt, A., Pejic, T., Dippel, A., & Znoj, H. (2008). Emotion-regulation skills as a treatment target in psychotherapy. *Behaviour Research and Therapy, 46*(11), 1230–1237.

Diedrich, A., Grant, M., Hofmann, S. G., Hiller, W., & Berking, M. (2014). Self-compassion as an emotion regulation strategy in major depressive disorder. *Behaviour Research and Therapy, 58*, 43–51.

Ebert, D., Christ, O., & Berking, M. (2013). Entwicklung und validierung eines fragebogens zur emotionsspezifischen selbsteinschätzung emotionaler kompetenzen (SEK-ES). [Development and validation of a self-report instrument for the assessment of emotion-specific regulation skills]. *Diagnostica, 59*(1), 17–32.

Ehret, A., Kowalsky, J., Rief, W., Hiller, W., & Berking, M. (2014). Effects of an intense affect regulation training on symptoms of major depressive disorder: Study protocol of a randomized controlled trial. *BMC Psychiatry, 14*, 20–31.

Evans, B. J., Coman, G. J., Stanley, R. O., & Burrows, G. D. (1993). Police officers coping strategies: An Australian police survey. *Stress Medicine, 9*(4), 237–246.

Gottschalk, J.M., Bleichhardt, G., Kleinstäuber, M., Berking, M., & Rief, W. (in press). Erweiterung der kognitiven Verhaltenstherapie um Emotions regulations training bei Patienten mit multiplen somatoformen Symptomen: Ergebnisse einer kontrollierten Pilotstudie. [Complementing CBT for somatoform symptoms with an intense emotion regulation training: Results from a controlled study] *Verhaltenstherapie [Behavior Therapy]*.

Schwarz, J., Kowalsky, J., & Berking, M. (2013). *A systematic training enhances self compassion in college students: A randomized controlled trial.* Poster presented on the 43rd annual conference of the European Association for Behavioral and Cognitive Therapy, Marrakesh, Morocco.

Velten, E. (1968). A laboratory task for the induction of mood states. *Behavioral Research and Therapy, 6*(4), 473–482.

Chapter 19
Limitations and Future Directions of the ART Program

The ART program has many positive features that make it an attractive intervention for a variety of populations. However, there are also limitations of this training program. This chapter will discuss these limitations, as well as the current efforts underway to improve and enhance ART in order to increase the training's effectiveness.

19.1 Transdiagnostic Nature of ART

One of the outstanding features of ART is that it has been developed as a transdiagnostic intervention, providing several distinct advantages for the program. For example, ART can be delivered in a diverse group setting without the need to ensure that everyone in attendance shares the same types of pathology. The applicability of ART in a diverse group setting enables the program to be delivered in a cost-effective manner. Additionally, the transdiagnostic nature of ART enables patients with comorbid disorders to receive treatment that is relevant for all of their various disorders, rather than participating in multiple disorder-specific treatments.

However, as a transdiagnostic intervention, ART may neglect important and unique characteristics of particular disorders. For example, a patient who develops panic disorder after erroneously attributing an accelerated heart rate to a serious heart condition may not be treated in the most effective and straightforward way with ART. We generally do *not* propose using ART as an alternative to disorder-specific, evidence-based interventions. Instead, ART should be added to such interventions whenever strengthening emotion regulation skills would help a patient better manage his/her problems.

We are currently investigating the feasibility of adding material related to specific mental disorders to the existing ART program to increase the effectiveness of ART when it is combined with other evidence-based treatments to address certain disorders. For example, we are currently developing a disorder-specific adaptation of ART for individuals suffering from somatic symptom disorder. Other disorders for which we are developing modified versions of ART include depressive disorders,

M. Berking and B. Whitley, *Affect Regulation Training: A Practitioners' Manual*,
DOI 10.1007/978-1-4939-1022-9_19, © Springer Science+Business Media New York 2014

eating disorders, substance use disorders, and tinnitus. The additions to the ART program in these disorder-specific versions will be rather small and will focus on (a) an explanation of why enhancing affect regulation skills is an effective means of coping with the specific disorder, (b) addressing factors relevant for the particular disorder as targets for change (e.g., fostering regular eating habits to reduce binge eating in binge eating disorder and bulimia nervosa), and (c) adapting the psycho-educational components and exercises to the cognitive capacities of the target population (e.g., reducing the length of exercises in response to attention problems that can occur in substance use disorders).

19.2   Utilizing Translational Research Findings to Explain Emotion Regulation Difficulties

ART heavily utilizes neuroscience to explain the mechanisms at work during emotion regulation. According to our clinical experience, this approach is particularly helpful when working with patients who have difficulty experiencing emotional states without attributing them to somatic experiences (e.g., "My stomach is upset" instead of "I am scared"). However, we have learned that it is very difficult to find the right balance between a clinically helpful teaching model and a scientifically valid, neuroaffective model of affect regulation. For example, anthropomorphizing relevant brain areas (e.g., "The amygdala only wants to protect you.") might be an effective psychotherapeutic intervention to help explain emotion dysregulation, but this expression is inadequate in the context of a purely scientific explanation. Additionally, we must acknowledge that remaining up to date with the latest findings and theories of the affective neurosciences while simultaneously conducting large, randomized clinical trials has resulted in a remarkable challenge. During the time it takes to research the latest neuroscientific findings related to emotion regulation, incorporate these findings into ART, write a treatment manual, raise the funds for efficacy trials, and conduct and publish the results of those trials, the original neuroscience research is likely outdated. Thus, we are currently looking for neuroscience experts who share our interest in translational research and with whom we can closely collaborate. With the assistance of these experts, we aim to enhance the neuroscientific translational approach used in ART by creating valid and understandable models that provide rationale for the interventions in the ART program.

19.3   Participant Engagement in Skill-Building Exercises

The effectiveness of ART can be partly attributed to its strong focus on building emotion regulation skills through the use of standardized exercises. According to our experience, participants benefit greatly from the program if they actively engage in the daily ART Skills. While experience has shown that the majority of ART participants can be motivated to engage in daily skills training, there are also a significant number of participants who have difficulties practicing regularly during and after the training and subsequently experience less benefit from the program. To address this, we are working hard to improve the ART repertoire of motivation enhancing techniques as well as exploring additional ways for participants to practice the ART Skills including the utilization of technology.

Since 2004, text messages and email have been used in ART to deliver short exercises to participants to support their daily skills practice. In a similar manner, we hope to use additional emerging technology to provide more practice resources for participants. For example, we are currently finalizing an interactive online version of ART as well as several "games" that can be used to practice the ART Skills in a leisurely fashion. Since ART participants will only be able to maintain and improve the regulation skills they acquired during the training with frequent and ongoing practice *after* the ART classes have concluded, we also plan to develop an online community for ART graduates. This online community will offer ART graduates support, encouragement, and additional tips for practicing and applying the ART Skills. We hope endeavors such as these will help additional participants more thoroughly practice the ART Skills and as a result experience more positive effects.

Chapter 20
Closing Summary

The world is not primarily geared to satisfy our needs, so we frequently find ourselves in situations in which our needs are not adequately met. Moreover, anytime our needs are met and our goals are attained, we are likely to become accustomed to the present situation and generate additional needs and more ambitious goals. Consequently, people will repeatedly experience negative feelings. These feelings are an indispensable aspect of the human existence. However, the manner in which we deal with these emotions is crucial to our success, health, and satisfaction in life.

Our goal in Affect Regulation Training is to provide assistance to anyone who would like to improve the skills needed to adaptively cope with undesired affective states. Effective regulation skills reduce the need to engage in dysfunctional emotion regulation strategies and contribute to a more successful, healthy, and satisfying life. These skills also enable us to truly appreciate the role our feelings play in facilitating rich and colorful experiences in our lives. Beyond this manual, interested readers can find more information at www.AffectRegulationTraining.com.

M. Berking and B. Whitley, *Affect Regulation Training: A Practitioners' Manual*, 215
DOI 10.1007/978-1-4939-1022-9_20, © Springer Science+Business Media New York 2014

Appendices

M. Berking and B. Whitley, *Affect Regulation Training: A Practitioners' Manual*,
DOI 10.1007/978-1-4939-1022-9, © Springer Science+Business Media New York 2014

ART-S & ERSQ	(Code-) Name: _____	Age: ____
Version SR 2010/2	Occupation: _____	Sex: ____

Dear Participant,

Below, are some statements about a variety of emotions you may have experienced in the last week and about how you dealt with these emotions. Please fill in the circle for the answer that fits the best for you. Don't spend a lot of time on each question. The first answer that comes to your mind is probably the best.

1. Emotions & Mood: In the last week I felt ...

#		not at all	rarely	some-times	often	almost always	#		not at all	rarely	some-times	often	almost always
1	courageous:	O_0	O_1	O_2	O_3	O_4	26	sad:	O_0	O_1	O_2	O_3	O_4
2	worthless:	O_0	O_1	O_2	O_3	O_4	27	disappointed:	O_0	O_1	O_2	O_3	O_4
3	thankful:	O_0	O_1	O_2	O_3	O_4	28	confident:	O_0	O_1	O_2	O_3	O_4
4	active:	O_0	O_1	O_2	O_3	O_4	29	cozy:	O_0	O_1	O_2	O_3	O_4
5	interested:	O_0	O_1	O_2	O_3	O_4	30	alarmed:	O_0	O_1	O_2	O_3	O_4
6	excited:	O_0	O_1	O_2	O_3	O_4	31	depressed:	O_0	O_1	O_2	O_3	O_4
7	strong:	O_0	O_1	O_2	O_3	O_4	32	unhappy:	O_0	O_1	O_2	O_3	O_4
8	inspired:	O_0	O_1	O_2	O_3	O_4	33	tense:	O_0	O_1	O_2	O_3	O_4
9	proud:	O_0	O_1	O_2	O_3	O_4	34	stressed:	O_0	O_1	O_2	O_3	O_4
10	enthusiastic:	O_0	O_1	O_2	O_3	O_4	35	hopeless:	O_0	O_1	O_2	O_3	O_4
11	alert:	O_0	O_1	O_2	O_3	O_4	36	optimistic:	O_0	O_1	O_2	O_3	O_4
12	determined:	O_0	O_1	O_2	O_3	O_4	37	anxious:	O_0	O_1	O_2	O_3	O_4
13	attentive:	O_0	O_1	O_2	O_3	O_4	38	disgusted:	O_0	O_1	O_2	O_3	O_4
14	distressed:	O_0	O_1	O_2	O_3	O_4	39	humiliated:	O_0	O_1	O_2	O_3	O_4
15	upset:	O_0	O_1	O_2	O_3	O_4	40	valuable:	O_0	O_1	O_2	O_3	O_4
16	guilty:	O_0	O_1	O_2	O_3	O_4	41	balanced:	O_0	O_1	O_2	O_3	O_4
17	scared:	O_0	O_1	O_2	O_3	O_4	42	content:	O_0	O_1	O_2	O_3	O_4
18	hostile:	O_0	O_1	O_2	O_3	O_4	43	satisfied:	O_0	O_1	O_2	O_3	O_4
19	irritable:	O_0	O_1	O_2	O_3	O_4	44	jealous:	O_0	O_1	O_2	O_3	O_4
20	ashamed:	O_0	O_1	O_2	O_3	O_4	45	love:	O_0	O_1	O_2	O_3	O_4
21	nervous:	O_0	O_1	O_2	O_3	O_4	46	peaceful:	O_0	O_1	O_2	O_3	O_4
22	jittery:	O_0	O_1	O_2	O_3	O_4	47	calm:	O_0	O_1	O_2	O_3	O_4
23	afraid:	O_0	O_1	O_2	O_3	O_4	48	envious:	O_0	O_1	O_2	O_3	O_4
24	safe:	O_0	O_1	O_2	O_3	O_4	49	happy:	O_0	O_1	O_2	O_3	O_4
25	embarrassed:	O_0	O_1	O_2	O_3	O_4	50	relaxed:	O_0	O_1	O_2	O_3	O_4

Affective States Relevant in Psychotherapy- Self-Report (ART-S); Emotion Regulation Skills Questionnaire (ERSQ)

© Berking, 2014

2. Dealing with emotions: In the last week ...

		not at all	rarely	some-times	often	almost always
1.)	... I was able to consciously pay attention to my feelings.	O_0	O_1	O_2	O_3	O_4
2.)	... I could consciously bring about positive feelings.	O_0	O_1	O_2	O_3	O_4
3.)	... I understood my emotional reactions.	O_0	O_1	O_2	O_3	O_4
4.)	... I could endure my negative feelings.	O_0	O_1	O_2	O_3	O_4
5.)	... I was able to accept my negative feelings.	O_0	O_1	O_2	O_3	O_4
6.)	... I could have labeled my feelings.	O_0	O_1	O_2	O_3	O_4
7.)	... I had a clear physical perception of my feelings.	O_0	O_1	O_2	O_3	O_4
8.)	... I did what I wanted to do, even if I had to face negative feelings on the way.	O_0	O_1	O_2	O_3	O_4
9.)	... I tried to reassure myself during distressing situations.	O_0	O_1	O_2	O_3	O_4
10.)	... I was able to influence my negative feelings.	O_0	O_1	O_2	O_3	O_4
11.)	... I knew what my feelings meant.	O_0	O_1	O_2	O_3	O_4
12.)	... I could focus on my negative emotions if necessary.	O_0	O_1	O_2	O_3	O_4
13.)	... I knew what emotions I was feeling in the moment.	O_0	O_1	O_2	O_3	O_4
14.)	... I consciously noticed when my body reacted towards emotionally charged situations in a particular way.	O_0	O_1	O_2	O_3	O_4
15.)	... I tried to cheer myself up in emotionally distressing situations.	O_0	O_1	O_2	O_3	O_4
16.)	... I did what I intended to do despite my negative feelings.	O_0	O_1	O_2	O_3	O_4
17.)	... I was OK with my feelings, even if they were negative .	O	O_1	O_2	O_3	O_4
18.)	... I was certain that I would be able to tolerate even intense negative feelings.	O_0	O_1	O_2	O_3	O_4
19.)	... I was able to experience my feelings consciously.	O_0	O_1	O_2	O_3	O_4
20.)	... I was aware of why I felt the way I felt.	O_0	O_1	O_2	O_3	O_4
21.)	... I knew that I was able to influence my feelings.	O_0	O_1	O_2	O_3	O_4
22.)	... I pursued goals that were important to me, even if I thought that doing so would trigger or intensify negative feelings.	O_0	O_1	O_2	O_3	O_4
23.)	... I was able to experience my negative feelings without immediately trying to fight them off.	O_0	O_1	O_2	O_3	O_4
24.)	... my physical sensations were a good indication of how I was feeling.	O_0	O_1	O_2	O_3	O_4
25.)	... I was clear about what emotions I was experiencing.	O_0	O_1	O_2	O_3	O_4
26.)	... I could tolerate my negative feelings.	O_0	O_1	O_2	O_3	O_4
27.)	... I supported myself in emotionally distressing situations.	O_0	O_1	O_2	O_3	O_4

Thank you!

Scoring Instructions for ERSQ

#	Scale	Items	Computation
1	Attention toward feelings	1, 12, 19	mean score
2	Body perception of feelings	7, 14, 24	mean score
3	Clarity of feelings	6, 13, 25	mean score
4	Understanding of feelings	3, 11, 20	mean score
5	Acceptance of feelings	5, 17, 23	mean score
6	Resilience: Tolerate and endure feelings	4, 18, 26	mean score
7	Readiness to confront undesired emotions (if necessary to attain personally important goals)	8, 16, 22	mean score
8	Self-support	9, 15, 27	mean score
9	Modification	2, 10, 21	mean score
10	Total of emotion regulation skills	1-27	mean score

See section 3.3 for applicable references on the ERSQ.

ART Skills and ART Sequence

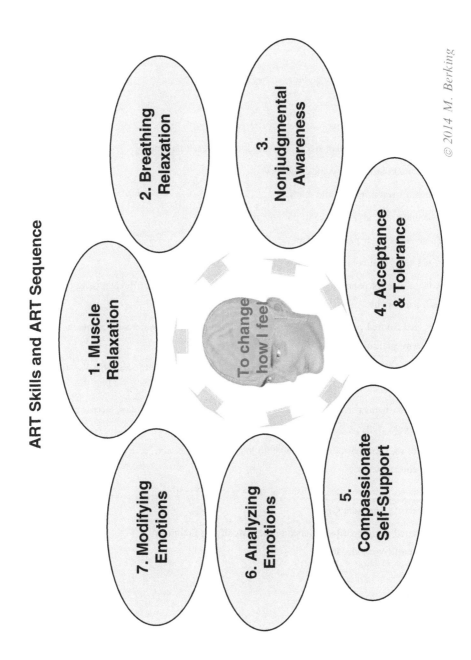

Classroom Materials List

- Meditation bell ("apps" are available for smart phones)

- Computer

- Computer projector

- Projector screen

- Computer CDs containing audio exercises

- One soft foam ball

- Pens for each participant

- Dowel rods (5/8 inch diameter x 20 inches long) for each participant

- Dry erase board and dry erase markers

- Flip chart stand, paper, and markers

- Relaxing music and a device to play the music

- Three index cards per participant

- A red and green colored pencil for each participant

- A large sheet of paper (e.g., 11" x 17" or 12" x 18") and a sheet of flip chart-size paprer for each participant

- Assorted colored pencils, crayons, markers, colored chalk, and watercolor paints in sufficient quantities for the participants to share

- Four to six items per participant that have an interesting texture or shape (shells, stones, feathers, etc.)

- Four to six items per participant that have an interesting smell (candles, incense sticks, play dough, etc.)

- Four to six items per participant with an interesting or pleasant taste (orange slices, dried fruit, chocolate, etc.)

- Laminated posterboard-size version of the Analyzing Emotions Worksheet (Appendix Q)

- Laminated posterboard-size version of the Modifying Emotions Worksheet (Appendix R)

Personal Insights

	What I learned ➡	How I can apply it
1)		
2)		
3)		
4)		
5)		
6)		
7)		
8)		
9)		
10)		

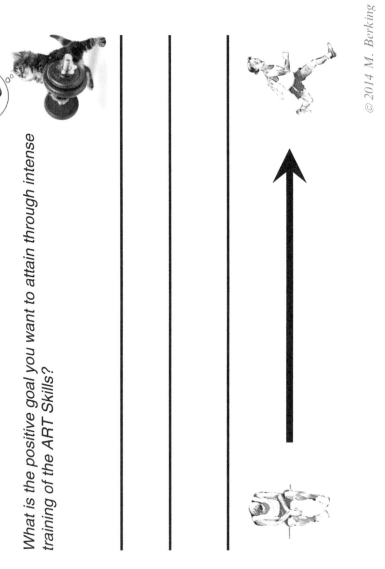

What is the positive goal you want to attain through intense training of the ART Skills?

My Personal ART Training Schedule

Time	Monday	Tuesday	Wednesday	Thursday	Friday	Saturday	Sunday
8:00 AM							
9:00 AM							
10:00 AM							
11:00 AM							
12:00 PM							
1:00 PM							
2:00 PM							
3:00 PM							
4:00 PM							
5:00 PM							
6:00 PM							
7:00 PM							
8:00 PM							

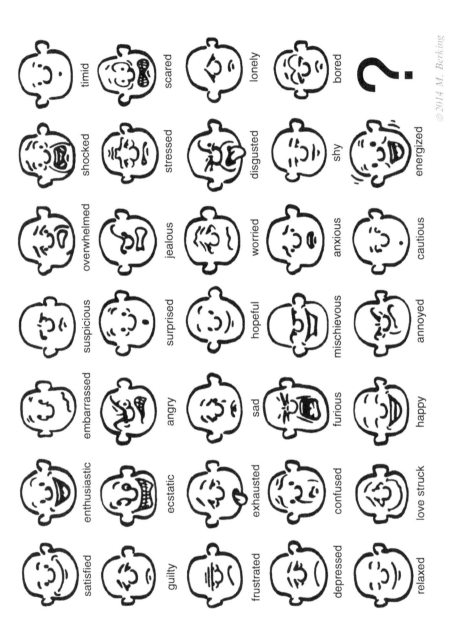

Understanding Acceptance & Tolerance

Acceptance & Tolerance does not mean...

• you have to like or enjoy the emotion you are trying to accept

• you have to accept everything always

• you accept the situation that triggered the negative emotion

• you give up and stop fighting to improve the situation

Acceptance and Tolerance does mean...

• intentionally permitting negative emotions to be present for the amount of time necessary for them to change, since fighting against emotions is likely to make them even stronger

5-Step Acceptance and Tolerance Plan

1. Set acceptance and tolerance as a goal

We must first intentionally decide to make acceptance and tolerance of our emotions our goal. For example you could say to yourself, "I will work to accept and tolerate my current emotion, even if it is difficult for me at the moment."

2. Give yourself a reason for focusing on acceptance

Since the brain typically prefers to get rid of unwanted emotions instead of accepting and tolerating them, we need to give our brain a good reason for engaging in this "second-rate" strategy. The most convincing reason is that fighting too hard to change your emotions might backfire and cue further negative feelings, whereas acceptance paradoxically often facilitates change. Thus, you could say to yourself, "Since trying to fight my emotions will only make them stronger, I will work to accept and tolerate them at least for a certain period of time to regain the calmness I need to eventually change them."

3. View your emotions as helpful

Viewing your emotions (especially challenging ones) in a more positive light can help you be more accepting and tolerating of them. One way to view emotions more positively is to see them as your allies, which are trying to give you important information and facilitate helpful responses. You could say to yourself, "Although painful, these emotions are providing me with valuable information. They are helping me protect my needs and goals. They are telling me ___. They help me by ___."

4. Remind yourself how tough and resilient you are

It can be helpful to remind yourself that you may be underestimating your ability to endure negative emotions. To strengthen this argument, it is often helpful to remember that you have been able to endure negative feelings in the past on numerous occasions. You could say to yourself, "I have frequently proven that I can endure negative feelings, so I can do it again. I can tolerate these feelings even though they are painful!"

5. Remind yourself that emotions are NOT permanent

In the final step of the plan you can remind yourself that emotions are not designed to last forever. Eventually every emotion will change unless it is maintained by desperately trying to avoid it. Reminding yourself that no emotion lasts forever can be a very effective way of fostering acceptance of an undesired emotion. You may find it helpful to tell yourself something like, "This emotion is only temporary. I will not have to endure it forever."

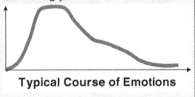

Typical Course of Emotions

Challenging Emotions

Triggered when ...	Function	Typical Thoughts	Typical Changes in the Body
Stress			
... important personal goals could be threatened.	Stress mobilizes additional mental and physical energy to facilitate goal attainment.	*This is too much. I am not sure whether I will be able to cope with this.*	Increased muscle tension Accelerated shallow breathing Accelerated heart rate Increased blood flow to larger muscles and reduced blood flow in the periphery of the body
Anxiety & Fear			
... important personal goals are threatened and I doubt whether I can cope with this challenge.	Anxiety & Fear, similar to stress, mobilize additional mental and physical energy to deal with the threat including flight and freeze responses.	*I definitely do not have the tools to manage this.*	Same as "Stress" but more intense
Anger			
... someone or something prevents me from attaining important goals, and there is no excuse for this.	Anger prepares the mind and body for battle. This preparation is very important in order to attain/protect our goals against resistance from others.	*Idiot! What a jerk!*	Similar to "Anxiety and Fear"
Guilt			
... I have broken an important moral rule that I have for myself.	Guilt encourages behavior to make amends, especially to others, for offenses we have committed, so we remain in good standing with others ·	*I certainly should not have done that.*	Loss of energy Reduced activity
Shame			
... I negatively evaluate who I am as a person.	Shame is an intense feeling that encourages us to withdraw from others when we have violated a major social norm, Withdrawal signals to others that we truly regret what we have done and should still be allowed to remain a member of the group.	*I am a bad person, because I acted that way.*	Similar to "Guilt" but much more intense
Embarrassment			
... I believe other people are judging me or my behavior in a negative manner.	Embarrassment encourages us to fix whatever we believe is causing people to judge us, so we are seen and accepted more favorably by others.	*I must have looked like a klutz when I tripped in front of them!*	Blushing
Sadness (& Disappointment)			
... I realize that I will not (ever) be able to attain a particular goal that is important to me.	Sadness & Disappointment cue physical and mental processes that help us disengage from an unattainable goal. Ultimately, these emotions enable us to redirect our energy in order to set new goals.	*I guess this just isn't going to work out ...*	Crying Reduced activity
Depression			
... I start believing that: 1) I will not attain any of the goals important to me 2) I am helpless to achieve my goals 3) I am hopeless this will ever change	Depression can facilitate a complete reorientation of our needs and goals, which can lead to substantial change.	*Nothing is working out for me.* *There is nothing I can do to change my situation.* *This will never end. I am worthless.*	Loss of energy Trouble concentrating Increased pain sensitivity Difficulty sleeping Multiple physical problems

©2014 M. Berking

Positive Emotions

Triggered when ...	Function	Typical Thoughts	Typical Changes in the Body
Relaxation			
... I am currently attaining my goals or at least I can't see any threats to attaining my goals.	Relaxation rejuvenates the mind and body.	*It sure is nice not having something urgent to take care of right now.*	Slowed heart rate Calm, regular breathing Decreased muscle tension Reduced sensations of pain
Safety			
... I am sure that my goals are not threatended or that I could defend them easily.	Safety leads to relaxation	*Everything is all right.* *I feel secure.* *Nothing can happen to me.*	Similar to "Relaxation"
Courage			
... I face dangerous situations with the belief that I can cope with them.	Courage counterbalances anxiety. Anxiety alerts to danger, while courage faciliates action to reach important objectives despite the danger.	*I am going to do it!* *I will succeed!*	Muscle tension Increased energy
Calmness			
... something at first appears dangerous but with more information or a different perspective, it becomes manageable.	Calmness allows thoughtfulness and objectivity in difficult situations.	*It is going to turn out fine.* *I understand it was not intended to be taken that way.*	Slightly increased heart rate Calm, regular breathing Slight muscle tension
Pride			
... I attribute successful goal attainment to my abilities and/or character.	Pride increases feelings of self-worth.	*I did this really well!* *I am valuable.*	Increased heart rate Quicker breathing Increased energy
Satisfaction			
... my present situation is congruent with my goals.	Satisfaction engenders a sense of peace and happiness in the present moment.	*All is well.* *I have everything I need right now.*	Similar to "Relaxation"
Joy			
... I assess a past or future experience as positive.	Joy is a signal that our goals have been or are going to be met soon. Joy gives motivation to continue the pursuit of important goals.	*Yes! It worked out!* *I am excited to see the light at the end of this tunnel!*	Similar to "Pride"
Optimism			
... I am convinced that I can achieve my goals even if it is not going to be easy.	Optimism is necessary to remain steadfast in the pursuit of important but difficult goals.	*I can make it!* *In the end it will turn out all right!*	Similar to "Pride", but with less physical arousal
Relatedness			
... I feel connected in relationship with someone else.	Relatedness increases feelings of safety, knowing that assistance from another is available.	*I am not alone.* *Someone is there for me.* *I know there are many caring people around me.*	Similar to "Calmness"

© 2014 M. Berking

5-Step Acceptance and Tolerance Plan

1. Set acceptance and tolerance as a goal

State your goal of accepting and tolerating your emotion:_____

_____

2. Give yourself a reason for focusing on acceptance

Describe your reason for setting the goal of acceptance and tolerance of your

emotions: _____

_____

3. View your emotions as helpful

List what your emotions are trying to tell you regarding your needs: _____

_____

_____

List the helpful response(s) they facilitate: _____

_____

_____

4. Remind yourself how tough and resilient you are

Write a sentence reminding yourself that you have tolerated challenging emotions in

the past: _____

_____

5. Remind yourself that emotions are NOT permanent

In your own words, state that this emotion will pass: _____

_____

Personal Acceptance and Tolerance Statement

In a few sentences, summarize the 5-Steps in a meaningful way that would

encourage you in times of stress to accept and tolerate your emotions: _____

_____

_____

_____

_____

Two Effective Strategies to Build Self-Esteem

1

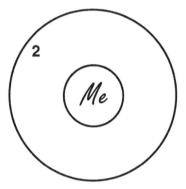

Self-Support Diary I: Appreciation of my Achievements & Strengths

Day	Achievements	My Strengths & Abilities that Contributed to my Achievements	Unconditional Self-Esteem Signal (✓)
Monday			
Tuesday			
Wednesday			
Thursday			
Friday			
Saturday			
Sunday			

Self-Support Diary II: Balanced Lifestyle & Appreciating the Positive

Day:

	Duties/Work	Leisure/Fun
08:00 – 09:00		
09:00 – 10:00		
10:00 – 11:00		
11:00 – 12:00		
12:00 – 01:00		
01:00 – 02:00		
02:00 – 03:00		
03:00 – 04:00		
04:00 – 05:00		
05:00 – 06:00		
06:00 – 07:00		
07:00 – 08:00		
08:00 – 09:00		
09:00 – 10:00		

When working on tasks or taking it easy: Try to appreciate the positive at least once every hour!

Positive Activities

get a massage	go to the movies
reflect upon how fortunate you are	go to a concert
practice mindful walking	practice muscle and breathing relaxation
sunbathe	eat ice cream
go hiking	go to a flea market
visit a museum or an exhibition	go see a play

attend a lecture	take a walk
feed ducks	go swimming
play table tennis	go cycling
play golf or miniature golf	go jogging
go boating	go fishing
practice a pleasure exercise (e.g.,consciously enjoy drinking coffee)	go dancing
complete a task you have postponed for a long time	play billiards

go bowling	play chess, Scrabble, or cards
smile at someone	call a friend
try a handcraft (knitting, sewing)	paint or draw something
look at old photographs	take care of your plants/pets
wash your car	prepare a tasty meal for yourself
watch animals outside	practice an ART Skill of your choice
think of one past achievement and identify your skills that contributed to the acheivement	read a book or the newspaper

listen to the radio	go the library and borrow a book or a CD
write a letter or a postcard	go out for a meal with friends
play an instrument	try a new food recipe
bake a cake	praise yourself for something you did well
go for a picnic	meet a friend
take a bath or a shower	give yourself a smile in the mirror
practice having compassion for yourself	fullfill a wish you have always had

plan an excursion for the next weekend	go for a scenic drive
mow the lawn	pracitice naming your feelings
watch other people, identify their current emotions and think of how these emotions can be helpful	listen to music
relax in a jacuzzi	go ice skating
say something kind to yourself	plan your next vacation
meditate	smell flowers
create more cards with pleasant acitivities	go shopping

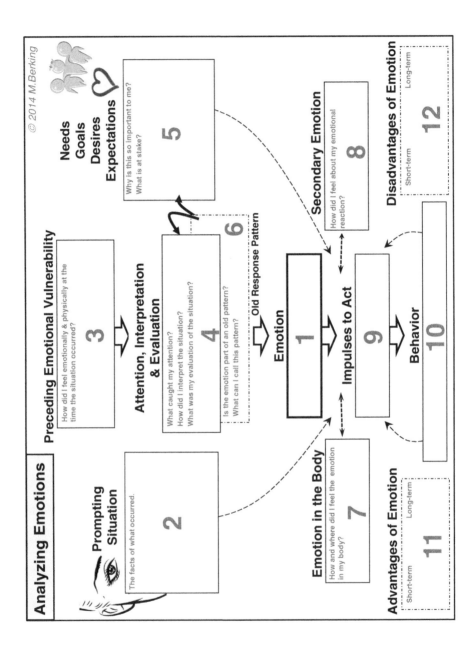

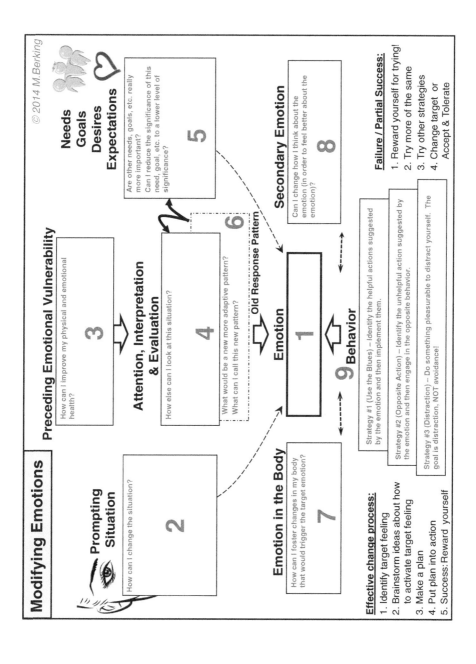

Modifying Emotions

Prompting Situation
2
How can I change the situation?

Preceding Emotional Vulnerability
3
How can I improve my physical and emotional health?

Attention, Interpretation & Evaluation
4
How else can I look at this situation?
What would be a new more adaptive pattern? What can I call this new pattern?

Old Response Pattern
6

Needs
Goals
Desires
Expectations
5
Are other needs, goals, etc. really more important?
Can I reduce the significance of this need, goal, etc. to a lower level of significance?

© 2014 M.Berking

Secondary Emotion
8
Can I change how I think about the emotion (in order to feel better about the emotion)?

Emotion
1

Behavior
9

Emotion in the Body
7
How can I foster changes in my body that would trigger the target emotion?

Strategy #1 (Use the Blues) – Identify the helpful actions suggested by the emotion and then implement them.

Strategy #2 (Opposite Action) – Identify the unhelpful action suggested by the emotion and then engage in the opposite behavior.

Strategy #3 (Distraction) – Do something pleasurable to distract yourself. The goal is distraction, NOT avoidance!

Effective change process:
1. Identify target feeling
2. Brainstorm ideas about how to activate target feeling
3. Make a plan
4. Put plan into action
5. Success: Reward yourself

Failure / Partial Success:
1. Reward yourself for trying!
2. Try more of the same
3. Try other strategies
4. Change target or Accept & Tolerate

Helpful / Unhelpful Emotions

When are these emotions helpful and when are they not?

	Helpful	Not helpful anymore
Stress/Tension		
Fear/Anxiety		
Anger		
Shame		
Guilt		
Sadness & Disappointment		
Depressed Mood		

How would I rather feel?

	What are potential **Target Emotions** for ...
Stress/Tension ⇨	
Fear/Anxiety ⇨	
Anger ⇨	
Shame ⇨	
Guilt ⇨	
Sadness & Dissappointment ⇨	
Depressed mood ⇨	

Cheat Sheet
Modifying Particularly Important Emotions

Goal	Short-Term	Long-term
Stress/Tension ↓ **Relaxation**	• Focus on your breathing. • Relax your muscles. • Switch into non-judgmental awareness mode and simply observe and describe the challenging situation, your thoughts, your emotions, and your bodily responses. • Engage in pleasant and/or physical activities. • Reprioritize tasks. • Get rid of tasks that are not important. • Reduce self-imposed demands.	• Properly balance demands/work with leisure/relaxation. • Practice relaxation on a daily basis. • Increase your physical fitness. • Reconsider your long-term goals if they are too demanding. • Get rid of goals that cause too much pressure. (e.g., Do you really have to excel at everything?) • Practice the ART Sequence.
Anxiety/Fear ↓ **Courage & Optimism**	• Relax your muscles. • Focus on your breathing. • Switch into non-judgmental awareness. • *Decatastrophize* the feared outcome by imagining the worst possible outcome, becoming more accustomed to it, & developing a plan to cope with this outcome in the best possible way. • *Estimate the likelihood* that the feared outcome will actually occur (give risk in percentages, then double check whether estimate is realistic) then determine if reduced risk lessens the threat. • Visualize other more positive outcomes • Take active steps to positively influence the situation (make a plan and put the plan into action).	• Continually expose yourself to situations that cause unhelpful levels of fear. Only exposure can provide evidence that you you can tolerate these situations and the anxiety they trigger. Also, exposure helps you become accustomed to the feared stimuli. • Practice relaxation every day • Practice non-judgmental awareness every day. • Increase your physical fitness • Reconsider the importance of unhelpful goals that often trigger dysfunctional anxiety (goals such as: to always be liked by everybody; to always produce the best results; to avoid conflicts at any price). • Practice the ART Sequence.
Anger ↓ **Calm & Kindness**	• Leave the situation (if you are likely to attack your opponent in an unconstructive way). • Distract yourself (e.g., count to ten). • Engage in physically demanding exercise. • Relax your muscles & focus on your breathing. • Express anger in assertive but constructive ways (e.g., "No, I am sorry, but I will not comply with your demand"). • Put yourself in the shoes of the person you feel anger toward. Try to understand why this person behaves the way he/she does. Try to let the feeling of compassion with this person arise in you. • Use opposite action: Be nice to the person who angered you.	• Try to reduce your stress level if this contributes to your anger. • Practice awareness of your wants and needs. • Practice the ability to fight for your rights in an assertive and skillful way if necessary. • Practice self-compassion and compassion with others on a daily basis (or even better: practice the entire ART Sequence).

Shame ↓ **Self-Approval** **&** **Assertiveness**	• *Estimate the likelihood* that others will (a) notice your mistake, (b) consider your mistake important, (c) always dislike you because of your mistake. • *Decatastrophize* the worst possible outcome: How could you cope with significant others (a) noting your mistake, (b) considering it important and (c) disliking you because of your mistake. Continue to imagine the worst case scenario for an extended period of time until you get more accustomed to it. Use effective self-support (compassion, self-care) to cope with the feared rejection. • If possible: Use opposite action and openly engage in the behavior the shame tries to suppress (e.g., expose your sweaty armpits on purpose).	• Purposefully expose yourself to sitations that cue (unneccesary) shame until your fear of rejection is reduced to an adaptive level (e.g., tie a toothbrush to a string and pull it behind you in a populated pedestrian area and let your body and mind become accustomed to the fear that others think you are crazy) Carefully watch how others react to your shame attacking exercises: Often they do not notice at all. Typically, they respond with amusement rather than rejection. • Engage in regular (ART) training to foster your self-esteem. If you learn to love yourself, you become less dependent on the opinion of others.
Guilt ↓ **Self-** **Compassion** **&** **Forgiveness**	• Clarify how much responsibility you had for the event you feel guilty about (e.g. by drawing a *responsibility pie* with different sized slices of the pie representing the amount of responsibility various people and circumstances have for the event) and elaborate on ways other people/factors contributed to the event. • Make amends for things you actually did wrong. If not possible to make amends to the person you wronged, make symbolical amends by doing something good elsewhere. • Use self-compassion. • Try to see the reasons why you behaved the way you did. • Forgive yourself. We all make mistakes. • Distinguish between your behavior (which might have been wrong) and yourself as a person (who is valuable regardless of your flaws). • Again: Use self-compassion.	• If you suffer from appropriate guilt resulting from a significant mistake that you made: Continue to make amends by doing good while also working to practice self-compassion on a daily basis. Consider self-disclosure to trustworthy others. Often talking about one's mistakes helps make them easier to cope with. • If you tend to experience dysfunctional guilt: Work to understand where this old pattern comes from. If you have copied the punishing style of your parents: Think about whether this is a fair way to treat yourself. Think about where this will lead you. Consider that you can decide to value yourself. If you decide to do so, practice being a caring parent for yourself on a daily basis, and defend yourself against unfair accusations from your own conscience. • Practice the ART Sequence.
Sadness & Disappointment ↓ **Acceptance** **&** **Comfort**	• Clarify what you have lost. Put your loss into words (e.g., "My husband left me. He will not be coming back. Our time together has come to an end. It will never be as it was before.") • Allow yourself the feelings of grief and sadness. Allow yourself to cry. • You can even work to cue feelings of grief and sadness purposefully by thinking of or visualizing what you have lost. The more you cue these feelings by active "grief work" the sooner they will become less intense. Examples of "grief work" include: looking at pictures of what you have lost, listening to music that reminds you of your loss, visiting the grave if someone died, writing a good-bye letter etc. while letting your tears flow freely for as long as it takes for them to stop flowing by themselves.	• Embrace loss and sadness as a fundamental aspect of the human existence. • Practice grief work on a daily basis. You may schedule regular sessions of grief work for at least 1.5 hours in length (for one or two weeks, or even more if neccesary). The systematic use of grief work is a very effective tool to disengage from something we would like to have but will not. • Consider practicing grief work through the Compassion and Loving Kindness Exercise on a daily basis. • Complement the Compassion & Loving Kindness Exercise with the Sympathetic Joy Exercise.

© 2014 M. Berking

	• Maybe express your feelings through words, music, paintings etc. • Complement facing what you have lost, with reminders of what you still have. • Focus on what you still have and work to appreciate and savor it. • Complement grief work with pleasant activities to recharge your mental battery. • Try to give yourself (and maybe others) a warm and friendly (inner) smile. If you fail to do so: Try again!	• Practice considering how fortunate you are every day (Exercise of Gratitude). You can do this exercise in the morning and the Compassion and Loving Kindess and Sympathetic Joy excercises in the evening. • Practice the entire ART Sequence on a daily basis.
Depressed mood ↓ **Constructive Sadness,** **&** **Comfort** **&** **Optimism**	• Accept your depressed mood. • Try to identify the problems burdening you. Make a list of your problems. Identify the most important one. Start working to solve it. Take one step at a time. Keep praising yourself for your efforts. • If the problem involves a loss, face what you have lost and engage in grief work for a certain period of time. • Complement problem solving and grief work with relaxation, leisure and pleasant activities. • Don't mistake how you see things when you are depressed with how things actually are. Try to see things from a more helpful angle. • Practice self-compassion and loving kindness towards yourself. • Give yourself a warm inner-smile. • Engage in positive activities and keep doing them patiently knowing that it often takes time until they affect your mood.	• Practice compassionate self-support on a daily basis by: Purposefully noticing and appreciating your achievements and identifying the abilities behind these achievements; Valuing yourself as a person with the help of your unconditional love statement; Continuous self-care through positive acitivities and focusing on positive things (use *Self-Support Diary I*). • Engage in positive activities on a daily basis (even if you do not feel like it). • Structure your day in advance to make sure that you find a good balance between task-related and leisure activities. If you do not feel well: spend more time on positive acitivities (use the *Self-Support Diary 2* to plan each day). • Engage in active problem solving. • Appreciate and focus on any positive experience (regardless how small it is). • Restore or maintain positive relationships with others. • Practice the ART Sequence. • Do not expect these exercises to work immediately. They usually take time to take effect. Keep doing them at least to some extent even when you feel better to sustain your well-being.

Index

CPSIA information can be obtained at www.ICGtesting.com
Printed in the USA
BVOW10*2147151214

379573BV00001B/11/P

9 781493 910212